The Deer Cry Pavilion

Pat Barr was born in Norwich and read English at Birmingham University and University College, London. She lived in Japan for three years before returning to Britain, and now divides her time between Norwich and the Hebridean island of Coll. *The Coming of the Barbarians* was her first book. This was followed by *The Deer Cry Pavilion*, *A Curious Life for a Lady*, *To China with Love*, *The Memsahibs* and *Taming the Jungle*. She then turned her hand to fiction with the immensely successful *Chinese Alice*, *Uncut Jade* and *Kenjiro*, all set in the nineteenth-century East.

The Deer Cry Pavilion

A STORY OF WESTERNERS IN
JAPAN 1868–1905

PAT BARR

PENGUIN BOOKS

PENGUIN BOOKS

Published by the Penguin Group
27 Wrights Lane, London W8 5TZ, England
Viking Penguin Inc., 40 West 23rd Street, New York, New York 10010, USA
Penguin Books Australia Ltd, Ringwood, Victoria, Australia
Penguin Books Canada Ltd, 2801 John Street, Markham, Ontario, Canada L3R 1B4
Penguin Books (NZ) Ltd, 182–190 Wairau Road, Auckland 10, New Zealand

Penguin Books Ltd, Registered Offices: Harmondsworth, Middlesex, England

First published by Macmillan & Co Ltd 1968
Published in Penguin Books 1988

Made and printed in Great Britain by
Richard Clay Ltd, Bungay, Suffolk

FOR MY MOTHER

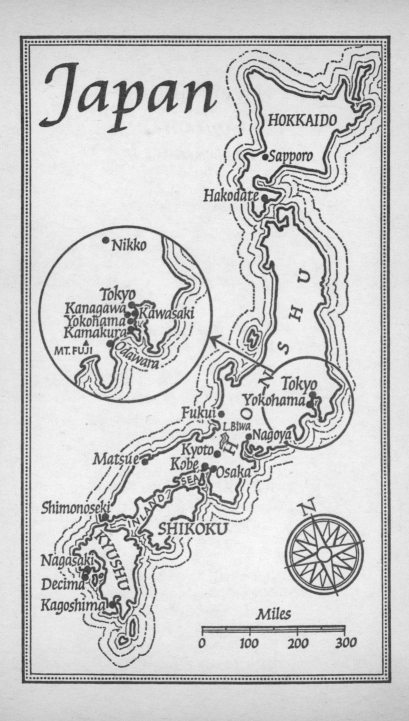

Contents

7

Illustrations

ACKNOWLEDGEMENTS FOR THE PLATES

Acknowledgements are due to Mr Tsuneo Tamba for permission to reproduce plates 1, 6, 9, 16, 17 and the endpaper illustration from prints in the Tamba collection of the Kanagawa Prefectural Museum; to the Japan Society (of London) Library for plates 2, 3, 5, from *The Far East Magazine*; to the Trustees of the British Museum for plates 8, 18, 23; to *Vanity Fair* for plate 20; to the Radio Times Hulton Picture Library for plates 4, 19, 21, 25, 27, 28; to *The Illustrated London News* for plates 24, 26; to Mr Paul Blum for plate 14 (from *Yokohama in 1872*); to John Murray Ltd for plate 13.

Author's Note

As I neared the end of my first book about the opening of Japan to the West, *The Coming of the Barbarians*, which covered the period between 1853 and 1870, it became increasingly clear that I was leaving a story half-told. In the course of my researches I had examined a very large quantity of books by Westerners about Japan after the Meiji Emperor's* restoration to power in 1868 and these now positively invited me to continue the same theme.

In writing this present book my first problem was how to select from the quantity of contemporary source-material available, for the whole picture of the West's relationship with Japan became much more complex and diverse during the Meiji period than it had been earlier. In order to tell what I hope is both an informative and an entertaining story, I have drawn most fully upon the works of writers who, in my view, describe most interestingly the ways in which the Japanese government's policy of modernisation and international communication affected their personal lives and the lives of the Japanese around them. The writers I have chosen are not necessarily the most rewarding from a purely literary or academic point of view, but they are still, I think, all very real people who lived through a historical situation of world-wide significance and who recorded most vividly and honestly what it was like for them.

I should add that, to keep this book within manageable proportions, I have confined my selection to words available in English, and I have seldom quoted directly from Japanese

---

*I am aware that the title of Meiji was granted posthumously to the Emperor Mutsuhito. The title is now always used to describe the man and the period and, for clarity, I have therefore availed myself of it.

sources in translation. The complex social and political development of Japan during this period has been most ably analysed by modern historians such as Sir George Sansom, Professor W. G. Beasley, Dr I. Nish and Dr E. O. Reischauer. I should like to acknowledge my debt to them and also to Captain Malcolm Kennedy, who has given me much useful advice and information. My own purpose has been different, however: to write a story of Meiji Japan through the eyes of Westerners who were involved in its process of rapid modernisation. I have also tried to explain some of the Japanese reactions to this process in so far as they help to set the westerners' stories meaningfully in context. I have started my narrative in the year 1868, as the Meiji Era officially began then, though the actual process of modernisation hardly got under way until 1870. I have chosen to end with Japan's military victory over Russia in 1905, and to describe the course of the war I have used eyewitness accounts of western observers or combatants. This has meant, naturally, that the scene shifts outside Japan itself, as western interest at the time focused principally on the forces in the field rather than on civilians. It seemed appropriate to conclude with some recollections of this first western experience of the aggressive effectiveness of Japanese military might – a demonstration, and unfortunately a portent, of Japan's new twentieth-century role.

My book has been named after the *Rokumeikan* (The Deer Cry Pavilion), a social centre opened in Tokyo in 1883. It was a spacious, pretentious building, its construction financed by the Japanese Government, its vaguely classical style suggested by a British architect. It contained a large dining-room supervised by a French chef, salons, parlours, games-rooms, ballrooms and 'a corridor for promenading'; at the bars English cigarettes, German beer and American cocktails were sold. At its opening the Japanese Minister of Foreign Affairs announced that the pavilion had been built to provide a place for international communication. 'The highest in the land can set an example of social intercourse with foreigners upon a grand scale,' he explained. This thought, added the Minister, was exemplified in the word *Rokumeikan* that had been borrowed from an old

Chinese banqueting poem to illustrate 'the harmonious social intercourse of persons of all nationalities'. This was the poem:

> Yu, yu, cry the deer
> Nibbling the black southernwood in the field.
> I have a lucky guest.
> Let me play my zither, blow my reed-organ,
> Blow my reed-organ, trill their tongues,
> Take up the baskets of offerings,
> Here is a man that loves me
> And will teach me the ways of Chou.*

I should like to express my gratitude to Matheson & Co. of Lombard Street, London, for permission to look at the Jardine Matheson archives of correspondence from the Japanese treaty ports; to Commander A. Newman and Mr Robert Scoales of the Japan Society Library for drawing my attention to so many welcome and unexpected items of interest and to Mr Tsuneo Tamba of Yokohama for allowing me to reproduce some of the late nineteenth-century prints from his unsurpassed collection. I should also like to thank all those who wrote to me either about possible material for this book or to express their appreciation of my first one. My biggest debt of gratitude is again to my husband, for his unfailing encouragement and understanding.

* Translation by Arthur Waley from his *Book of Songs* (1937), No. 183. The 'ways of Chou' are foreign ways.

Prologue

Stories about modern Japan begin with the name of Commodore Matthew Calbraith Perry, that competent, tenacious, morose American naval commander whose four ships sailed into Tokyo Bay on a July day in 1853 bringing demands for the establishment of trade relations, and who, in this fashion, without an arrow or a cannon being fired, 'opened' the country. In one sense the process was as ticklish as the handling of a newly discovered fossil, for Japan had been immured in almost total political, social and economic isolation from the rest of the world for nearly 250 years until Perry's sudden arrival. Yet in another sense the process was as easy as drawing a cork from a bottle for the Japanese were ripe for release, fermenting restlessly against that policy of isolation imposed upon them by their rulers, the Tokugawa Shoguns – they were a people eager and ready to run out and meet the world half-way.

The long pent-up eagerness of the Japanese to explore, understand and emulate fresh ideas and unfamiliar productions was manifest from the very beginning of this new East-West relationship. It was clear from the moment when Commodore Perry, having returned to Tokyo Bay early in 1854 to learn how the Japanese would reply to the American cannon-supported 'request' for commercial intercourse, allowed a number of native officials to board his steamers. The officials, naturally, wore their traditional ceremonial habit – loose-sleeved brocade jackets, wide silken trousers, stiff lacquer hats tied on their heads, cumbersome clogs on their feet. But this hampering, essentially unadaptable garb did not prevent them from showing, even in that first tentative, bewildering encounter, the national zest for discovery and assimilation that was to take them so far so quickly during the next fifty years. They 'went about peering into every nook and corner', recorded Francis Hawks, the chronicler of Perry's expedition, 'peeping into the muzzles of guns, examining curiously the small arms, handling the ropes, measuring the boats, looking eagerly into the engine room and watching every movement of the engineers and workmen as they busily moved in and about the gigantic machinery of the steamers'. Hawks was encouraged by their keen receptive interest, a promise, he felt, 'of the comparatively easy introduction of foreign customs and habits among them, if not of the nobler principles and better life of a higher civilisation'.

Further evidence of America's 'higher civilisation' was Perry's gifts to the Japanese: a small telegraph system and a steam locomotive with carriage and tender. The latter were on a lilliputian scale: the carriage, said Hawks, 'could hardly carry a child of six', the little engine ran in a 350-foot circle on a narrow-gauge track. It was a demonstration model, designed to suggest something of what the wideawake West had been up to while Japan slept. But, miniature or not, the Japanese were determined to mount this wonderful steed, and, as soon as the track was laid, they queued for hours to take a ride. 'As they were unable to reduce themselves to the capacity of the carriage,' Hawks explained, 'they betook themselves to the roof' and, clinging to its edge, went whirling round, their robes flapping in the breeze, 'grinning with intense interest' and crying out with enthusiasm every time the steam whistle sounded.

When the rides and the diplomatic negotiations were over, the foreign ships sailed triumphantly away, bearing with them a preliminary agreement of friendship between America and Japan which permitted the beginning of a closely regulated trade. But, once the excitement of the 'peaceful invasion' had died down, many Japanese grew sad with envy, for they well understood what the magically powered vessels and the smoky whistling chargers could do for a country like theirs, where everything had to be carried on pack-horses, push-carts or junks. For these were the only methods of transport available to the Japanese, who since 1636 had been kept as virtual prisoners, forbidden on pain of death to go overseas or communicate in any way with foreigners. And foreigners, in their turn, had been forbidden access to the country, except for a few Dutch and Chinese merchants allowed restricted trading rights at Naga-saki. During this period of isolation Japan had remained a haven of peace compared to Europe, free from any serious internal upheaval or external war. It had become, in some ways, a wealthy land – rich in its artists and craftsmen, its gracious cultural and family traditions, its gay, affluent town life, its beautiful shrines and castles, its docile hard-working peasantry, its lovely, obedient women. But the country had also been starved – starved of fresh outlets for the resourcefulness and energy of its people, of fully-informed dynamic leadership, of the free cross-fertilisation of social, political and technologi-cal ideas. As a result, where America now had trains and steamers, Japan had only junks and carts.

The visit of Commodore Perry had brought into sharp focus the feelings of discontent, insufficiency and claustrophobia that had, for years, haunted the nation's educated classes. These men – officials, scholars, politicians, clan leaders, some active in the Shogun's government, others secretly against it – had by then learned of the recent humiliating defeats of the Chinese by western powers. Cultural and historical links with the Chinese were close and their evident weakness in the face of foreign aggression both frightened the Japanese and encouraged them to look elsewhere for a model. They looked, hesitantly at first, towards the strong western world, and at once realised that by its standards theirs was a backward country. They had coal, but no locomotives; iron and steel, but no sophisticated machinery; paper, but no survey maps or constitutions; gold and silver, but no international currency. They had people in plenty, but none of them were scientists or engineers, machine-minders, tele-graph-operators or engine-drivers. And they wanted to learn all these jobs as soon as they could.

But they had to wait, for there were a number of political and social questions which it took Japan the next fourteen years to sort out. For instance, was the country's government willing to make adjustments, to co-operate with the foreigners, or was it safer and wiser to obstruct them in every possible way, to fight them to the death if necessary? And who was best fitted to rule now that this first western impact had revealed the political disunity, moral insecurity and timorous conservatism of the Shogun and his ministers, who had vacillated, temporised and eventually agreed to the American demands?

A principal cause for the frailty of the Tokugawa Shogunate was the historical fact that the Shoguns were really 'generalissimos'. Military and administrative authority lay with the Shogun and his counsellors, but there was also another power in the land – an Emperor living in Kyoto with his family. The Emperor was closely guarded, often in the past he had been a practically impotent figurehead, yet he could always command a great deal of spiritual and moral allegiance, he was an ever-ominous focus for all those who opposed the dominant Tokugawa regime. The existence of the Emperor and his court was of vital importance during the next stage of Japan's history, but it was a sort of national secret and one to be most carefully shielded from the prying eyes of arriving westerners.

Consequently the American, Townsend Harris, in 1856, the first foreign consul to reach Japan, had no inkling that the Shogun to whom (after much prevarication) he was allowed to present his credentials and with whose ministers he hammered out details of a full American-Japanese commercial treaty, was not the absolute and unquestioned ruler he purported to be. The secret was also kept at first from the diplomatic representatives of other western countries – Britain, Holland, France, Germany and Russia – who, taking advantage of the American initiative, hastily arrived to conclude similar treaties with the Shogun's ministers.

As a result of these treaties, none of which received the assent of the Emperor, the first three Japanese 'treaty ports' were opened at Yokohama, Nagasaki and Hakodate in 1859. These were the only places in the land where foreigners (except diplomats) were permitted to reside, and in the early years the settlers who came to trade were strictly penned inside the twenty-four-mile 'treaty limits' by the Japanese authorities.

The pioneering American and European merchants who rented plots along the empty Yokohama shoreline and built wooden bungalows and warehouses on them, had, therefore, rather a cloistered time of it – and any excitement which came their way was frequently undesirable. For, within a year of the ports' opening, a number of Japanese reactionaries – a few noblemen, warriors from the ancient clans, xenophobic patriots, many of whose prime allegiance was to the Imperial family – had rallied to the cry of 'Revere the Emperor, expel the barbarians!' Some adherents of this chauvinistic royalist cause were fanatical swordsmen who, during the early 1860s, assaulted and even assassinated innocent western residents, so that on a few occasions European and American gunboats were hastily summoned to Japan's shores to protect their nationals against the onslaughts of the murderous natives.

These attacks were symptoms of the political and ideological dissensions that racked the country during this period – dissensions which did not always follow clear-cut lines of party or clan membership. On the one hand were the progressives, who positively welcomed the westerners' arrival, or accepted its inevitability or saw in it a chance to enhance their own power; on the other hand were the conservatives (not always advocates of violence), who feared and loathed the invasion of the 'barbarians' because they realised it would permanently alter the *status quo* and probably undermine their own authority. To progressives, reactionaries and fence-sitters alike, however, certain facts were undeniable: firstly, that the Shogunate was incapable of either mollifying all the dissenters or guaranteeing the safety of foreigners against xenophobic attack; secondly, that support for the imperial cause was growing as people realised the ineffectuality of the present government; thirdly, most important of all, it was hurtfully apparent that the westerners had achieved mastery of certain technical and scientific skills that enabled them to subdue their environment, increase their wealth and exploit their national potentials in a more direct and effective way than the Japanese had ever imagined possible.

It was also plain that, if Japan was to muster the resources of manpower and money necessary for the acquisition of these enviable skills, it had to be united, firmly governed, geared to a common purpose. But between 1859 and 1866, a time of almost limitless potential, the national energies were largely frittered away in inter-clan skirmishes, in occasional acts of violence against westerners and reformers within the government, and in arguments about how to expel 'barbarians' whom, in any case, no group had the military strength to expel. Militarists and ministers of the Shogunate, the Emperor's advisers and loyal clan-leaders all saw this, and in 1866 the latter seized the political initiative by agreeing to bury their traditional rivalries and fight together to restore the Emperor to power.

As the incidence of overt strife increased it was no longer possible to keep secret the growing power of the imperial line, and representatives of the major foreign powers in the country watched events anxiously, wondering to which side they should ally themselves. Most of them, remembering that the Shogun's ministers had signed the trade treaties and that at first xenophobia had centred round the imperialists, supported the Tokugawa cause; the British, who learned that in fact there were as many pro-westerners within the imperial party as on the other side, supported the Emperor.

Between 1867 and 1869 there was intermittent fighting between the two factions, but it was fairly bloodless and surprisingly half-hearted; clearly the country was socially and psychologically ready for change. Realising this, the young Shogun (who had only been in power for about a year) voluntarily resigned his authority to the young Emperor (who ascended the throne on his father's death in 1867). During the last days of 1867 there was a subdued, almost polite, palace revolution, and two and a half centuries of Tokugawa rule came to an end. Early in 1868, though fighting was not yet over, the imperial line was securely restored.

The nominal head of the new regime was Mutsuhito, the sixteen-year-old Emperor; the actual rulers of the country during Mutsuhito's minority and, to a still-debatable extent, for his entire reign, were the ministers and leaders of the royalist clans who secured the throne for him, and young, progressive *samurai* from both factions. One of Mutsuhito's first public acts after his accession was to proclaim to his followers and his people the Charter Oath of Five Articles. The Oath recognised the need for a more liberal interpretation of individual rights and freedoms, for the establishment of deliberative assemblies along democratic lines and for the country's leaders to look outward and seek inter-action with other nations. This progressive, enterprising, radical proclamation was an appropriate herald for the reign of one who was to grow up to be the great Meiji Emperor, whose long period of 'Enlightened Government' was that remarkable, vigorous, experimental Meiji Era.

Part One

1868–1877

Of railwaymen, schoolmasters and things that were done in a hurry

The capital of Meiji Japan was Tokyo, where everything that was modern, foreign and challenging began. A year after the proclamation of the Charter Oath the Emperor and his ministers moved there from Kyoto, the former imperial seat, and began to reorganise many aspects of the national life along new western-style lines. To implement this reorganisation the Japanese had to call upon foreign advice and expertise and so, during the 1870s, about three thousand professional men from Europe and America – engineers, scientists, teachers, military officers, doctors and lawyers – came to the capital as employees of the government. In addition, and mainly because of the outward-looking policy of the new administration, more diplomats, traders and missionaries also arrived, to swell the number of those already residing in the treaty ports. A large percentage of the newcomers however, particularly the professional experts, were based in Tokyo, the 'Eastern Capital' and so it was in Tokyo that the first western-style ministerial departments and legislative offices opened, many of the military, medical and technical colleges were founded, the early postal and telegraph services operated and to which the first railway lines stretched.

For the Japanese had not forgotten the wondrous circles made by Commodore Perry's miniature locomotive and within a year of the Emperor's restoration to power, negotiations were in progress to raise sufficient capital to get the first trains rolling between Tokyo and Yokohama. Yokohama was the largest treaty port in the country, where some nine hundred foreigners lived. Two other important ports, Kobe and Osaka, opened for trade in 1868 and soon their foreign settlement areas, like those of the first three treaty ports, became living examples, exhibitions almost, to the provincial Japanese of the western way of life.

Appropriately then, the miracle-engine was to run between the most thriving treaty port and the bustling new capital and that it failed to do so almost on the instant provoked much sarcasm and irritation from Japanese and foreigner alike. The delays were indeed frustrating, but understandable enough, considering the complete novelty of the enterprise. For a bad start, the first British contractor failed to produce the amount of capital he had promised; then a few of the foreigners employed by the Japanese as qualified engineers turned out to be simply loafers enjoying a free oriental holiday; it was difficult, in any event, to use quickly and effectively the local labourers to whom the whole railway world was totally unfamiliar. To allay public impatience, the authorities staged a number of 'trial runs' for privileged persons in the autumn of 1871. They all bought tickets at the brand-new Yokohama ticket office, had them snipped at the barrier by a guard in a peaked cap, and then boarded a train that travelled over rails which, according to a reporter, 'had a disturbingly wavy appearance'. After four and a half miles the tracks ended in the middle of fields and the passengers got out to watch some navvies bolting down the next section of line under the eye of an English superintendent. 'They all worked with a will and very rapidly,' commented the reporter, 'but it was very plainly seen how absolutely necessary is the overlooking by foreigners'.

Eventually, just over a year later, the line was well and truly opened. An American scholar, Professor William Griffis, was one of several foreigners present at the inaugural proceedings and he was quite carried away with enthusiasm. 'The 14th October was a day of matchless autumnal beauty and ineffable influence. The sun rose cloudlessly on Sunrise Land...' he began. 'On that auspicious day the Mikado (Emperor), princes of the blood, court nobles, the "flowery nobility" of ex-*daimyo*, and guests representing the literature, science, art and army of Japan, in flowing and picturesque costume, the foreign Diplomatic Corps in tight cloth smeared with gold; ambassadors of

Kiu Kiu, the Ainu chiefs and officials in modern dress, made the procession that, underneath arches of camellias, azaleas and chrysanthemums, moved into the stone-built depot and, before twenty thousand spectators, stepped into the train. It was a sublime moment when, before that august array of rank and fame and myriads of his subjects, the one hundred and twenty-third representative of the Imperial Line declared the road open.' As the train left the station to the weird notes of Japanese western-style music, Griffis concluded that 'today Japan, fresh and vigorous, with new blood in her heart, was taking an upward step in life'.

After such a send-off, the whole country wanted to share in the railway marvel. During the next year some twenty-five railway engines, twenty-four cases of tickets, boxes of peaked caps and station-masters' jackets, several miles of track and 158 carriages were imported and snapped up with joyous enthusiasm in every province. As a Japanese reporter put it in an English-language newspaper when announcing the beginning of line-surveys in his area: 'Arrivals from far distant places will be quick as thought – like going to a neighbour's house! Transactions done in a breath! Let us fly over a thousand miles without wings. Let us hurry through space without using our nimble feet. Isn't it a jolly world! ! !'

Into this jolly Japanese world of 1873 there arrived, among other foreigners, a Mr E. G. Holtham. Mr Holtham was an Englishman of normal appetites: he liked eating oysters, hunting, singing in groups, drinking, playing billiards, and in his book *Eight Years in Japan* he writes with appropriate seriousness and gusto about all these pleasures. There was, however, one thing he enjoyed doing more than all these, and it was this that made him such a useful person to have around at that time and in that place – he liked building railways.

Nothing in his life could quite compare with the first moment he saw some pristine stretch of land – a few mountain crags, perhaps, an inconveniently long lake, a sharp decline into a narrow valley – and knew that he, and he more or less unaided, was to decide where and how the 'iron road' would traverse that stretch, how it could coil down the quiet valley, curve over the spine of the farthest spur, wheel along the margins of the unsuspecting lake. And so he was just the man to set down upon the untouched country west of Tokyo with instructions to survey the fifteen miles between Shiotsu and Tsuruga, the town on the coast whose enthusiastic mayor had already designated a plain near by as the site of the grand railway-station-to-be.

Holtham had come to Japan in the *Avoca*, a comfortable steamer whose captain had the delightful habit of producing anchovy toast and hot grog about midnight and with whom one could always share a glass of tropical grapefruit juice at sunrise the next morning. After the *Avoca* had, in Holtham's words, 'dropped contingents of Egyptian merchants, chaplains and frisky matrons, the last presentable maidens at Calle, all mothers and babies at Penang, the tea-men and missionaries at Hongkong' there were few remaining male passengers to gather in the 'smoking tent erected half-way up the main hatch' for the last night's singsong. The grog flowed easily, voices churned out the unprintable ditties, 'Old Noah', 'O Kafoozleum', 'Sandy, he Belongs to the Mill' until the early hours and when they awoke next morning with aching heads and dry throats they were sliding into Yokohama harbour.

Holtham, with Tom, his engineering companion and friend, headed straight for the Grand Hotel on the Bund and were 'speedily outside a light repast of oysters and Chablis' followed by a game of billiards and a couple of whiskies, doubtless drunk as the hair of the proverbial dog. Considering that 'E. G.' had never been in the Orient before, his lack of interest in its manifestations was truly exceptional. In retrospect this is a gain, for while there are many who tell us about the local temples and curio shops, there is no one else to tell us, in an honest and direct manner, what it was like to be employed by the Japanese government in the building of some of the country's first railways.

Apparently, it was all rather a hit-and-miss business at first. When Holtham got to his headquarters at the treaty port of Kobe, he discovered to his surprise that the straightness of the tracks being laid there depended primarily on the accuracy of the foreman's eye, and the result, as the resident engineer confessed, was that the line 'had many quite unnecessary curves in it'. Nor had it been clearly decided whether to lay single or double tracks – two tunnels in one stretch of line would only accommodate one track, while two others were wide enough for three. Further along the tracks, excessive caution had prevailed and, in order to cross a stream eighteen inches wide, 'a couple of walls big enough for a fifty foot bridge' had been built to span 'the yawning gulf below'. Several other British engineers and surveyors were already on the job, but Holtham is careful not to say how the mistakes had been made.

At last, two days before the Christmas of 1873, 'E. G.' and Tom left Osaka by river for up-country, taking with them the usual contingent of attendants – six coolies, two coolie masters, two body-servants, one native surveyor and two students 'of English engineering and foreign character'. They travelled first by *yaka-bune*, a low barge with a flat-roofed, shuttered cabin along half its length and a deck space in the stern where crew cooked rice and fish, smoked, chattered, slept. A *yaka-bune*, as Holtham soon discovered, was not made for westerners in a hurry. They were hauled upstream at an average of three miles per hour by crew-members who plodded along the bank attached with webbing lines to the main tow-rope. Frequently obstacles blocked the path or an adverse current swirled in the water, and at a shout from the steersman, the towing party would jump aboard just as the vessel veered clumsily off towards the opposite bank. For two cold days the railwaymen travelled thus, in bored silence broken only by the ripple of slow water and the occasional thunderous thudding of a dozen or more bare feet on the roof just above their heads as the tow-gang leaped aboard and, a few minutes later, took off again. At long last, they landed on the shores of Lake Biwa, near Kyoto, and E. G., impatient as a bridegroom, was able to take his first tramp across the first virgin stretch of country where the railway was to be laid.

As Basil Hall Chamberlain, scholar, linguist and author of

that most reliable and useful handbook, *Things Japanese*, explained, 'Japan is not naturally suited to railway construction: the country is too mountainous, the streams – mere beds of sand today – are, tomorrow, after a heavy rain, wild surging rivers that sweep away bridges and embankments'. Mr Holtham, exploring the unaccommodating terrain before the bridges and embankments were actually there, duly noted such future impediments. Dense woods and outcrops of bleak shale clawed the steep hillsides, debris-laden streams pelted through precipitous gullies – the whole was traversable only along sodden tracks rutted by the wide wheels of the peasants' carts bringing sacks of fish manure from the shore. For the last mile or so the line was to run across the badly drained coastal plain to Tsuruga, a plain of exactly the character Chamberlain described. Mountain waters sloshed over the banks of its irrigation canals and river tributaries during the spring rains; each midsummer it was a mosquito-ridden desert, its blistered earth crumbling away underfoot. It was in fact a challenge, what he and Tom had come for.

Back at the starting-point the Englishmen commandeered part of a local priest's house adjoining the village temple, stuck some glass in the windows instead of paper and unpacked their luggage – an iron stove for the main room, a creaky roll-top desk, choppers, thigh boots and a barrel of beer in the most convenient corner. And then, seated at the desk, E. G. 'reduced to order and planned upon paper the main ridges, the valleys, the gullies and obstacles' on his proposed route. The actual surveying, 'hillwork' as E. G. called it, was bone-wearying. Each morning the party set out early, their two dogs, 'Mr Dick' and 'Mrs Bella', leading the way, then the foreigners carrying their charts and instruments, the students, and the coolies laden with poles, chains, staves, axes, ropes and their little wooden lunch-boxes. There were, of course, difficulties of communication, particularly with the students who were trying to learn the techniques of railway survey work in a language that had no technical terminology. 'Dimensions, angles, lines and planes all became mixed, like an approaching nightmare,' Holtham admits, 'and many a hopeless fog did these hapless cadets get into in the morning and wander through all the rest of the day.' The coolies fired with the general enthusiasm for the enterprise, but with less demanding roles, were, Holtham noted, 'uncommon quick' at interpreting orders. They sat and watched quietly but eagerly as E. G. and Tom made their calculations and then, at a sign, jumped up and mimed the driving-in of a pole, the cutting-down of a tree, the rattling-out of a length of chain and so learned by a process of rapid elimination what was required of them.

Nevertheless the work was slow. In places the ground was a rubble heap of boulders and gravel; on other stretches, thirty woodcutters had to be employed to cut a swathe through the forest and then only managed to progress a hundred and fifty yards in a day. Later there was the problem of the 1¼-mile-long main tunnel whose end faced out on a steep ridge from whence the rail would, one day, ride 'high on the shoulders of transverse spurs, winding round or piercing them and spring across gullies and ravines of a very precipitous character'.

But that was in the future; meanwhile the snows melted and the land was softer. Tom went off to get married and one Charlie came instead. During the midsummer heats they rose at dawn and worked with compass and theodolite until noon, when the sun pierced through their shirts and the coolies and the students all keeled over in siesta under the shade of the trees. Back at base, Charlie and E. G. threw water over their sunbaked shoulders, took a nip of sherry to introduce the fried ham and eggs and then had a nap on the veranda, with pipes and tea, the dogs panting and dozing at their feet. Towards sunset when the forest birds perked up, they went for a swim in a bamboo-shadowed pool near by; then more 'desk-work', more grog and bed. It was a simple life, but it had purpose, its progress could be charted and 'we were not so badly off, Charlie and I, this sweltering July, and we each thanked the powers above that the other didn't snore'.

To E. G. and his mates it mattered little that they were in Japan; the actual physical land they knew and understood, but the people of the land remained totally unpredictable and unloved. Most of the coolies were 'swindlers', older Japanese women 'simply frumps' and as for those colourful native festivals he'd heard about, well, Holtham couldn't see it himself. One day, to his annoyance, none of the labourers reported for work. Holtham tramped back to the village in search of them and found a religious holiday in full swing. The young men, 'in a kind of uniform tunic of scanty dimensions, were whooping and leaping about the road, and the female part of the community were standing around, clapping their hands and singing out *"omishiro"* to signify their joyfulness . . .' and what was so fascinating about that? Moreover, they all made a hell of a shindy that evening when the 'shrine deity' was returned to the near-by temple and, Holtham assumed, was 'comfortably tucked up again by his ministers'.

No, the hectic mysteries of the native rituals could remain mysterious as far as E. G. and Charlie were concerned, they preferred to make their own amusement. They went fishing, and grilled fresh salmon and sweet potatoes over a wood fire; they went hunting and 'Mr Dick' and 'Mrs Bella' helped in the retrieving of many a golden-feathered pheasant and painted snipe. Officially, shooting outside treaty limits was forbidden and E. G. was heavily sarcastic about a circular issued by 'the bigwigs in Tokyo' which threatened 'consequences of the most heartrending description' to any of their employees who pursued game with a gun or 'any other engine'. Occasionally, they took a longer break – for a merry meeting with Billy and Christopher who were working farther down the line. And then how the paper screens of the native inn shuddered to the sounds of Billy's 'growler' (portable harmonium) and the songs and the gossip about preferments, salaries and headquarter-stupidities, as large quantities of Bass were poured 'down the red lane'.

And then, rather suddenly, before Holtham realised it, came the end of the 'First Year's Work'. The next year he got a promotion; Billy and Christopher moved to Nagoya; Ned arrived with a pretty wife and 'had to be made pretty comfortable in consequence'; Charlie got smallpox and survived; another new arrival, 'young Smith', was drowned while bathing. Each year's work brought greater responsibilities, more exacting duties. It was E. G. who had to get hold of the right smooth-faced granite for the clock-tower and entrance arcade of Kyoto station, who had to direct the extinguishing of a fire that broke out on the newly thatched roof of the goods yard down the line, who had to keep a sharp eye on all 'the scamps of riveters' who had the habit of cradling themselves to sleep among the struts of the bridges in the afternoon sun.

And then at long last, and yet still in a sense, too soon, came the Greatest Day of all – 5 February 1877, culmination of much of the work done by E. G., Tom, Charlie, Billy, Christopher and all their unnamed mates during the last five years. On that day Kyoto station and the whole forty-seven miles stretching from it to Kobe was declared open and the Imperial Emperor himself came to his erstwhile Imperial City to make the declaration. By this time, the Meiji Emperor looked rather like other modern young men of New Japan, with a few royal embellishments. His last public appearance in full national court dress had been five years earlier, when he had boarded one of the warships of the visiting Russian Pacific Squadron wearing loose satin robes of crimson and white and large lacquer sabots, his head bound by a fillet of fluted gold with a tall gold plume springing from it at the back. But what, at that time, had caused the young ruler even more disquiet than the obvious incongruity of his attire in that modern naval setting, had been the hesitant and disorganised manoeuvrings made by his small national fleet compared to those of the disciplined, impregnable-looking foreign ships.

The insufficiency of the Japanese vessels and the anachronism of the court robes made a deep impression on the Emperor and his ministers. Soon afterwards, the building-up of the navy was made a national priority; from then on, for public ceremonies at which westerners were present, the Emperor normally wore a black coat lined with purple silk, a military-style suit with a high collar, a dress sword and a cocked hat of English naval shape. It was for this comparatively muted personage that the station offices and reception rooms at Kyoto station were 'carpeted and hung round with tapestry and equipped with a gorgeous throne all proper', the interior of the railway-carriage in which he sat was padded with satin and furnished with chairs, tables and a lavatory 'ingeniously disposed' and the engine to pull the royal carriage along the shining rails was 'painted and silvered up until she looked almost quite too beautiful' and the driver and stoker who ran the engine which pulled the carriage wore their best Sunday clothes, but even then were considered not quite lovely enough and were decorously concealed behind 'a grove of evergreen cunningly attached to the cab'.

And so the train with His Imperial Highness aboard left for Kobe to a roaring send-off of fireworks, bands, gun salutes and with the resident engineer, Mr E. G. Holtham in the staff carriage at the back, most uncomfortably fitted out in a dress coat, white choker and chimney-pot hat and 'blushing like a pickled cabbage' because just before the train pulled out, he had been presented to the Emperor. The whole length of the track was gay with floral arches, national flags and country people who lowered their heads in homage as the strange engine approached, 'changing a bright field of expectant faces into an expanse of black polls' and then 'breaking out again with the flush of accomplished ceremony as the entourage vanished in the distance'. 'Now and then too,' writes another passenger who experienced that first triumphal trip, 'some little temple would be discovered buried in the woods from which as the train approached a priest would step out clad in the brilliant garments of Old Japan and bow reverently as we passed.'

Many Western observers probably found a certain irony and pathos in that little scene – but not Holtham. Musings on the incongruous clashes of Japan's modernisation process were not in his line nor were dress coats and 'functions' or choosing stone for station clock-towers. In fact, when he looked back and decided to write about it all a few years later it was very clear that there was nothing to touch the First Year of 'hillwork', with Tom and Charlie and the dogs and the wood fires and the evening bathes and the uncharted land and the first moment when the gradient line was staked along the earth and the first time he looked back at the route he had just marked out – the route that the trains would ride.

II

'It is not easy,' remarked John Black, former editor of *The Japan Herald*, one of the country's first newspapers, and author of a haphazard vivid history of Japan's modern progress... 'it is not easy to follow the government's movements at this period [the early seventies] with perfect regularity, on account of the frequent changes that were constantly occurring in the departments, sub-departments and offices of state as well as in their names, and in the names and titles of their officials. There was a restlessness, I might almost say an irritability, perceptible in the management of public business that showed all was not working smoothly. Men had not yet found their proper grooves.'

That this should have been so was not surprising. The Japanese were trying to absorb and use, within the space of a decade or so, techniques, practical knowledge and experience that western nations had accumulated during almost a hundred years of industrial revolution. The government was trying to graft on to its country and its people a number of alien political, social and cultural institutions that had evolved within the specialised framework of western technological development.

And yet, during the seventies, only a few conservative aristocrats and intellectuals totally rejected the idea of modernising the country; but there was a great deal of disagreement as to how quickly and how extensively this should be done. In the political sphere, liberals were advocating the establishment of a popularly elected representative assembly as early as 1871 and their views gathered supporters throughout the decade. These radicals saw the wisdom of beginning to educate the public at local level for the responsibilities of constitutional elections and wanted this to be started immediately. The government however, which was mainly in the hands of the ruling oligarchy that had come to power at the Emperor's restoration, refused to be pushed and pursued a policy of alternate suppression and gradual reform. It did not concede a great deal to liberal agitation until 1881, when it was announced that a national assembly would be established by 1890.

In the social sphere however, the policy of encouraging the people to accept westernisation was pursued more vigorously. So vigorously indeed that, in the words of one historian, 'A sort of mania for issuing decrees and regulations now took possession of the government and they were issued in their thousands.' It was no wonder that, as Black commented, civil servants were somewhat irritable. Certainly the ordinary people were somewhat confused.

First of all there were the things that people used to do quite naturally, but were now forbidden or discouraged from doing. For instance, married women were discouraged from blackening their teeth and shaving their eyebrows as they had done for centuries to indicate their conjugal state; their husbands were discouraged from wearing top-knots. This latter injunction was a real headache, as variations in hair-style were traditional identification marks of authority and rank. Nevertheless, in 1871, the government announced the top-knot was an optional accessory from now on – for one thing it looked pretty silly underneath the chimney-pot hats and military caps that were just becoming fashionable. Two years later the Emperor himself had his top-knot off; most of the court dutifully followed suit; soon students and bright new men-about-town all had cropped hair – older men and reactionaries kept theirs long. Two hundred barbers stormed along to the Governor's office in one province shouting that this decree would ruin their livelihood as people would not need the customary daily top-knot dressing any more. In the event, their fears proved unwarranted, shorter hair required more clipping and soon Tokyo sprouted modern-style barbers' shops with signs that read 'An Hairdresser for Japanese and Foreigner'.

But westernisation crept slowly from the head downwards, so that though foreign hats became very popular, simple native robes were still preferred, especially in summer. 'The adoption of foreign dress has been much retarded by the recent hot weather,' snarled *The Japan Mail* crossly in August of 1873, 'and many of those who had been inclined to commence its wear have subsided into their ordinary garb'. Considering that with the temperature in the high eighties, the choice lay between one loose cotton garment (the *yukata*) gathered at the waist and a pair of airy pattens, or stiff white shirt, jacket, trousers, tie, underpants, socks, gloves, shoes etc. the natives were surely wise thus to subside. It took people as immune from outside influence as most nineteenth-century western business men to refrain from lapsing into *yukata* themselves in a particularly heated moment. But the business men, of course, had a considerable vested interest in the matter. It had been too quickly assumed that the Japanese would shed their native dress as, it seemed, they had discarded a number of their other feudal habits – and large quantities of cheap foreign clothes were poured into the country. 'The ragbags of Europe', commented one western observer, 'were ransacked to supply last year's fashions to orientals who had too much taste to buy them.' And in fact for many years the Japanese business man's western wardrobe remained small and tight – one suit, one hat, one pair of all necessary accessories. Sometimes it resulted in rather odd oriental-occidental sartorial combinations, but only foreigners sniggered at these.

In the matter of food and drink however, the Japanese, having perhaps, less to lose, were much more amenable to innovation. Ever since 1853, when the first native officials boarded Commodore Perry's flagship and were given a glass of champagne, the people decided they liked foreign drinks. Not only champagne, but whisky and gin, brandy and wine soon became popular and of course beer, which they quickly started to manufacture for themselves. 'Fuji Beer' was one of the early brands, a wholesome beverage. Announced its maker, 'The efficacy of this Beer is to give the health and especially strength for stomach. The flavour is so sweet and simple that not injure for much drink.' And with the good beer – bread. The *Mail* felt that the country should turn over to wheat production on a grand scale: it was nutritious, easy to grow, and 'the replacement of endless rice marshes by a succession of golden cornfields would, we are persuaded, prove a sanitary boon to the dwellers in the valleys, over which so often, as evening draws on, we see a heavy and not seldom poisonous mist hanging like a grey pall'. A few convinced farmers grew grain and stall-holders in Yokohama sold bread at half a *rin* per slice. But at first they did not appreciate the need for freshness and cleanliness and some of the loaves, warned the *Mail*, 'are covered with a mould that would be a rich green colour but for the great quantity of dust with which it is mingled'. The Japanese added to the bread's various flavours by sprinkling soy sauce over it, and then decided to go back to rice, in spite of the pall that shrouded its growth.

In the old Buddhist days, the flesh of cattle was considered quite unfit for human consumption and shopkeepers who sold any sort of meat were liable, so the tale went, to have crippled children born to them as a punishment. But now the central government itself could not find enough kind and gracious things to say about meat. It was a fine food which would strengthen the physique of the nation, make men out of boys and provide built-in immunisation against cholera – a disease which foreigners, who ate meat, contracted less frequently. Encouraging pictures were issued showing a strong, new Japanese youth tucking into a sturdy, body-building beef stew and gazing reverently at a gilt watch lying on the table beside him. (Watches, like meat, were all the rage. 'A good omen for future punctuality among the natives,' commented a local reporter.) Soon, the Emperor ate his first steak and there was the usual rush to follow the royal example. Shops advertising 'cowmeat and pigmeat' multiplied and the interior of the deep woods, into which only makers of charcoal used to venture, now cracked to the sound of rifles and hunters dragging back the carcasses of deer – the flesh of which was often called 'Mountain Whale' by the Japanese, a fishier and therefore more palatable name. Meat prices increased and steak-hungry foreigners called for more stock farms. 'It is lamentable', complained the seldom-satisfied *Mail* reporter, 'to see the beautiful hills which might be rendered capable of supporting incredible members [*sic*] of sheep and cattle as deserted and unutilised as they are.' Best-seller of the day was a cook-book called *The Secrets of Western Cuisine*, which explained, with clever illustrations, how to eat with a knife and fork, roast a joint and even prepare a ram for slaughter.

Multifarious and marvellous indeed were the secrets of the West and the Japanese wanted to try them all – post offices, brass bands, cameras, the Gregorian calendar (introduced in 1873 to replace the old lunar calendar), banks and billiards for example. The first native billiard club was opened in Kobe in 1875; there was a table with a red and white squared cloth, the balls were of *kiaki* wood, the cues tipless and all the 'mods' of Kobe gathered there to roll the balls along, eat steak and smoke in the sophisticated western manner. Tobacco for pipe-smoking had been introduced by the Portuguese over two hundred years before, but the modern cigarettes were, apparently, much better for you. 'Of smokes,' announced an advertiser in an English-language newspaper, 'our Cigarettes is preasure to the Tongue and give the Healthiness to Hers and Hes'.

A few copywriters' mistakes were excusable enough, for, to the Japanese at the time, not only the concept of advertising but the institution of the press itself were new. One of the first vernacular newspapers, mainly a government mouthpiece, appeared in the early seventies and was called *Shimbun Zasshi* – 'a Budget of News'. In its prospectus, the editor hoped that his readers would 'find much to wonder and rejoice over in the things between heaven and earth which are foreign to their own experience, then they will see that those who only know one corner cannot help being rustics, and that the summer-insects are laughed at for disbelieving in the existence of ice'.

The paper went on to express concern for those who, 'living at a distance, do not know how the general government is carried on, and will be likely to be led into doubt and error'.

The important function of explaining political action to the people soon got the newspapers into trouble. Other papers appeared during the seventies and sometimes they were vehemently, even slanderously, critical of official government policy. This led to the passing of laws which seriously restricted press freedom and the beginning of a long and bitter battle between the reactionary members of the government who favoured suppression of many forms of public debate, and those, both inside and outside the political sphere, who agitated for popular rights and the liberty of free speech. The editors of liberally oriented newspapers were often arrested and spent almost as much time in prison as they did at their editorial desks.

However, when the first newspaper appeared few challenged its right to existence nor its contention that it was essential to develop understanding of the country's modernisation process in the outlying provinces. It undoubtedly was easier for people in the cities and treaty ports who could actually see westerners wearing watches, enjoying healthy cigarettes, reading newspapers, and who were in contact with their own progressive civil servants and administrators. To the rustic 'summer-insects' however, not words like 'ice' exactly, but certainly terms like 'bank', 'advertisement' and 'telegraph' were utterly mysterious – it was rumoured for instance, that when the first telegraph lines were erected across their fields, the peasants stared at them for hours hoping to see the messages go by.

Even the vitally important rural matter of the rice harvest was suddenly subject to change. For centuries, the way to thresh rice had been to pull the stalks through a comb of iron plates – slow but sure, and everyone did it. But now some of the more prosperous farmers were getting hold of these new-fangled machines instead. You tipped your harvest into this gadget, turned a handle and the rice was threshed in a trice.

It was simple enough, but the peasants were suspicious of it at first.

Nor was this all. Those same wealthy farmers were suddenly permitted to ride horseback along the public highways and wear loose silk jackets and trousers – two prerogatives of *samurai* and other noblemen for as long as anyone could remember. Now, it seemed, *samurai* were not nearly such important people as you had been brought up to believe, while *eta* on the other hand were suddenly of more consequence. *Eta*, in fact, had not been people at all until 1871, but untouchable outcasts who had done the country's dirty work, such as slaughtering animals, burying the dead, assisting at executions, making leather goods from old hides. Traditionally, *eta* had had no human rights to existence and they had lived in segregated villages which also did not officially exist as they had always been ignored when measuring road distances. Thus, in Tokugawa times, a twelve-mile stretch of road which went through a mile of *eta* habitations was posted as eleven miles! But in 1871 the government announced that *eta* could now live and work where they liked and that they were even to share the same class-name (*heimin*, meaning commoner) as the peasants themselves.

In short, the idea seemed to be that everyone was to enjoy these new phenomena called 'rights and freedoms of the people' – as one political philosopher of the time, Ueki Emori, emphasised by addressing his tract on the subject to 'Mr Farmer, Mr Merchant, Mr Fisherman, Mr Samurai, Mr Doctor and Mr New Commoner'. A man who thought along similar lines to these was Fukuzawa Yukichi who had visited Europe and America in 1862 and was already established as a leading authority on things western. Fukuzawa understood that if the Japanese were fully to reap the benefits from the new technologies, they must change, or at least modify, many of their most deeply rooted moral and social attitudes. The ethical, social and political laws of western nations were founded, Fukuzawa realised, on concepts such as the liberty of the individual, personal equality and the desirability of material self-advancement.

But these concepts were only half-understood or even totally unfamiliar to many Japanese who unquestioningly accepted the moral teachings of Buddhism, Shintoism and Confucianism. Simply to borrow the modern amenities and outward forms of western society without understanding its basic philosophies was like wearing a fancy-dress costume and mask all day – ultimately an unsatisfactory and uncomfortable practice. Having reached this conclusion, Fukuzawa felt that his function and that of his fellow intellectuals was to reform, redirect and illuminate the minds of the ordinary people in order truly to fit them for the modern world.

And so, to return to the puzzled peasantry, then the great bulk of the ordinary people of the country, it was clear that they needed more education, more explanation, for it was misunderstanding and misinformation that caused trouble. A classic case in point, quoted by Sir George Sansome, was that of military conscription. It was announced that all male commoners between certain ages were to be conscripted for a spell of military service – the Blood Tax, as the government rather tactlessly termed it, meaning the readiness to give one's blood for one's country. But surely, the peasants reasoned, they who had never been permitted to as much as carry a sword, were not now to be allowed to fire a cannon or sight a rifle? Of course not; the Blood Tax they decided, meant something much more sinister. It so happened that one of the few foreign articles country folk were familiar with was the cheap red woollen blanket which they wore round their shoulders in cold weather. Clearly, the government's plan was to draw their good peasant blood from them in pailfuls and sell it to the foreigners who needed it for the wonderful fast colour of their red blankets! A bloody tax indeed.

The peasants tried to remedy matters. They took up their stoutest staves and collected a few large stones and they went in a bunch to the residence of the Governor of the province and they handed in petitions which stated that, for instance, they 'did not wish to change the calendar, to cut off their topknots, to have foreign education, books or customs introduced among them'. And when no one paid much attention, they belaboured a few officials with their staves and threw their stones at the local offices of administration, and that was about all they could do. About two hundred peasant uprisings occurred during the early years of the Meiji era, but they were all ill-organised and politically ineffectual.

These uprisings were not, however, actively directed against individual westerners whom country folk seldom saw and whom, when they did see, they sometimes treated with an awed deference that was reminiscent of the Japanese approach to foreigners when they had first come to the country twenty years before. The experience of an ordinary British traveller who arrived at the remote mountain village of Teradomori in 1874, would have seemed more appropriate some two decades previously. 'We were waited upon by six *yakunin* (government officials) who were each armed with a small sword, portable inkpot, pencil and pipe and tobacco pouch in his girdle and a small stick in his hand. One of them walked before us, the others following. The foremost cleared, as it were, the street with his stick; children were taken up and put down softly in the neighbouring houses, inhabitants standing in front of their houses were ordered to kneel down; by the incessant cry of "*kassa, kassa*", horseleaders were ordered to take care of their horses, which were as quiet as possible, but, frightened by the noise of the *yakunin*, began to kick and trample, passers-by were ordered to take off their hats at the cry of "*oashi, oashi*". ... The most curious incident of our progress was the furious look and cursing, "*chiku-sho*" (damn you!) which a *yakunin* cast upon a cock that dared to crow at the moment we passed!'

But behaviour like this was something of an anachronism even in 1874 and, within a few years, the number of foreign travellers to remote areas increased to such an extent that no one bothered any longer to hush the cocks as they went by. Peasants soon discovered the advantages of riding horses and using threshing-machines; they found that their sons did not return from military service drained bloodless; by the end of the decade overt unrest among the commoners had died away. The only really consequential uprising against the central government's policy of modernisation was one of the last, but it was instigated not by the peasantry, but by leaders of the southern Satsuma clan in 1877. Bitter fighting between groups of rebellious warriors and government forces went on for a few months before the insurgents were defeated and their strong chief, Saigo, was killed during their last stand.

Perhaps the most vital single factor that helped to dissolve the rebelliousness, the myths and awe, the reactionary fears, was the government's enterprising educational policy. Before the Meiji era a quite high percentage of commoners' children had received at least a short rudimentary education; more advanced knowledge was imparted mainly to the sons of the nobility and *samurai*. This higher learning, however, involved a great deal of rote memorisation of ancient Chinese classics and history – as a secretary at the British Legation put it, perhaps a little unfairly, 'The tendency of the whole system of education among the Japanese in the past was to magnify the memory of things imparted through the senses and minify the reasoning powers.' Now, everybody's intellectual powers were to be magnified by the Ministry of Education's magic wand that was to wave over the Old and make it New. The Ministry, formed in 1871, was given the task of eradicating illiteracy throughout the country within a decade. 'It is intended', stated an official government address to the people made the following year, 'that henceforth education shall be so diffused that there may not be a village with an ignorant family, nor a family with an ignorant member.'

School attendance was made compulsory for all children over six, American text-books and teaching methods were introduced and English adopted as a required foreign language in secondary schools. These measures resulted in the first of several heydays for qualified English teachers, or indeed, for any wandering unemployed foreigner who cared to lay claim to pedagogical talents. And there were too many in the latter category, as a report in *The Japan Mail* of 1873 points out: 'It is unalloyed truth to say that the majority of the "Professors" in

44

the schools of Tokyo were graduates of the dry-goods counter, the forecastle, the camp and the shambles, or belonged to that vast array of unclassified humanity that floats like waifs in every seaport. Coming directly from the bar-room, the brothel, the gambling-saloon or the resort of boon companions, they have brought the graces, the language and the manners of these places into the school-room.'

Illustrative after-dinner tales current at the time support the *Mail* correspondent's contention. For instance, a semi-literate American sailor had jumped ship, started an English Academy in Yokohama with himself as Principal and made a fortune in a couple of years, and the Board of Public Works in Tokyo, which was charged with the unenviable task of importing somehow from somewhere everything that new Japan suddenly wanted, had sent a memo to its London agent asking for

1 Professor of Electric Sciences,
1   Do   Mining
2 Blast Furnaces

Well, perhaps – or perhaps it didn't happen quite like that. The main drift was certainly clear, however: practically any young man of some education from America or Britain who turned up in Japan during the 1870s was pretty sure to be offered a job in the teaching profession. It was a fairly painless way of seeing the country; the word got around, and many who heard it went.

III

One of the westerners to climb upon the educational bandwagon of the 1870s was Arthur Maclay, a smug young American from New York without academic qualifications, who went to Japan in 1874 'on spec' and was soon offered a well-paid teaching post in one of the northern provinces. Much impressed with his own sudden rise in status, Maclay described his new situation in gloating terms: 'A foreign teacher's house is generally the best in the city and occupies a site where only the relatives of *daimyo* (noblemen) were formerly permitted to live, and he finds himself decidedly the leader of fashion. All the scholars pattern after him as closely as possible and receive no small amount of social distinction from being under the tuition of a foreigner. The head men of the city will be proud to visit and receive visits from him' . . .

Maclay and others of his stamp relished all this greatly at first – the intimacies with the local 'head-men', the personal retinues of cooks, grooms and 'boys', their rank, particularly in the remote provinces, as the high priests of enlightenment and modern culture. Students, hungry for crumbs of western wisdom escorted the foreigner on all his walks, gently bribed him with generous presents to teach them after school-hours, besieged him, in fact, with a feverish, puritanical industriousness that impressed, but soon unnerved, the less dedicated pedagogue. 'There are the Idleness and the Industrious in the world,' explained an earnest pupil to Maclay in his weekly composition. 'In Japan, Idleness are there great, but Japan commenced to civilisation, therefore Idlemen became of little number and there began to go to school.' 'This composition', concluded the writer, a sorry linguist but capable of grasping the moral essentials, 'is mistaken and I was sick and cannot so good, but always Idleness is Wrong.'

This stringent principle also ruled the lives of the students at Tokyo's new Imperial College, as William Dixon, a much-in-demand professor of engineering there, describes with reluctant admiration. His pupils, youths in their late teens, were forbidden on pain of instant expulsion to drink any kind of liquor, or 'amuse themselves in tea-houses with the singing girls', or go out after dark, except for a nine-o'clock extension on Saturday. They studied after classes, in bed at night and, when the lights were turned out in the dormitories, Dixon remembers seeing them crouched under the dim lamps in the corridors, wearing coats and mufflers over their nightclothes, text-books in their numbed hands, muttering English verb conjugations to each other. Dedication mastered the classrooms; no further

A concert at the Rokumeikan or Deer Cry Pavilion, a social club devoted to the dissemination of western manners and customs

Yokohama's Gaiety Theatre where dramatic scenes 'set in a rich gold frame' delighted western audiences

Yokohama's race-course—a photograph taken in 1870

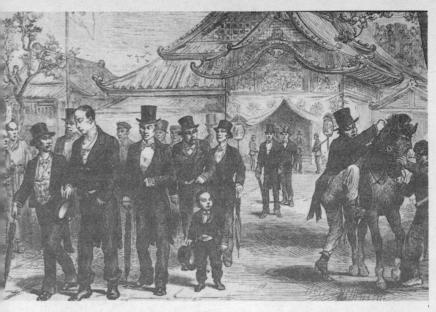

Western dress replaces traditional Japanese wear for formal occasions: here government officials leave after an audience with the Emperor

Young Japanese instrumentalists in Mr Fenton's 'Satsuma band'

The opening of the Yokohama Post Office in 1875

Consulates and ships — a typical treaty port scene

A Japanese station, western style

The British Consulate at Yokohama — one of the most impressive official buildings

A church at Sapporo, Hokkaido, with converts

A 'Japlish' sign of the times

A missionary disappearing into the hinterlands with bundles of texts, and a bicycle

Isabella Bird

Public-spirited Smith: 'one of the most energetic and indefatigable men who ever went to Japan'

An elaborately decorated 'Pullman car' or jinrikisha

discipline was required for students like these, who sought proficiency in Chinese and Japanese, English and German, mathematics and engineering, physics and military tactics all at once.

The same conditions of spartan industriousness prevailed in most of the provincial secondary schools. Lacking more appropriate buildings, these schools were often established in temples, empty fortresses or former *daimyo* residences. Wind whistled bleakly through unheated rooms; piles of tattered books mildewed against damp walls; at noon, schoolboys bolted down cold rice-balls and then got on with extra study; if they were lucky, there were benches to sit on, if not, they squatted on stone floors. And, like their elder brothers, how remorselessly avid they were for understanding! Every westerner who taught them seems to have recalled with a shudder the sound of hundreds of skinny-legged, wideawake boys as they scrambled and clattered in their wooden clogs across the cobbled courtyards the moment the school gates opened at eight o'clock – literally panting to reach their desks!

Not surprisingly, the turnover in foreign teachers was rapid; and many broke their contracts, either to flee homewards or to accept a yet more lucrative post. Still, there were a number of foreign professors who did all they could to meet the country's need and who, sometimes, stayed for years, fascinated by the sheer magnitude and intensity of its educational ambitions, eager to take part in its great leap forward. One of these was William Eliot Griffis, a lecturer at Rutgers College, New Brunswick, who was invited by the Lord of the province of Echizen, in western Japan, to go to his provincial capital, Fukui, and there to 'organise a scientific school on the American principle and give instructions in the physical sciences'.

It was a considerable trek in those days from New Brunswick to Fukui. There was for a start, the journey to San Francisco by Central Pacific Railroad across the wild lands of the American West. There were no proper stations between Omaha in Nebraska and Ogden in Utah and Griffis took a four-day stock of cooked provisions to see him through. The train did halt occasionally at various desolate watering-places, where Griffis saw 'plenty of wild Indians with scalp locks, one or two scalped white men . . . and squaws who, not knowing what a nickel coin was, but not ashamed to beg, would throw away as a joke and fraud, money fresh from the mint at Philadelphia'. The empty spaces lurched tediously past the carriage windows; antelopes and prairie dogs, bears and buffaloes seemed their only inhabitants. And then the monotony of the train journey was obliterated in the longer monotony of the twenty-seven-day Pacific crossing, when every traveller, Griffis suspected, 'however seaworthy, yearns in his secret soul for the sight of land again'.

Griffis reached land at last just after the Christmas of 1870 and soon began the last stage of his jumbled, arduous journey – from Yokohama to Fukui. The travellers – Griffis, an interpreter and a seven-man escort – went by steamer to Osaka and there boarded a *yaka-bune*. Poled gently over the icy waters of the Yodo river, Griffis watched the thatch-roofed villages slide past, the creaky turnings of the grist-mill wheels that were anchored on rafts at the stream's edge, the white flash of heron and stork among the undergrowth on the bank, the occasional baleful hawk flapping a protesting wing overhead. It was oriental time now; there was no hurry. Griffis was taken to see the great Shinto shrine on Pigeon Peak near Fushimi and its atmosphere of lofty, uncluttered calm impressed him deeply – as foreigners were often impressed, perhaps against their wills, by the dignity of this alien faith. He was, the priests said, the first westerner ever to pass that way and so he was shown all the temple treasures – carvings, ornaments and the battered remains of a 'golden gutter' which the famous warrior Hideyoshi had bestowed 'to collect from the birds the sacred droppings of the Sanctuary'. The next halt was to point out to Griffis, an historian by inclination, the site of the biggest battle in the civil war of the Meiji Restoration which had taken place just outside Fushimi only two years previously. Here the army of the last of the Tokugawa Shoguns was routed, its men felled by the hundreds, Griffis relates, as they stumbled along the narrow causeways across the paddies, only to 'receive into their bosoms the canister from the [enemy] cannon' and soon, he was told, the fields around Fushimi were 'piled with dead men like bundles of firewood'.

At Fushimi, Griffis was greeted by his new bodyguard of five *samurai*, with their attendants, who had travelled over a hundred and thirty miles to escort him to their capital. And a very long one hundred and thirty miles it seemed, so leisurely was the pace, so increasingly wild and icy the open countryside. They stopped at the home of a mountain hunter to see the enormous carcasses of three wild boar lying, still tusked and damp, on the floor, while the owner proudly demonstrated the light, bayonet-like spear with which he had transfixed over a hundred other victims so far that winter. At many, too many, other places they just stopped – to drink tea, to gossip, to show the foreigner off to the villagers and warm themselves by the fires that were lit in the middle of the house-rooms and hung about with pot-hooks and iron-racks for smoking bean-cheese, trout or monkey meat.

Twelve miles from their destination came the final night's halt, for the formal greeting by one of the Lord's officers (who presented Griffis with a duck and a box of green and yellow sweetmeats) and for the first of many celebratory dinners, with waiting-girls 'acting as Hebes' and his *samurai* companions performing 'what might be called stag-dances, from their novelty and vigour'. The next day Fukui appeared rather casually on the horizon, not the 'vaguely grand, mistily imposing' city of Griffis' imagination, but 'a dark vast array of low-roofed houses, gables, castle towers, tufts of bamboo groves' – a gentle, quiet place in fact, which after all that long journeying seemed to the westerner to be at the uttermost ends of the earth.

With their customary solicitude the Japanese had 'foreignised' a house for their first American guest. It contained a Peekskill stove, a bed, washstand, chairs; knives and forks were supplied for the next celebration feast. Nothing was too good for the newcomer. He was presented with a coal-black charger called Green Willow and a *betto* (attendant groom), who, in the traditional fashion of *betto*, was 'tattooed from neck to heels with red and blue dragons'; he was also offered 'the fairest and brightest maiden in the town' whom, Griffis explained, 'I might bring to my house and make my play-mate'. But her, of course, he refused and proudly tells us so, in the manner of many nineteenth-century male travellers who enjoyed not only preserving their unimpeachable virtue in such circumstances, but telling their readers about it afterwards.

And so, fairly well-equipped, William Griffis from New Jersey settled down to a teacher's life in Fukui. It was a typical provincial city of its time, containing some 12,000 inhabitants, 2,849 houses, 25 inns and 34 streets along the centres of which clear mountain water was conducted through stone channels and in these the citizens washed their dishes and their clothes. The city was known for its ironworkers who wrought plough-coulters, hoes and broad flat knives, and for its makers of noodles, hempen cloth and sound straight arrows. Griffis taught in a school stuffed with some eight hundred students who were studying their own, English and Chinese literature as well as medicine and military tactics. They were nearly all the sons of *samurai* and, when Griffis first arrived, were still proud and stalwart upholders of their hereditary status. They were adept at fencing, wrestling and trials-of-strength and, in addition to their scholarly equipment – inkstones, brushes and sticks of ink wrapped in silk – they all came to school wearing a short ornamental sword and a vicious-looking long sword tucked in their girdles. Rather to Griffis' relief, they deposited the latter in the school's 'sword-room' while they were in class. This particular cause of foreign unease was soon to be removed. In 1876 the government announced that the wearing of swords by *samurai* and their sons was forbidden – an injunction which dealt a heavy blow to their self-esteem, for sword-carrying had been a traditional and treasured *samurai* right for centuries. But, early in 1871, Griffis' pupils were happily unaware of the changes that were so soon to overtake them and, as he says, 'with their top-knot, cue and shaven mid-scalp most of them with bare feet in their clogs and with their characteristic dress, swagger, fierce looks, bare skin exposed at the scalp, neck, arms, calves and feet, with their murderous swords in their belts, they impressed upon my memory a picture of feudalism I shall never forget'.

But however feudal their mien and their social attitudes, these boys, like all their compatriots, yearned for western knowledge. When, with the help of his interpreter, Griffis demonstrated chemical experiments, the lecture-hall was jammed with spectators – students, staff, local officials – who watched with fascination the mysterious glow in the test-tube, the mingling of the seemingly incompatible elements. The craving for instruction among practically the whole population of Fukui was impossible to quench, and Griffis soon found himself giving lectures, both in and out of school hours, on just about everything – 'physical and descriptive geography, geology, chemistry, physiology, microscopy, moral science, the science of government, the history of European countries, various arts and manufactures and our social system . . .'. Bearing in mind the limitations of Griffis' own knowledge, the intellectual background of his students and the insufficiencies of his interpreter, this seems a rather ambitious programme and one can imagine that the notes which were indefatigably scribbled as he talked contained some pretty weird interpretations of western life and institutions.

However he was trying to help and the people of Fukui were embarrassingly grateful. Every morning, Griffis tells us, his desk was laden with gifts – not merely the conventional sweetmeats, sponge cakes and bouquets of plum blossom, but boxes of persimmons or salmon-trout, coils of water-blue or peach silk corded in red and white, bronze carvings, glass sponges, legs of venison, shoulders of wild boar, a goose just plucked or a duck caught over the hills at dawn in one of the huge triangular nets set in a bamboo frame that skilled hunters could toss twenty feet in the air. Griffis was surprised and warmed by their liking for him. 'From the prince and officers to the students, citizens and children who learned to know me and welcome me with smiles and bows and a "good-morning teacher", I have nothing to record but respect, consideration, sympathy and kindness', he wrote.

In spite of the cordiality that surrounded him and the satisfaction he gained from teaching those who wished to learn, two matters bothered William Griffis considerably during his stay in Fukui. Firstly, he was a religious man and the complete absence of the anchor of Sunday as a day of meditation and community worship fretted his soul. He was allowed to keep the day as a holiday, but what to do with it in this 'Sabbathless land' where there were 'no church-bells pealing, no church, no pews, no pulpit, no streetcars, no pavements, no Sunday school and no familiar friends'? On his first day of rest Griffis walked the heathen-busy streets feeling totally alien and bereft; later he was able somewhat to assuage his need for Sunday-style activities by holding Bible-classes for his more earnest and pliable students (a tacit concession allowed him as a lonely foreigner, for the edicts against the preaching of Christianity were not yet removed).

The second matter which troubled Griffis admitted of no such even half-way satisfactory solution; it was intangible, and anyway, he was probably wrong to worry about it. The point was that Griffis had been installed in a beautiful, two-hundred-year-old 'shaggy-eaved' Japanese house of some twelve spacious, quietly-matted rooms which had, in the past, been the setting of many time-honoured family festivals and gracious household rhythms. The house was enclosed within a ten-acre estate and the long garden contained trees planted in the sixteenth century which had grown into 'tall and grave sentinels of mighty girth and widespread limbs that measured their height by rods and shadows by furlongs'. In that garden, down the years, 'children caught their first butterflies, began their first stratagem by decoying the unwary fish with the hook and picked off the lotus petals for banners, the leaves for sun-shades and the round seeds to eat or roll like marbles'. The noble mansion was encrusted and redolent with memories of this ordered, insulated, feudal family life which, Griffis was very aware, he and others like him had come from the West to destroy. He loved the place, especially the sad whispers of the ancient garden at night, moonlight sifting through the firs and silvering the surface of ivy leaf and moat. And as he strolled among the lotus-lined paths he kept asking himself the same question: 'Why not leave these people alone? They seem to be happy enough; and he that increaseth knowledge increaseth sorrow.' Should he have come here at all? Having come, should he leave at once? And he winced to remember that his dining-table had once been the family oratory, that his stiff shirts now hung to dry on the bamboo poles from which, in days gone by, bright paper carp had flown on Boys' Festival Days in honour of the sons of the house. But in his less melancholy moments Griffis understood that the patterns of the past for which the house had stood were doomed in any case, whether he stayed there or not; the most effective and helpful role he could play was to teach his pupils what to expect from the future.

And the future overtook Fukui with great rapidity and force during that year of 1871. One summer day a messenger arrived from Tokyo bearing a laconically brief but dire proclamation: the former divisions of the fiefs were abolished, and sinecure offices were to be reduced; feudal domains were to become prefectures under the administration of the central government; officials were to be appointed direct from Tokyo. To the provincial *samurai* and their sons the news came as a thunderbolt; 'there was commotion in the school', Griffis recorded; teachers, officials and students grew pale-faced and some of them 'strode to the door, thrust their swords into their belts, stepped into their clogs and set off with flowing garments and silk coat-tails flapping to the leeward in a manner quite theatrical, just like the pictures in Japanese books'. But the drama of protest was denied these men and the far-sighted among them understood that many of the changes were beneficial to the country. Legions of lackadaisical minor functionaries, 'the lazy rice-eaters' Griffis calls them, were made redundant; Fukui's municipal affairs were managed by seventy civil servants instead of the five hundred officials formerly employed; four instead of fourteen administrators ran the school; Griffis found himself with two instead of eight gatekeepers and welcomed the reduction.

Just in case active rebellion was contemplated in remote areas such as Echizen, a further proclamation soon followed the first: the Lords of every province (who would probably have been the ringleaders of any organised revolt) were at once to relinquish their estates, titles and their attendant *samurai* and retire to private life in Tokyo. Griffis, who is adept at giving flesh and spirit to the bare outlines of the country's political upheavals at this time, movingly describes the farewell ceremony held for the Lord of Echizen, who obeyed the proclamation without overt protest. From dawn on the day preceding the Lord's departure the streets of the town were filled with processions of *samurai* and their attendants moving, like funeral cortèges, towards the ancient castle. At nine, Griffis also entered the main hall to watch the scene. 'Arranged in the order of their rank, each in his starched robe of ceremony with shaven crown and gun-hammer top-knot, with hands clasped on the hilt of his sword resting upright before him as he sat on his knees, were the three thousand *samurai* of the Fukui clan.' Griffis, a sympathetic observer, fancied he could read their dismal thoughts: 'Must we whose fathers were glorious knights and warriors and whose blood and spirit we inherit be mingled hopelessly with the common herd? What are we to do when our hereditary pensions are stopped entirely or further cut to a beggar's pittance? Is the *samurai* to become less than a trader? What is the future to bring us?'

There was a sad resigned hush as the Lord of Echizen, uprooted like his warriors, entered the hall. He was a stern-faced man in his mid-thirties, wearing wide purple satin trousers, an 'inner robe of white satin and outer coat of silk crape of a dark slate hue embroidered on sleeve, back and breast with the Tokugawa crest. In his girdle was thrust the usual side-arm or dirk, the hilt of which was a carved and frosted mass of solid gold.' The *daimyo* moved silently to the centre of the hall and his chief minister, in a subdued voice, recounted to the rows of bowed heads before him the clan's glorious history of past achievements, ending with an explanation of why the lord was now forced to leave his people and an adjuration that the *samurai* would completely transfer their allegiance to the Emperor. The next day, watched by crowds of weeping citizens, ranks of immobile warriors, the Lord of Echizen left his castle and his province.

Once the *daimyo*, the king-pin, had gone, the old structures collapsed as quickly and unresistingly as sand-castles at high tide. Three companies of Imperial troops wearing smart French-style uniforms arrived to occupy the city barracks; the military school for young *samurai* and the arsenal which supplied it were closed; the outer walls of the castle were demolished and its moat filled up, its entrance gates were broken down and their copper ornamentation stripped off and sold. Many of the spacious and wealthy town houses, similar to the one in which Griffis lived, were converted into shops, and the shopkeepers, pleased with their larger premises were also delighted to sell 'all the paraphernalia of the feudal days' as Griffis termed it. Studded harnesses, leather and iron suits of armour, bronze stirrups, burnished spears, silver-horned helmets, lacquer boxes containing jewelled hair ornaments, ivory carvings, goblets – all these treasures were 'going dirt cheap'. The remaining servants of the remaining *samurai* brought them along to the shops on horseback and then went to market to auction the remaining horses.

Suddenly, it seemed to Griffis, Fukui had become a city of remainders, as had many of the former provincial capitals at this time. When the feudal lords left, many of their ablest retainers left with them and they in turn, of course, took away their sons who were often the cleverest students in schools such as the one where Griffis taught. 'I have not over half my best students left,' he complained. The capital and the treaty ports were the places for forward-looking people; the provinces were inhabited by ice-disbelieving 'summer-insects'. Clearly too, a man such as William Griffis, expert in science and English, with a smattering of Japanese and a year's experience in a good native school, was a pearl who need not long remain buried in Fukui. The Minister of Education and the Mayor of Tokyo themselves wrote to offer him a professorship at a newly established polytechnic school, he accepted and was relieved to leave his loneliness behind. 'The ruin of temper and principle which such a lonely life threatens, are more than I wish to attempt to bear, when duty and pleasure seem both to invite me to the capital,' Griffis wrote, in defence of his abrupt termination of what was originally intended to be a three-year stay in Fukui.

After his time in the hinterlands, Griffis noticed many changes. The new telegraph poles along the Tokaido highway were promises of the future, possessors of a 'bare, grim, silent majesty as eloquent as pulses of light', and he rejoiced in the thought that their 'electric wires will soon connect the sacred city of the Sun Land with the girdle that clasps the globe'. However, the hirsute foreigners who conjured the wires into existence and who frequented, in ever-increasing numbers, the streets of Yokohama, seemed to him especially ungainly intruders upon the light-textured Japanese scene to which he had become accustomed. 'These proud fellows with red beards and hair look hideous.... How ugly those blue eyes!... How proud, how overbearing and swaggering many of them appear, acting as if Japan was their own!'

That wasn't quite fair. Most of the 'hairy barbarians' did not want to take over Japan. But as to who should have legal jurisdiction over the settlers and who should conduct municipal affairs within the treaty ports – well, these were troublesome matters.

IV

People who saw Yokohama for the first time in the early 1870s were often quite rude about it. For instance a medical missionary, Doctor Henry Faulds, makes a very cool assessment of its attractions and detractions. It is a place, he reports, 'which stands on a low swamp, ditched all over at right angles with broad shallow tidal canals filled with a concentrated essence of sub-tropical drainage which the sea does its humble best, twice a day, to assist the authorities in rendering tolerable; and bridged over at very frequent intervals with unpainted wooden structures not of a very endurable character; a town of rapid weedy growth, choked up with closely built hongs or warehouses, some really fine and well-stocked western shops, a good hotel or two, acres on acres of bonded and free stores, custom-houses, banks, shipping offices, poisoning grog-shops, two well-built churches, tiny shops of Chinese money-changers, tasteful bungalows with pretty gardens, riffraff lodging-houses . . .'.

Faulds, as it happened, was on his way to live in Tokyo and the romance of Yokohama quite eluded him. But some of the foreign merchants, who had been living in the port for nine or ten years perhaps, were fond of it and, given the chance, were wont to wax quite nostalgic about its good old days – when a fellow could walk to the marsh just behind the settlement and easily bag a brace of wild geese or duck before breakfast. It was strictly against the law, but the Japanese usually looked the other way. A quiet, easy life it was then, if confined and monotonous. The mail-packets only called about once a month and there was a race meeting at least once a week. Everyone owned a pony in those days – even if they could not rub two silver dollars together. Respectable western women (and even the other kind) were as rare as roses in January, but that famous institution the Gankiro teahouse (later known as 'No 9') was already in business. Three hundred or so pretty Japanese lasses were in attendance there, to bring tea, sweetmeats, *saké* and play *chonkina*, a game of forfeits in which every time a girl lost a round, she took off another piece of clothing. . . . Whisky was marvellously cheap too in those days, because the Customs duties were very low. And, all in all, a certain journalist from one of the London newspapers wasn't far wrong when he wrote a piece for the folk back home saying that 'the practice of sending a young chap to Yokohama to sober him up and make a respectable citizen out of him was like sending him to Hades to cool off'.

But nowadays more men had their wives and children with them and lived in proper family households, and numbers of missionaries had arrived who, in the words of one approving observer, 'did much to elevate the moral tone of the settlement'. And this was as it should be, nearly everyone agreed. For Yokohama was the country's showplace of western-style living and as such had to set an example of sobriety and wholesome morality. Peasants came from miles around to gape at bungalows with glass in the windows instead of paper, shops that sold marmalade and antimacassars and whose customers wore chimney-pot hats or flowery bonnets. And Yokohama of the early seventies had to become respectable, if only because it (just) contained one Mr W. H. Smith.

Mr Smith was himself an 'old Japan hand' by then. He had come to the country as a lieutenant in the Royal Marines during the sixties, had liked the place, taken his discharge there and stayed. He was a sturdy fellow with a broad grin who wanted people to get together in groups and be jolly with each other. He helped to form the Yokohama United Club for a start and, in 1873, became managing director of the brand new Grand Hotel on the Bund, a building which, wrote an admiring reporter, 'possesses various modern contrivances to increase comfort and diminish labour; the rooms are lofty and the furniture appropriate'. It was an appropriate setting for Mr Smith, who loved arranging functions. Tiffins were a speciality – for the members of the Cricket Club (whose committee he happened to be on and for whose turf he imported supplies of grass and clover seed from Shanghai) and even, he enthusiastically proposed, tiffin for the Emperor, who happened to arrive unexpectedly at Yokohama one day that August. But this 'public-spirited offer', as the local newspaper somewhat sarcastically called it, was declined. The reporter was well aware that, as a result of his tireless efforts for the common weal, Smith was known as 'public-spirited Smith', the man with a dream of Yokohama.

In Mr Smith's dream, the port looked almost exactly like Eastbourne: well-lit streets free of rubbish, a nice open front uncluttered by drunken sailors or ne'er-do-wells, proper parks with paths and rose-trellised entrances – a place, in short, fit for ladies and children to promenade and where they need have no fear of meeting anyone disorderly or smelling anything unpleasant. And, as, at the time, these things could not honestly be guaranteed for any lady so promenading, Mr Smith took action. He formed or chaired, or sat upon or spoke to, or voted for or quarrelled with a large number of committees whose members were of varying nationalities and, often, of very different opinions. There was then, and for many years afterwards, a preponderance of British, American and German residents (the Chinese – who outnumbered all others, seem to have taken no part in civic affairs); there were also Frenchmen, Danes, Peruvians, Swiss, Australians, Portuguese, Dutch, Russians, Belgians and Austrians on the Consular Lists so that there must have been some linguistic confusion at committee meetings, in addition to the confusion caused by the prickly, vexing nature of the matters under discussion.

There was, to cite a particularly knotty case, the question of street lighting. Whose responsibility was it to illuminate the Yokohama streets? This had never been clearly defined. The Japanese considered it was up to the foreigners – it was they who wanted the lights after all, the natives had managed quite well without them in the past. The foreigners felt it was up to the Japanese – they owned the streets and they wanted to have all the bright new western conveniences, didn't they? So, at length, they reached a compromise: the Japanese were to light most of the town, but the westerners were to light the 'Settlement' (where the foreign business houses were) and the Bluff, the high hill overlooking the port upon which most of the merchants lived. On 3 September 1870, Mr Smith, an ordinary member, attended the first meeting of the 'street-lighting committee', and it was agreed to draw up estimates and start a public subscription among residents for the one hundred and thirty-seven lamps needed. In December, the first lot of lampposts ordered by the Japanese arrived and were duly erected by them in the native quarter – 'the first rebuke to foreigners', commented the editor of *The Far East Magazine* sourly. In January the Japanese began to build a gasworks near the railway station which was ready to provide ample gas supplies a year later.

But the foreigners were determined to make a good bargain, so they delayed for several months while two companies, one Japanese, one German, vied for the concession which would give a monopoly over the supply of gas for a number of years. Each company circulated a prospectus that lauded the super-excellent quality of its gas-pipes and the unsurpassable business acumen of its manager; the German company offered to do the job at four dollars per thousand feet, the Japanese quoted three dollars and seventy-five cents. The latter, Takashima, naturally got the contract and began to increase the mire in the winter streets by laying its praiseworthy pipes. 'Light by New Year's Day, if not before', *The Japan Mail* predicted joyfully. Unfortunately however, it had not, as the committee supposed, been agreed that the company would also supply all the lamp-posts at a certain price and in the course of an acrimonious correspondence, it transpired that one of those occidental-oriental misunderstandings had occurred. The next lot of posts were to cost more and the foreigners were supposed to make up the difference. Negotiations broke down utterly when the committee received a letter from Mr Takashima ending: 'and although the contract has been entered into and completed but the term of one year is not consent for myself even as those lamp-posts and others which I bought previously were sold all, so that none is left, I can't sell so cheap, what I bought at present being thirty per cent dearer.'

Now they were really in the mire: there were some of the posts in one street and some of the mains in another and no money to bring the two together. The whole business, growled the *Mail*, its optimistic forecasts withered, 'affords fresh evidence of the thankless and fruitless nature of a task undertaken by those who enter upon matters affecting the welfare of this settlement'. Well, whatever happened, the foreigners were not paying more than the agreed price. They would finance a European Gas Company; they would form a Consumers' Association for Gas; Mr Takashima could keep his expensive posts – which he did, and used them to light the rest of the native quarter. In the autumn of 1872 huge crowds gathered in its narrow streets as the lamps flared for the first time and seemed to melt the night.

But the foreign settlement, mourned the *Mail*'s disillusioned reporter, was still 'doomed to Stygian darkness'. About three years later, its benighted residents approached another Japanese company and new subscription lists were circulated. The funds raised were still insufficient to finance a year-round lighting system, so it was agreed that the company should trim costs by 'extinguishing the lamps during such part of the night when the moon is, or should, shine, re-lighting them again as necessary'. A fellow who took an unsuspected canal-tumble on a pitch-black night could then comfort himself in the knowledge that he should have been all right as the moon should have been shining.

The only people to benefit from the continuing darkness of the settlement were the local thieves, of whom there must have been a legion, for the one-sheet evening paper ran a regular column headed 'Today's Burglaries'. Godowns, the large warehouses that were situated in the settlement away from the merchants' living quarters, were particularly vulnerable, and, in due course, a Police Committee was formed whose task was to check the rising crime-rate. The committee mustered a full-time police force of twenty men – French, British and Chinese. Four men did four-hour shifts, one on the Bund, one each for Main Street and Water Street, one for the Swamp, that low-lying area behind the town which, in spite of repeated efforts over many years, still existed and still stank. It must have been a fairly nerve-racking job to go clumping alone along Main Street at three o'clock on a November morning with fog swirling in from the sea, scuttle of rats down by the canal, creak of ancient junk, shuffle of bundle-of-rags beggar under the bridge, whine of homeless yellow mongrel and thudding pad of footsteps down a side-alley – a ship-bound sailor, a clerk returning from a 'tea-house' or a thief with a cloth over his mouth and a dirk in his belt? 'The size of the police force', groaned the *Mail*'s harassed reporter, 'is quite inadequate'; the number of robberies continued to increase.

For example the godown of Messrs Kirby & Co. was broken into for the fifth time in December 1874. Thieves pounded to pieces a large brass Chubb padlock, cut a hole big enough for a man to get through in the inner door and stole plate glass and bales of silk-waste. The police, commented the papers next day, 'were as usual in blissful ignorance until the affair was reported to them next morning'. Merchants, arriving at their business premises after leisurely breakfasts up on the Bluff, became increasingly angry to discover that yet another roll of brocade, bundle of shirtings or pile of silk-waste had been spirited away through gaping holes during the treacherous hours of darkness. They became increasingly sarcastic about the rather moribund Police Committee and its police force, which was a zealous enough little band over such matters as making sure each *betto* (groom) carried a lantern at night, but 'sinks into apathy and is perfectly powerless to assist us when people require real aid'. 'What we want,' roared 'Mr Third Time Victim' in the columns of *The Japan Herald*, 'is our own Vigilance Committee to shoot down or hang up every criminal caught.' Some of the adept burglars must also have been good at reading English, for, a few days later, the *Herald*'s offices and its editor's house were neatly burgled on the same night. From the former little was stolen, but the editor (and he gives very full details) lost, among other things, 'a marble dining clock, various silver spoons and one set of pickle castors on an electro-plated stand'.

Undoubtedly, if a Vigilance Committee had been formed, Mr W. H. Smith would have been a member thereof. But 'Mr Third Time Victim's' scheme did not materialise and Smith was able to conserve his energies for his favourite and foremost project – the creation and later the maintenance of the Yokohama Public Gardens. Smith was a very enthusiastic gardener; he had been the first to import vegetable and flower seeds from

Europe and was always inviting people to come and admire the plot behind his bungalow, upon which, he explained, grew the fattest cauliflowers in the country and the longest, sweetest beans and the most voluptuous peaches. But not content with this, Mr Smith wanted everyone to have a garden, a public one with rose-bushes, lawns and a bandstand. And, in the summer of 1870, after two years of planning, the Gardens duly opened and every Sunday evening the band of the Tenth Regiment clustered on the bandstand to 'discourse sweet sounds for the general delectation', as a reporter put it.

The sounds were delectable because they were conjured by Mr Fenton, the generally acclaimed regimental bandmaster to whom the Prince of Satsuma sent his sons to learn western-style music. The boys, with other young men from aristocratic families, were fastened inside tightly buttoned jackets, thick serge trousers and given horn, bugle, fife and drum to explore. And so inspiriting was Mr Fenton's leadership that, after three months' tuition, the boys were able to render a number of lively cotillions for the Garden's first 'outdoor soirée' – an event which also included fireworks and a magic lantern show, whose views were, unfortunately, 'dissolved by the excessively bright moonlight on that particular evening'.

For the first month, the delights of the Gardens were offered free to Yokohama's foreign citizenry, but it soon became clear that, to finance maintenance, either an entrance fee must be charged or the Gardens must be made available for private hire. This caused a royal row on the Public Gardens committee and Mr Smith was among those who resigned – the Gardens must manage without their creator. Without him, in spite of flower shows and dog shows and botanical shows and a pond with a rustic bridge, the Gardens were three hundred and fifty dollars in the red only a year after the opening. Mr Smith, smilingly, offered four hundred dollars to keep them open, a gesture which was considered during another waspish committee meeting. And suddenly, there was a new Managing Director of the Public Gardens, Mr W. H. Smith, appealing for funds. So much could go on there – croquet, bowls, archery, quoits – 'Come now,' he pleaded, 'let persons form clubs for these amusements and go into the affair heartily as in other places.'

The Gardens did, eventually, become a permanent feature of the local landscape open to respectable westerners and Japanese alike, and people began to form clubs and play there as they were bidden to do; the committee had still, in 1882, to count the pennies carefully however. A young clerk, writing in the satirical *Japan Punch* is pretty scathing about the attractions of a forthcoming Flower Show: 'Tea without milk or sugar, twenty cents a cup. Donuts ditto. Barrel organ ground by the celebrated musician "Doleful Jimmy" will play a selection of popular airs to the tune the old cow died of. Extra charge for listening to music. Extra charge for looking at flowers. No flirting allowed. The Gardens being unprovided with seats, visitors are requested to bring their own. . . .'

In the absence of seats, vagrants could often be found taking a nap under the bandstand, whence they were sent shuffling on their way by the Keeper because they lowered the tone of the place. Rudderless, homeless men these, the drifting flotsam of the East – ex-seamen, ex-soldiers, ex-stevedores, wanderers simply – who floated into Yokohama as into all the large ports between there and Bombay. For example, take Old Joe: he had first seen Yokohama in about 1860 when it was just opened for foreign trade; those were the days when 'a piece of land was cheaper than a piece of skirt', as he put it. He had bought a nice little plot for next to nothing and set up a coffee-bun-and-liquor stall there and had done quite a trade with the sailors who had nowhere much to go. But the consul and the authorities had cheated him out of his land, according to Old Joe. So he hung around in Yokohama waiting for a break, for he was a first-rate seaman and he had taken the ship's wheel in more force ten gales than he cared to remember and brought her safely through. He wasn't much at letters, but he could make the strongest sennit this side of Tilbury, he could repair lines that other fellows would have thrown overboard, he could sniff a storm brewing fifty miles away.

Men such as Old Joe usually pinned their hopes on adventurers like themselves, who had been more successful than they, but who also scorned the dull routine of regular and secure employment. For, particularly in the 1860s and 70s, Yokohama was a base, not only for large and thoroughly reputable trading companies, but for undertakings by speculators willing to gamble on the chances of the time in the hope of making quick money. There were a number of one- or two-man, one- or two-ship 'companies' in operation that would try any enterprise, load any cargo, employ any labour available, all without asking too many questions. And it was on this sort of footing that, in 1873, Old Joe was hired by Mr J. H. Snow as a mate on his schooner, the *Snowdrop*. It was a satisfactory arrangement for both parties: Old Joe found a good berth for several years and Snow had a competent man for the job.

The job, in this case, was hunting the sea-otter off the Kurile Islands and the northern coasts of Hokkaido. It was a lucrative but risky trade that demanded men with muscle, verve and stamina, a quick eye, steady nerves and a passion for adventure – all of which qualities the young Snow possessed. He had taken his first trip north the year before in a weather-battered fore-and-aft rigged schooner called the *Swallow*, with a Japanese crew and a couple of amateurs like himself, who had done a bit of whaling, but hardly knew one end of a sea-otter from the other. Luckily, Snow used to say, the sea-otters diving around the wild northern seas in those days didn't know one end of a hunter from the other either. There were few hunting-boats about, so the otters came right up alongside and stared at them with their beady eyes, just 'standing' as the term was, with heads and forepaws out of the water, 'offering the easiest target imaginable'. Snow and his companions made a tidy haul, some eighty pelts, and enjoyed every minute in spite of the filthy storms that almost broke up the old *Swallow* on the Hokkaido coast. So, with the proceeds from the trip, Snow bought his *Snowdrop*, a tight, bright, galeworthy little schooner fitted with three hunting boats. He found a couple of other fellows who were not 'of the bank clerk mentality', he found Old Joe, the best seaman in port, and the next season they returned to the north and began 'running' otters in earnest. And this was the way it was done, Mr Snow used to explain to the members of the Yokohama United Club many years later, when he had been so successful that there were not many otters left to 'run'.

The weather had to be calmish and if there was a touch of lifting fog over the water so much the better, for then the sea and sky were all milky and an otter showed up like a black dog in a snow-field. When the *Snowdrop* came within a mile or so of the coast, she dropped anchor and the small boats were lowered, each with its hunter, a couple of rowers, steersman, and a supply of Winchester rifles, ammunition, oilskins, food and a brass foghorn in case of emergency. You had to use the boats because otters keep fairly close in by the reefs and rocks usually, 'lying up in comfort in the kelp beds where it is always smooth'. And when a hunter – standing firm in the bow – had a sighting, he got the first shot, but it was seldom you bagged an otter that easily. For when the animal heard the sound he'd be off and away, diving and turning, now a long dive, now a couple of short ones, and if it was breezy he'd head upwind, and if it was sunny he'd rush straight up the sun-streak on the surface, for he seemed to know you could not see him in the glare. And then, most likely, he'd start to 'breach', that is, he'd jump clear of the water like a salmon and go tearing away at a great rate. And the nearest hunter would have to stand steady and aim just ahead of him so that he'd double back into the circle that all three boats would now be covering with their guns. Hardest to get was a three-parts grown pup that would dive again and again under the boats and 'breach' constantly – Snow had once spent three hours and three hundred shots chasing one of those and lost it. But he didn't usually lose, and he'd come back to Yokohama with more than a couple of hundred pelts aboard in his time, all carefully brushed and staked out in frames on the deck to dry. And what's more, Snow used to say, there was nothing lovelier on this earth than a good sea-otter fur, dense and thick and silky soft, pearly white near the roots, darkening to deep sheeny-black on the surface, with silvery hairs distributed evenly over it – perfect, too good for any woman's back to tell the truth; but there you were, a man had to live.

There had been some fifty-two foreign ships engaged in sea-otter hunting around the north coasts of Japan and the Kuriles between the early seventies and the mid-nineties, and they had caught several thousand otters between them and made a lot of money. But it was a dangerous trade and of the forty European hunters Snow had known during his twenty hunting years, just half had died young of drowning, shooting or suicide, and of those fifty-two ships no less than forty had been wrecked and five captured by the Russians, which was what happened to Snow himself in 1883. He and his men had been kept in Vladivostok for a couple of months, a really back-of-beyond little place in those days, he recalled, whose inhabitants mostly lived in log-cabins, and where there wasn't a bank, a hotel or, fortunately, a prison.

The trouble was the Russians wanted the otters for themselves and maintained that they were being over-hunted, which was true enough. As time went by, the otters got more and more 'educated', you might say; they learned all manner of sly tricks, and bigger boats with more rowers were needed to get within firing range of them, and you'd never catch a mother-otter napping, as you occasionally did in the early days. And that reminded Snow of a weird story that old Werner, one of his fellow-hunters, used to tell, which went after this fashion: 'Off a cluster of rocks opposite what has since been called the Naibo Shanty, we sighted an otter swimming leisurely along on her back and holding a small pup to her breast. We soon got within shooting distance and two shots simultaneously fired told her that enemies were near. The otter made a backward dive towards the shore, but as she was encumbered with the pup she made but a short stay under water and on her reappearance she was again greeted with two shots. This time the pup was wounded, but still clasping it to her breast she made continuous dives towards the friendly shelter of the rocks which were now close to us, and all our efforts to cut her off with the boats were fruitless. For two hours we chased the otter, pursuing her between the rocks. The pup had been killed during the first hour but she was holding it firmly as ever until a shot struck one of her paws and made her drop it and, in trying to regain it, she was once more wounded. Again and again she made the attempt, all the time giving utterance to the most plaintive and sorrowing cries, but to no avail. To our mortification however, we had to abandon the chase and be satisfied with the body of the dead pup which we picked up.' But that wasn't the end, as Snow explained, for no sooner had they turned back towards the big ship that lay a mile or so out, than a really wicked squall blew up; the sky went dark and the wind and waves charged against the little boat threatening to crash them all on to the rocky shore. And all the time, through the whistle of the wind and the slashing of the rain, the men could hear the shrill, mournful shriek of the mother-otter screaming for her pup – a spine-chilling, piercing note that 'sounded like a spirit crying out for justice', was how Werner put it. And then suddenly, for the men were all 'in a kind of frenzy' of horror by that time, Werner seized the dead pup and flung it out in the direction of the mother's cries. 'Then followed one tremulous wail from the watery wastes and all was still.' The wind and waves calmed almost as rapidly as they had sprung up, and the men returned safely to their ship. But Werner used to confess that he was never quite sure if it was a mere sea-otter whose child he killed that wintry day.

And that was the sort of yarn that Mr H. J. Snow used to spin to the members of the Yokohama United Club in later years, when he was grey-haired and portly, with a walrus moustache and a gold watch-chain spread across his ample waistcoat. And he used to stick his thumbs in the waistcoat and, looking defiantly round the room, say in conclusion, 'I found life worth living in those days all right, whatever other people may say about the morality of the trade.'

In the early 1870s, most of the footloose and unprofessional men who shifted in and out of Yokohama in search of work and a fortune were not over-particular about the morality of a trade, especially if, unlike Snow, they had no money behind them, no flair for making any, and no particular skills or aptitudes. And many of the weaker among them slid downstream instead of up the golden road to fortune. They ended by doing casual labour, gambling, drinking and some of them were eventually hauled in front of their national consuls, charged, perhaps, with vagrancy or pilfering grog.

As in the case of poor Bill Collins, for instance, whose sorry story, unrolled in *The Japan Mail* of September 1874, was typical of many of those chaotic, shiftless, ever-hopeful lives. Collins, the Consul was informed, 'had come to Yokohama on the P.M.S.S. *Nevada* to get employment. He did not however obtain any. He was employed on the *Golden Age* in July last. He had been to America, but not since 1855. He had been to the U.S. Consulate to see if he could get over in the *Japan* to San Francisco. He knew Captain Coy of the *Nevada* and hoped that he might do something for him. He had been some time in China trying to get some compensation from the government for a thrashing he had got in Shanghai on May 3rd last year. He was a clerk and could read and write well; he could also sweep or clean decks; he could also take in and discharge freight.' Her Majesty's Consul, one imagines, sighed wearily. He dismissed Collins and gave him fifty cents, telling him not to spend it on liquor, as he could see from the man's nose that he had a fondness for it.

The chances are that the Consul's diagnosis was correct, for he heard only too often about how most seamen and ex-seamen behaved once they were freed from the heated bowels of their overcrowded ships. They made straight for Blood Street, which was lined with bars, the 'Welcome Inn', the 'British Queen', the 'Pacific Saloon' that was run by a strong

and surly Finn. And leaning over the stained tables they drank
and grumbled. There was, perhaps, the second fireman from
the U.S.S. *Yantic*, the steward of the barque *Etta Loring*, the
local pilot of the *White Cloud*, a couple of deckhands from
the *Swanee River* and the ex-sailmaker of the *Forward Ho*.
The latter's sailmaking days were temporarily suspended, he
was saying, because he'd been accused by the Cap'n of making
a real botch up of the sails – he, who'd worked in a sail-loft in
good old London town for five years before joining that stinking ship. And one morning, as they were rounding the Cape it
was, the Cap'n went stark mad, raised his boot, kicked him
right in the face and broke his bloody nose, for no reason at
all, that he could tell. And the sailmaker had sworn he'd take
the —— Cap'n to court when they got to port. And he had,
here in Yokohama. But they were all against you, all the bleeding Consuls and bleeding Cap'ns all on the same side. So he'd
got his papers, that's what. And now he was dossing down in
the Mission and how in Hades was he to get back to London
and the missus and the sail-loft that he should never have
bloody well left? Well, at least, they said comfortingly to the
crooked-nosed sailmaker, at least they hadn't put him in irons,
like they had poor Alf Lang and his mates who had been accused of insubordination on the *Imperial*. The victuals were
awful, for a start Lang had explained to the court. 'We have
had only salt beef twice a week, pork, hard bread and pea or
bean soup or alternate dumps [*sic*]. We have had flour duff
twice a week. If we had soft bread we had no duff.' There was
also the occasional slab of gingerbread which he 'never
touched'. Worse yet, the water ration was cut to two and a
half quarts a day and that was 'stinking rainwater, while the
cow got the best water from the tank'. Then the mate knocked
down a bloke on the wheel with a pair of brass knuckles and
they had to work a twelve-hour shift in Shanghai, from six to
six, and the night before they got to Yokohama the Captain
was so wild he threatened to shoot the lot of them – except
the officers of course. But nevertheless, it was Alf Lang and
his fellow rebels who were put in irons and the *Imperial*, after

taking aboard a few not-too-fussy new men and fresh supplies of flour for duff, had sailed away.

And as the seamen contemplated the hardness of their lot in this fashion, they drank more of the 'vile compounds of cheap liquor' in which the saloons specialised and they began to want to take it all out on someone. And so there were more melancholy tales for the Consul to hear: about the two sailors who drew knives on the barman who, they said, overcharged them; about the stoker who was pushed drink-sodden into the canal, in which he drowned; about the cabin boy who punched a baggage-coolie nearly to death; about the marine who threw live coals from the stove at everyone in the saloon and then took off his shoes and began to dance; about the merry trio of British jack-tars who split each other's heads open with beer bottles until blood lay in gobs over the sawdust and spittle floors.

From the summaries of local court hearings, it seems that fights such as these were almost daily occurrences, and it was to salvage a few bodies and souls from the demon drink that, in 1873, 'nine gentlemen of the town' banded together to form the Japan Total Abstinence Society. Sundry gentlewomen of similar persuasion congregated soon afterwards to form the Ladies Benevolent Society. As a result of their joint efforts – which included the holding of Japan's first Charity Bazaar – a Temperance Hall and an American Sailors' Mission were opened the following year.

The Hall's opening was jubilant. Lots of little flags fluttered from the rafters and under them one hundred and twenty 'sailors, marines and others' sat down before tables which, 'under the superintendence of the Ladies of Yokohama, were everything that could be desired', the editor of *The Far East Magazine* declared. Songs were sung by Mr Cope at the harmonium; a speech on the joys of temperance was made by the Rev. Mr Loomis, who had laboured long among the *saké*-loving Ainu in the north. In the nearby Mission, bagatelle and draughts boards, domino tables and a reading-room were provided to give sailors an alternative occupation to drinking.

'Vagabonds' were given baths and a bed; discharged sailors found temporary berths and in 1876 the Good Templars proudly claimed that nearly two hundred had signed the Pledge Book during the previous year.

Members of the Church Committee, one of whom was, inevitably, Mr W. H. Smith, were very active in these charitable matters, and they were also deeply involved in the affair of the church organ. The first Protestant church for foreigners had been founded during the sixties, but within a few years the congregation had so swelled that a more effective musical instrument was needed to guide its singing. Mr Smith proposed that the community be asked to subscribe for a larger organ to be sent from Shanghai. But here, unfortunately, the committee over-reached itself. The volume of noise made by the new organ when it arrived was 'out of all proportion to the size of the church', opined the *Mail*, and it could 'only be used in exceptional circumstances'. Moreover, the builder had omitted to fix composition pedals so there was no way of mellowing its 'blatant tone'. A special recess had to be made to house the obstreperous instrument and the congregation were requested to sing as lustily as possible to compete with it. A few years later, however, the committee realised that the root of the trouble lay in the church not being splendid enough for the organ. A new vestry was built and Messrs Tattershall & Co. of London were called upon to perform a long-distance decorating service. In place of the bare white walls which, a church-goer complained, 'left nothing for the eye to rest upon', there came a Gothic window, lots of blue and gold curtaining, a 'peculiarly beautiful lectern', a gilded lid for the font and scriptural scrolls upon which the commandments were inscribed, 'all overhung with clusters of ripe grapes'.

Now both organ and congregation had something to celebrate and every Sunday all the residents on the Bluff donned their sprucest clothes, and the skippers and chief officers from the respectable Protestant ships in port put on their smartest uniforms and whitest gloves, and they all went to morning service and the rafters rang with their praises. When it was

over and they came out under God's own sky, bright in the
heathen land, they stood and chatted by the church gate as if
they were in Somerset or Massachusetts, and some drove off
in neat traps or even broughams, as if they were going down
a quiet English lane. But some of them hailed a very odd-look-
ing vehicle, a most comical contraption which would have
caused a real sensation in an English lane, or in New England
or, indeed, anywhere west of Suez; but in Japan they were as
commonplace as butterflies. . . .

V

They were like perambulators and you felt like a baby in them,
or royalty on a little portable throne, or an old lady cosseted
in a Bath chair, with a rug or oilskin to keep the cold from
your knees as you were wheeled along. *Jinrikisha*, literally
'man-power-carriage' was their usual name, often corrupted
by ignorant tourists to 'rickshaw'; linguists and the Japanese
upper classes called them *kuruma* – a wheel; an American
saw the aptness of 'Pullman-car' and that was their jovial-
uncle name. You stepped up into them as into a buggy; the
seats were comfortably padded, if sometimes a bit tatty;
when the runner lifted the shafts you were thrown backwards
if you were not prepared, and forward again when he put
them down.

When it rained, a hood 'of almost untearable and evil-
smelling oiled paper without opening for light or ventilation is
drawn over the guest – as the hirer is delicately called', explained one habitual passenger, 'while he is perhaps trundled
rapidly along in a direction quite opposite to that desired by
him'. Jolting down the dark roads on wet nights with these
black hoods raised, *jinrikishas* looked like 'corpulent beetles
in full scud'; but when the sun shone, radiant Japanese ladies
emerged from them 'like butterflies from a chrysalis'.

Tall runners tended to hold the shafts at an uncomfortable tilt, so short ones were most popular. *Jinrikishas* always travelled in single file, the runner in front calling out particulars of various hazards – quagmires, rice-laden carts, narrow bridges – to his comrades behind. In sudden emergency, the first *jinrikisha* stopped sharply and the following passengers were, in the words of one who had experienced it, 'shot out like the contents of a dust-cart'. Usually you rode alone, but two passengers could be accommodated fairly comfortably, as long as they were not both six-feet tall, fourteen-stone 'barbarians'. One man did the pulling, usually, but if the load was large or the country hilly another coolie pushed from behind. If you really wanted to go like the wind you could hire two runners roped to the front as well as one behind.

But even if your *jinrikisha* was rather tatty and your iron-rimmed wheels made a rare old clatter on the stony roads and even if your coolie was too tall and went in the wrong direction, it was a grand way to sightsee – bowling along on a blue day with the white mushroom-shaped hat of the coolie jerking rhythmically ahead and the sights and sounds of the fabulous Orient unfolding before your very eyes.

The *jinrikisha* was probably invented in 1868, though some suggest the summer of 1870. According to a Mr Thrapp who wrote *The History of Coaches* they weren't an invention at all but merely a revival of the old French *brouette* popular in Paris about two hundred years previously and then described as a vehicle 'compounded of a wheel-barrow and a sedan-chair with long shafts and a man running between them'. Invention or not, the *jinrikisha* made as great an impact in Japan of the 1870s as the Model T Ford in the United States some forty years later. By the end of 1871, fifteen thousand were licensed in Tokyo alone; the next year there were forty thousand and the government refused to grant any more licences because they were ruining the trade of the boatmen on the canals. But boats were slow and *jinrikishas* were helping to speed the pace generally. The British Consul in Nagasaki wrote to Sir Harry Parkes, British Minister in Japan at the time, 'these little vehicles will urge the Japanese out of their former *dolce far niente* existence so that they will now devote less time to ceremony, will appreciate its value more and will think and decide quicker than they have been accustomed to do'.

The person who introduced the *jinrikisha* to Japan then surely had a lot to answer for; but he certainly did not make a Ford-size fortune out of it, because no one quite knew who it was. The most common explanation is that the vehicle was the brainchild of an American missionary in Yokohama who wanted a convenient mode of transport for his invalid wife. Sometimes, the inventive missionary is identified as the Rev. Jonathon Goble. The odd thing about Goble is that there hangs to his name another tale which has nothing to do with *jinrikishas* but is nonetheless interesting and well authenticated.

This tale goes back nearly twenty years, to Commodore Perry's second visit in 1854. On board one of the American ships anchored in Yokohama Bay was a certain Sam Patch and, according to Clara Mason, a Baptist missionary who came briefly into the Patch story near its end, 'Sam's life was historic'. Sam had been an ordinary Japanese fisherman called Sentaro until the year 1851, when he was rescued by an American brig from a rudderless junk drifting in mid-Pacific. He was taken to San Francisco, but when he heard of Commodore Perry's expedition he begged to return to his native land aboard one of the ships. His request was granted, but, apparently, the nearer he got to Japan the more he kept complaining of *shimpai, shimpai,* which actually meant 'trouble', but which sounded to the sailors like Sam Patch. The reason for Sam's *shimpai* was his increasing fear of what his xenophobically-inclined countrymen would do to him for being so friendly with the 'hairy barbarians'. When he reached Japan everyone, including the Governor of Yokohama who came aboard the ship, assured him that he would not be ill-treated, but Sam, whose head, according to William Griffis, had 'never been ballasted with over two thirds the average quantum of wit', was, by now, as determined to stay with the Americans as he had once been to return to his homeland. So the crew agreed to keep Sam as a sort of mascot and during the rest of their long and adventurous voyage he was taught a little English and instructed in the rudiments of Christianity by a sympathetic sailor called Jonathon Goble. On returning to New York, Goble, says Mrs Mason, 'tried to make a minister of Sam, but he was a man of small intellectual ability'. Soon, Goble left the navy, made a minister of himself instead and returned to Japan during the 1860s, bringing with him a wife – and Sam, to help him in his labours. By this time Sam was quite safe in his native land, but, Griffis sadly noted, his 'notoriety has somewhat spoiled his pristine modesty'. He quarrelled with Goble and ended up as a cook in a foreigner's household. The last news of Sam is from Mrs Mason who, while visiting a Tokyo hospital, was surprised to hear him speak a few words of English and learn his story from him. She and her husband took Sam to their home where, in 1874, he ended his 'historic life'. And the *jinrikisha*? Well, Goble was certainly in Japan at the time; he had a wife; she may have ailed; he may have invented the *jinrikisha* for her. It is a nice tidy theory.

Whatever their origin, *jinrikishas* were now an established fact, and they multiplied throughout the seventies in spite of the conflicting interests of the boatmen. Their fame spread: 'the Japanese modification of the Bath Chair', announced *The Japan Mail*, 'has been adopted by the residents of Shanghai and a company has been formed there to manufacture it'. During the next few years the little vehicle wheeled gaily south – to Singapore, Colombo and Bombay. In Japan, the *jinrikishas* grew in size as well as number and privately-owned ones became very grand. Some were boat-shaped (a final insult, perhaps, to the boatmen) and their 'prows' were in the shape of dragons' or cockerels' heads; some were gaudily painted with designs showing pheasants pluming themselves on branches of cherry-blossom or hares jumping over silver moons; some were of plain white wood with rich, silk-lined interiors; some grew fringes on top, like Oscar Hammerstein's surrey. In spite of such embellishments, *jinrikishas*, as the wife of one British diplomat remarked, 'correspond to omnibuses in London. The private *jinrikisha* may be a very dainty and luxurious little affair, but as we ourselves always go by carriage, we only keep one such private perambulator for our English servants.' The best people, in short, both western and Japanese, did not use them.

There were not enough 'best people' to endanger the *jinrikisha*-runner's trade, but what did bother him was the ever-growing number of competitors, all seeking a 'guest', especially a foreign one. Professor William Dixon remembered that on his way home from the Imperial College he passed a corner where a group of *jinrikisha* coolies habitually congregated. On seeing his familiar, easily-identifiable figure approaching, they drew lots by means of cords of unequal lengths to see who would first offer him a ride. Sometimes Dixon would have preferred to walk, but the disappointment on the face of the 'lucky' runner was so keen that he usually took the unwanted trip. Dixon's coolies seemed resigned to the system, but some were very importunate and an irate writer to *The Japan Times* claimed that no less than one hundred and four runners clamoured to give him a ride during a two-hour walk through the streets of the capital.

What with the rigorous competition, the long hours and the pay, the average *jinrikisha* coolie's life was a hard one. Often the vehicle he pulled was his whole world. He leaned against it and gambled with his mates while waiting for a 'guest', he slept in it when exhausted, sat in it while eating the meals of noodles and seaweed he bought at the nearby street-stalls and kept his meagre possessions under the seat: a spare pair of straw sandals, a pipe and tobacco pouch and a paper lantern which he lit and hung on the shafts at night, so that the little carriage looked like a firefly darting through the dark. When it rained he splashed barefoot through puddles and sometimes donned a raincoat made of straw which gave him the appearance of a bedraggled porcupine; in the summer countryside he peeled off all his clothes down to a loin-cloth and stowed them under the seat too. He would have liked to do the same in the stuffy towns, but in 1871 an edict had been issued stating that coolies were to work in a suitably clothed state so as not to offend the sensibilities of the foreigners.

A coolie's rate of pay averaged about a penny-ha'penny per running mile, which was not princely, even by nineteenth-century Japanese standards. The precise amount was a matter for direct negotiation, which meant, as another peeved writer complained in a local paper, that a fellow was no sooner aboard, than he had 'to devote all his intellectual energies to the question of how much he was to pay for his ride when it was finished'. Foreigners, in particular, always felt they were being 'gypped'; one of them felt so strongly that he wrote a verse on the subject:

I went and hired a ricksha man to wheel me to the Bund
I paid him twice the native fare and straight my ears he
    stunned
Importunately clamouring, protestin' it was right
For me to shell out 'ten cents more' because my face was
    white.

The coolies' attitude was understandable because, for one thing, those with 'white' faces usually did have more money and, for another, they were more frequently in a hurry and sometimes positively enjoyed testing the speed and endurance of the runners as if they were indeed animals between the shafts. *Jinrikisha* races were held at the end of the Yokohama Race Meetings, and elsewhere one Daniel Pidgeon, a globe-trotting engineer, used stopwatch and notebook to record his coolies' running times. They ran the first twenty miles in two hours and fifty minutes without stopping, he informs his readers; they then ran in ten-mile stages with fifteen-minute breaks for tea only. They covered fifty miles in less than eight hours.

Another Englishman, the Hon. Lewis Wingfield, who visited Japan during the eighties, was so enamoured of the *jinrikisha* that he refused to travel in anything else, even when going up a volcano. So he hired five of them, one for himself, one for the guide and three for his luggage – which included a *batterie de cuisine*, a folding bed and a 'goodly store' of whisky – and proceeded to have the lot hauled eight thousand feet up the crumbly side of Mount Asama, into whose crater he wanted to peep. There were four coolies for each *jinrikisha*, one in the shafts, two harnessed to the front with ropes and one behind, and they lifted the vehicles, their occupants and the baggage up 'a veritable Jacob's ladder of stones', trembling, often, on the verge of precipices, with the outer wheel of the vehicle spinning in mid-air.

Not surprisingly, considering the hard conditions of their lives, numbers of runners died early from heart and lung diseases. Nevertheless, they were invariably cheerful and obliging men, always ready to sew a button on for a helpless male wayfarer or cook an omelette for lunch during a long journey. 'A fine lot of fellows', decided one lady traveller, 'who take a pride in their work. And it is pleasant to see their muscular legs running before you.'

The legs ran, the steam-whistles blew and Japan had two new transport miracles: the train and the *jinrikisha*. Outside the railway stations, *jinrikishas* waited to whisk away arriving passengers, the one supplementing the other. On the whole, the Japanese most enjoyed riding the trains, the foreigners adored the *jinrikishas*, because they were so quaint. There was room for both in a country which seemed less confined nowadays and in which people moved around more frequently. The frontiers were pushed farther back: governors went on tours of inspection through their provinces; officials went to investigate sites for the development of docks and factories; youths from the countryside travelled to the cities in search of work and excitement. And, as the horizons of the Japanese began to extend, so certain westerners became very impatient of the restrictions which still confined them to within about twenty-four miles of each treaty port, unless they had a special passport that allowed them to travel farther. (An easy way to obtain such a document, incidentally, was to plead that, for reasons of health, one was in urgent need of mountain air. Doctors ran a lucrative side-line in ten dollar fees earned for writing notes to this effect which aspiring travellers could present to the passport-issuing authorities!) As time went on, these passports became more or less a formality, but during the seventies the rules were still quite strict and most foreigners stayed within the treaty limits, unless their work took them farther afield. Some of the westerners who came however were not so easily controlled: the true 'world travellers' for instance, determined to discover and explore for themselves the remotest parts of the land, and the missionaries, equally determined to recover and claim for God the souls of its people.

Part Two

1878–1888

Of travellers, missionaries and things that were sometimes disastrous

The dumpy, intelligent-eyed lady who capably got herself off the ship from San Francisco and on to the Yokohama Bund during the spring of 1878 was one of the most remarkable western women ever to go to Japan. She was, in fact, one of the nineteenth century's remarkable women, though the century did not yet acknowledge this. Her name was Isabella Bird and when, at the age of forty-seven, she reached Japan for the first time, the really exciting part of her life had only recently begun.

Isabella was the sickly elder daughter of a Yorkshire clergyman, and had spent much of her youth reclining on various rectory sofas suffering from a spinal complaint, which was never really cured but which she learned to bear. She was devoted to her immediate family, father, mother and above all her sister Hetty. She first left the beloved family circle in 1854 when, for the sake of her health, she visited Nova Scotia and America. But this was a mere preliminary canter and she was nearing middle age when she began to travel in earnest – to Australia, New Zealand, Honolulu and back to America, where she took her famous ride over the Rockies, described in her quaintly-entitled, *A Lady's Life in the Rocky Mountains.* When this book was published, a few unkind reviewers slyly suggested that its author was no lady because it contained a picture of her in wide trousers and a loose jacket. This costume, Isabella tartly explained in a preface to a later edition, was a Hawaiian riding dress and was perfectly suitable feminine attire. In any case, as she added in a letter to her publisher, 'Travellers are privileged to do the most improper things with perfect propriety.'

Isabella founded her two lives on this principle. In the one she was a dignified and gracious spinster lady of Edinburgh devoted to her ailing sister and an ardent pursuit of good works, such as the provision of fishing-boats for the crofters of the Western Isles, of washing-rooms for city slum-dwellers and shelters for the local cabbies. Her other life was uncluttered by her own sense of duty or other people's difficulties: 'no door bells, no "please mems", no dirt, no bills, no demands of any kind, no vain attempts to overtake all one knows one should do. Above all no nervousness and no conventionalities, no dressing for dinner...' she wrote with relief to her sister, describing her slow voyage across the Pacific between two unknown lands.

It was the second Isabella who came to Japan, a calm, resourceful woman possessed of an inexhaustible curiosity about places, their inhabitants and the various perfections and idiosyncrasies of the natural world, and an inexhaustible courage to face both the unknown and the physical pain of her spinal disease. She was driven, too, by a masochistic urge to reach the boundaries of her own endurance and, in so doing, to escape from the ordered tempos of civilised urban life that she partly envied, but among which she could not rest for long.

Like most confirmed travellers, Miss Bird could not abide Yokohama, a 'dead-alive place' of 'irregularity without picturesqueness' was her verdict in the first of many letters to her sister Hetty, and added, 'how I long to get away to the *real* Japan'. But getting away to the real Japan presented certain difficulties, even to her intrepid spirit. There was, firstly, the crucial business of hiring a Japanese guide-interpreter for the journey northwards – for she was determined to explore the least-known parts of the country. She wanted a strong, resourceful young man with a working command of English and a willingness to endure the tough comfortless conditions she intended to impose upon herself. Rightly, therefore, she rejected the first applicant on sight. He wore 'a suit of light-coloured tweed, a laid-down collar, a tie with a diamond pin and a white shirt so stiffly starched that he could hardly bend low enough for a bow of even European profundity. He wore a gilt watch-chain with a locket, the corner of a very white cambric handkerchief dangled from his breast pocket and he held a cane and a felt hat in his hand.' The New Japanese Dandy, in fact. Isabella shuddered; there were no facilities for shirt-starching and handkerchief-laundering where she was going. Applicant number two had been used to travelling with a large retinue of servants and 'his horror at finding that there was to be "no master" and that there would be no woman-servant was so great, that I hardly know whether he rejected me or I him'.

And then, as she was about to despair, Ito appeared. He was a short, bandy-legged youth of eighteen with a 'singularly plain face', an air of stolid stupidity, a furtive glance and no recommendations whatsoever. But some strange spark passed between the two, for Miss Bird hired him on the spot, paid him his monthly wage of twelve Mexican dollars in advance and thus gained a trusty, energetic companion for her travels, who soon became 'cook, laundryman and general attendant as well as courier and interpreter' and without whose care she might not have survived the next few months at all.

The engagement of Ito took place at the home of Doctor Hepburn, the Yokohama missionary and linguist with whom Isabella was staying. Dinner parties were held for her there, and during them the local community offered her a considerable amount of gratuitous advice on what she should take with her and how she should tackle the multiple perils of the way. There was general agreement that the greatest trial of all would be the omnipresent flea and Isabella was advised 'to sleep in a bag drawn tightly round the throat' and to make profligate use of carbolic acid, insect powder and dried fleabane. The 'Food Question' was also plumbed. Tinned meats, soups, clarets and coffee were deemed indispensable; but in a footnote written after the event, Miss Bird advises the traveller to encumber himself with none of these, 'except Liebig's extract of meat'. At Lady Parkes' instigation, Isabella did take 'an india-rubber bath' with her, for which she was soon duly grateful.

And so they set off. Isabella perched on the first of many recalcitrant mares and dressed in a serviceable habit of 'dust-coloured striped tweed', high-laced leather boots and a 'light bowl-shaped hat of plaited bamboo'. Behind her rode Ito, his horse led by the first of many puzzled but helpful grooms. A pack-horse and a *jinrikisha* (which was later dispensed with) completed the procession. In addition to the bath and other sundries, they were loaded with 'a travelling bed or stretcher, a folding chair, two baskets, an air pillow', candles, 'a loose wrapper for the evenings', numerous volumes of the English-Asiatic Society *Proceedings*, 'Mr Brunton's large map of Japan, Mr Satow's Anglo-Japanese dictionary and some brandy in case of need'.

After a short stay at Nikko to see its famous temples, they plunged steadily northwards into 'the real Japan'. This, at first, was a hilly, wet land where the horses slithered across insecure muddy bridges, rivers 'crystal blue or crystal green' bounced and boomed along the ravines and steep-roofed, russet-coloured dwellings were bunched together among dark hedges of camellia, orchards of persimmon and pomegranate. Village women, 'lugging on their backs gristly babies whose shorn heads are frizzling in the sun and wobbling about as though they must drop off', came to stare at this strange foreigner and wonder if it was male or female; when, to satisfy their curiosity, Ito read out the details of Miss Bird's pass-port, they gasped in admiration. In some places, crowds waited all night in the courtyards of inns where she stayed, they clambered over adjoining walls and verandas to watch her eating, when she left they followed her to the village boun-daries in droves, 'their clogs clattering like hailstones' behind her along the cobbled main street. But Isabella was soon so weary of this 'great melancholy stare', the gawking, mopish faces. 'I should be glad', she confessed, 'to hear a hearty, aggregate laugh, even if I was its object.'

Nevertheless, the passive, undemanding curiosity of the

native people was an easy cross to bear in comparison with the active malignancy of the native horses. These animals belonged to the local transport offices which did a brisk trade in hiring out, not only pack-horses, but *kagos* (the Japanese version of the litter), *jinrikishas* (in the more civilised areas), coolie-porters and grooms. In each large village there was such an office and when large loads needed carrying to the next 'station', the clerk would summon his casual labour by beating a wooden hammer on a hollow piece of wood that hung outside the door. The harsh tattoo banged along the dusty street; coolies rolled sleepily off their siesta mats, put on straw sandals and grunted with resignation as they shouldered their burdens. Miss Bird needed but one coolie at each station and she usually found them cheery, co-operative companions; but not so the horses. Either she must have been extraordinarily unlucky in her selection of them or there was something about her that made even the most docile Japanese steed restive – although she was a very accomplished horsewoman. She went over her horse's head on the first day out from Nikko and from then on it was a continual and painful battle against the lumpy, sullen mares or the positively vicious stallions. One of the latter, whose head was 'doubly chained to the saddle-girth' nevertheless ran at every person he saw with his ears back and ready to bite them. Nor was this all. Isabella continues, 'The evil beast made dashes with his tethered head at flies, threatening to twist or demolish my foot at each, flinging his hind legs upward, attempted to dislodge flies from his nose with his hind hoof, executed capers which involved a total disappearance of everything in front of the saddle, squealed, stumbled, kicked his old shoes off, resisted the feeble attempts which the groom made to replace them and finally walked into Yokote [a remote mountain village] and down its long and dismal street mainly on his hind legs, shaking the rope out of his timid leader's hand and shaking me into a sort of aching jelly.'

The system of shoeing to which Miss Bird refers did nothing to help relationships between a horse and its rider. Iron shoes had been introduced into the country in 1856 by Townsend Harris, the first American Consul, but over twenty years later the medieval straw-shoe was apparently still used in the remote districts. The shoes were tied on the beast's feet with wisps of straw and, even if they did not untie themselves in less than two miles, they would soon become so thin that the horse would begin to stumble. A halt would be called while the groom took four new shoes from the supply dangling on the saddle-girth, soaked them in water and fitted them over the unwilling hooves. As Miss Bird remarked, 'Anything more clumsy and temporary could hardly be devised.' Thousands of shoes were plaited each year by the villagers as they sat on their doorsteps in the summer evenings; thousands of shoes were strung up for sale at every transport-station; thousands of shoes, dirty and torn, lay discarded along the bridle-paths and were collected by children and put in heaps to decay for manure.

As if the horses and their shoes were not trials enough, there was also the business of a saddle. 'Imagine,' writes another westerner, who, similarly traversing unfrequented ways, similarly complains of equestrian discomforts, 'imagine an extremely steep and sharp gothic roof of small size on which is placed, for humanity's sake, a small cushion with a handful and a half of cotton wool on each end and nothing whatever in the middle' . . . Mounted upon it, one experienced 'a see-saw rickety-rackety movement which produced a frightful sensation of nothingness in the interior and a feeling that the exterior would part asunder and fall on either side of the severing saddle'.

Those were the words of a mere male tourist. Miss Bird was made of sterner stuff; she did not come apart in the middle. But she was soon on extremely unfriendly terms with the whole Japanese equine kingdom. 'I have now ridden, or rather sat, upon seventy-six horses, all horrible,' she told her sister, after a month's travelling. 'They all stumble. The loins of some are higher than their shoulders, so that one slips forward and the backbones of all are ridgy. Their hind feet grow into points which turn up and their hind legs all turn outwards, like those of a cat, from carrying heavy burdens at an early age.' In spite of their manifest intractability, Miss Bird recorded that she never saw a horse being beaten and that 'when they die they are decently buried and have stones placed over their graves'.

The farther north Isabella and Ito went, the more appalling were the places in which they had to spend the night. In one farmhouse the only food obtainable was pickled cucumbers and mouldy black beans – washed down with their own condensed milk – and another was already over-occupied by roomfuls of silk-worms and five tobacco merchants thrumming on that 'instrument of dismay' the *samisen* (a kind of banjo). At an exceedingly isolated country inn each wall and rafter was filthy with the soot from a wood fire burning in a trench in the kitchen and Miss Bird was offered – by an apologetic landlord – 'a dark, dirty, vile, noisy room poisoned by sewage odours' and shaken by the thud of drums celebrating the end of rice-planting. Perhaps the worst lodging of all was in a room where fleas hopped in myriads over her bedding, food and the letter she was writing, where the walls were made 'of hairy mud with living creatures crawling in the cracks', where, when she lay down to sleep, parties of 'beetles, spiders and wood-lice held a carnival', horseflies buzzed in from the adjoining stable to swell the rout and clouds of mosquitoes left the malodorous pond below her window to thrum hopefully against her protective sleeping-net.

At the beginning of August the travellers were overtaken by unseasonable floods. Rivers burst across the hillsides and thundered down the forest tracks, carrying loads of gravel, uprooted trees and timbers of bridges with them into the valleys – and also Miss Bird, tied on her saddle, clutching at a noose of rope and up to her shoulders in water as they forded the bridgeless torrents, slithered up their crumbling banks and finally squelched into an isolated hamlet called Igarigaseki. Here they were marooned; boots, bags and books covered with mildew, the remainder of the precious condensed milk dissolved in water, the bed a sodden mass of mud, even the meat lozenges turning to gravy. Isabella passed the time by reading damp Asiatic Society papers, applying zinc ointment to the sore eyes of the village children (which brought them relief and made her very popular) and writing, perhaps, some of her more ponderous sentences: 'The forest trees are almost solely the *Ailanthus Glandulosus* and the *Zelkowa Reakii* often mated together with the white-flowered trailer of the *Hydrangea* genus.'

Five days later, more or less dried out, they rode the last fifty miles to Aomori, from whence they spent fourteen uncomfortable hours on a very old paddle-boat going across the Tsugaru Strait which separates the Japanese mainland from the island of Yezo, now called Hokkaido. In a dry, cosy, proper bedroom in the Church Mission House at the town of Hakodate, Isabella triumphantly records in her letter home the trail of obstacles overcome and concludes, 'How musical the clamour of the northern ocean is! How inspiriting the shrieking and howling of the boisterous wind!' And, one feels, how truly indefatigable was Miss Isabella Bird.

And for Yezo which she looked upon as the real 'real Japan', Miss Bird needed every ounce of her indefatigability. For Yezo was a wild land which even the Japanese, with all their energy and resource, had never tamed. It was an island for animals, birds and fishes. Along the hundreds of miles of storm-plagued uninhabited coasts porpoises tumbled, sea-otters dived and nosed into caves, high-finned cachelots drifted close looking for cuttlefish among the rocks and seals snoozed by shallow pools. White-tailed eagles bred on grassy ledges among the crags, the scarlet beaks of oyster-catchers flashed, pairs of albatross, plovers both grey and ringed, wild geese, waders, swans and scaup-duck cast their winged shadows over the waves when the watery sun shone, and inland, across the high, yellowish prairie grass of the plains, wolves, deer and fox roamed undisturbed, with only each other for enemy.

As for the people, as the editor of *The Japan Mail* said, when commenting on the annual trade report from the British Consul in Hakodate: 'A taste for algae, crustaceae and marine oddities are essential to happiness there. No man is fitted to live there or can be trusted not to find his mind being gradually dwarfed, who cannot glow with enthusiasm over the great oyster, the *bêche-de-mer* and the thousand varieties of seaweed which embroider the Yezo coast. It is a place which makes the good better, the wicked worse; for people there are thrown entirely on themselves.'

The writer was describing the situation there five years before Isabella's arrival, but not a great deal had changed during the interim. The 'Office of the Commissioner of Colonisation and Development of Hokkaido' had been formed as early as 1869, when the old name for this remotest province – Yezo – was officially, though not popularly, discarded in favour of Hokkaido, meaning 'The Northern Sea Circuit'. From then on, various development schemes were initiated by the Commissioner's office: any farmer or ex-*samurai* discontented with his lot was given encouragement, in the form of a free passage, several acres of land and a couple of blankets, to go there and begin farming; gangs of convicts were sent there to hew down forests and cultivate more fertile areas; a grand new northern capital was founded at Sapporo. Sapporo was provided with a Capitol – an imitation of the one in Washington, with cupola, flag and pillars – and with several florid Public Buildings round an empty square where nightjars shrieked sadly after dark. An Agricultural College was opened and so was a museum, to which, wrote Reginald Farrer, a botanist who later visited it, 'no one went except dogs in search of mates'; the only items he could find in the Botanical Gardens opposite were 'a clump of forget-me-nots, one debilitated peony and an obese polyanthus of a common kind'. The whole town, Farrer continued, was 'pompously laid out in rectangles, with splendid boulevards at right angles and over the splendour of their spacious schemes meander only shepherd's purse and dandelion interspersed with a few desultory human beings'. Sapporo, in short, was one of those disastrous projects which never really 'took' in a land that remained inhospitable and withdrawn.

Yezo's winters were long and exceedingly cold. Snow-drifts curled up to the eaves of isolated houses and people scudded along in snow-shoes made from ash-bark to pick up the birds that had frozen solid on nearby trees during the night; ink, in the pots of Her Majesty's solitary Consul in Hakodate, turned to black lumps of ice; missionaries, arriving at remote hamlets, had to thaw out their moustaches and beards by the fire before they could open their mouths to preach the Word. Inland, during the short, insect-infested summers, scattered groups of Japanese peasants cultivated areas of millet and beans; the more ambitious among them worked in the sulphur and lead mines for part of the year and came back richer, but ingrained with yellow or black dust.

Along the shores, fishermen caught herring which were so numerous in some parts that, according to one visitor, 'those nearest the beach are pushed out of the water, and the shore for miles was thus kept constantly replenished with fresh fish'. Birds of all kinds and even wolves, bears and foxes visited the beaches for tasty, free meals and, the writer continued, 'the way the seagulls just picked a titbit from the back of the neck and left the remainder of the fish, showed how well they knew the supply was constant'. Fishermen used two-hundred-foot-long nets with wide-mouthed bags at their ends into which the herring jostled each other and from which they seldom escaped. Such massive hauls provided work for months afterwards: deep iron cauldrons stood in every village street wherein the fish were boiled down to extract their oil, and tons of fish-manure was laid out on the rocks to dry in the sun. In fact, as every foreign visitor there mentioned, the typical inhabitant of Yezo smelled permanently of fish – fish gutted, fish boiled, dried, salted and stewed.

In addition to the Japanese fishermen and peasants and the few disconsolate officials who rattled round the half-finished, half-filled buildings in Sapporo, there was a small group of foreigners – shipping agents, consuls and missionaries –

92

most of whom found, after a time, that their minds were indeed 'being gradually dwarfed' by the stunning emptiness of it all. Generally speaking, the only people who seemed to really belong to Yezo in those days were the Ainu, and it was the Ainu that Isabella Bird had come all that way to see.

The Ainu were a docile, dirty, lugubrious, primitive people, forgotten and unresilient, and from whence they came anthropologists could not quite decide. At any rate, they had for centuries been pushed northwards by the vigorous Japanese until, in Yezo, they found a haven. Some dwelt in fairytale-pretty forest clearings and worshipped the gods of the trees and bushes most punctiliously; some lived near the banks of the great rivers and, in early summer, floated off in their dug-out canoes with nets made of twisted vines fastened to bamboo poles which they first whirled round their shaggy heads and threw and scooped the quick salmon up from the water, and then tossed the fish to their wives – who sat in the boat's stern and smashed the thrashing heads with stones until they were still; some lived in stilt-high huts on swampy plains dense with tall, razor-edge grasses – horse-flies, blow-flies and mosquitoes multiplied merrily there and fastened thick as plague-sores on the flesh of any horse and rider tough enough to pass their way. Others yet had fled to the extreme north where rolling fogs blotted out the sun for days on end even in summer and it was so perpetually damp that, according to one traveller, the saturated atmosphere made even the Ainu go bald.

And, if this were so, it must have been wet indeed, for the Ainu are an extremely hirsute people. And because of this and on account of their wayward lethargy and habitual grubbiness, they were despised by the Japanese who invented the legend that this hairy race had sprung from an unnatural union of a mermaid and a dog. And the Japanese avoided them when they could, denied them higher education and paid them for any services rendered in *saké* rather than money, so that they could get drunk often but never rich or powerful. And the Ainu smiled resignedly at this and obediently drank the *saké* in large quantities on every possible occasion and called it their 'official milk'.

And so, for all these reasons, when Miss Bird's guide, Ito, heard that she was absolutely determined to visit the Ainu, he 'whimpered very much' and made such a fuss that, as Isabella tartly remarked, 'you would have thought that he was going to the stake'. And when it was plain that he had no option but to accompany her, he insisted on taking for his special comfort a bed-roll, a clean kettle, some soy sauce, a stewing-pan, a chicken and 'a supply of French beans'.

The tribe they visited first dwelt in the forests and to reach them Isabella and Ito slashed and scrambled through tangled undergrowth, 'coarse reedy grass, monstrous docks, the large-leaved *polygonum cuspidatum*, several umbelliferous plants and a ragweed which, like most of its gawky fellows, grows from five to six feet high'. Here Isabella experienced a new form of equestrian mishap. Her horse sank up to its chest in a more than usually glutinous bog and she was obliged to 'scramble upon his neck and jump to *terra firma* over his ears' (and what happened to the horse she does not say). At length they came to a clearing on rising ground and there was the Ainu village, a group of thatched huts surrounded by small patches of ill-cared-for millet, tobacco and pumpkins. The Ainu chief, a sad-eyed powerfully-built man with long, thick, soft, black hair, beard and moustache, greeted them courteously and led them into his house to rest.

Inside the dim, smoke-laden room a fire constantly burned which was presided over by the chief's formidable mother, 'a weird, witch-like woman of eighty, with shocks of yellow-white hair and a stern suspiciousness in her wrinkled face'. After a day or so of this chatelaine's company, Isabella decided that she probably 'had the evil eye, as she sits there watching, watching – always and for ever knotting the bark thread like one of the Fates'. However, Miss Bird hopefully ignored this uncongenial influence and allowed herself to be installed upon the raised seat of honour at the fire's head – for which she was grateful, 'as the fleas on the floor beneath were legion'.

Soon, the evening meal was prepared by the chief's principal wife, who tipped into a sooty pot swinging over the flames a mixture of wild roots, beans, seaweed, shredded fish, dried venison, millet paste, water and fish-oil and left the lot to stew for three hours. After watching these culinary activities and smelling the odour that the pot emitted, Miss Bird would doubtless have agreed with the Rev. John Batchelor, a missionary who preached to and ate with the Ainu for about twenty years, when he feelingly remarked, 'In no sense are the Ainu epicures.' He went on to describe some of their delicacies: sea-slugs, the roots of the dog-tooth violet, which they boiled, pulped and shaped into desiccated cakes for the winter, choice parts of horse cooked in heavy bear grease and stringy, ancient slabs of dried fish.

Several Ainu men arrived to share the feast (of which Isabella and Ito declined to partake) and after it was over bowls of *saké*, across which lay strips of carved wood, were handed round. Before drinking each man dipped his stick into the wine and sprinkled a few drops on the floor as a libation to the gods; he then used the stick to keep his drooping moustache out of the bowl as he drank. Apparently one of the few really odious *faux pas* at an Ainu gathering was for a man to get his moustache wet. While they drank, Isabella, through Ito and another interpreter who knew both Japanese and Ainu, plied the men with questions about their way of life, their religious beliefs and general philosophy and took copious notes of the replies. Time scarcely mattered and, when darkness fell, the slow exchange long continued by firelight, 'aided by a succession of chips of birch bark with which the women replenished a cleft stick that was stuck into the fire-hole. I never saw', Isabella affirms, 'such a strangely picturesque sight as that group of magnificent savages with fitful firelight on their faces and, for adjunct, the flare of the torch, the strong light, the blackness of the recesses of the room and of the roof, at one end of which the stars looked in, and a row of savage women in the background.' At last they all bade her a courteous good night and Isabella climbed into her hammock which had been strung in a secluded corner, pulled her mosquito-net over her and prepared to sleep. In the flickering glow she could see one of the women still sitting by the fire sewing a robe of elm-bark for her lord; dogs whined and prowled among the refuse outside; fumes of fish-oil, smoke and *saké* caked the air; the thatch rustled with vermin above her head; it was very cold. But never mind, it was all so exciting, so weird and wonderful. 'I can only say', Isabella concludes, 'that I have seldom spent a more interesting evening.'

Miss Bird's interest in and liking for the Ainu continued unabated for the next month, during which she and Ito journeyed from one small settlement to another. By now, this really rather ill-assorted pair had established a relationship based on mutual respect and the constant sharing of privation and discomfort. If she was agreeably surprised at his resourcefulness and reliability in times of stress, he must have been perpetually astonished at her behaviour. It had fallen to the lot of few Japanese males of his time to know such a woman as Isabella Bird and he probably thought she was awe-inspiring, marvellous and not a little mad. Of course, he concealed his admiration for her, and sometimes, boy-like, he tried to taunt her firm imperturbability. He tells her on one occasion that 'Japanese men have only one lawful wife, but as many others as they can support, just like Englishmen'. At which Miss Bird calmly comments that Ito's 'frankness is sometimes startling, but probably I learn more about things as they really are from this very defect'. No considerations of propriety or prudence could, in the last resort, deflect Isabella from her hunger to know about things 'as they really are'. She continued, 'Ito is not a good boy. He has no moral sense, according to our notions . . .' Yet she liked him, he was so quick, he understood that she could teach him much – more, perhaps, than he could absorb.

One thing Ito could never understand was why this fearsome foreign woman bothered with the Ainu at all. She wanted to know so many silly things about them – the names of their gods, their family customs, the circumference of their skulls, the meaning of the designs which ornamented their pipes, arrows and cooking utensils and were tattooed on their bodies. Ainu females, in particular, were subjected to an extremely painful and disfiguring tattooing process, and Isabella describes the scene as the mother of a 'dear little bright five-year-old' made a series of horizontal cuts along the child's upper lip, following the curve of the mouth. Soot was then rubbed into the wounds and, three days later, the scars were washed with a solution made from tree-bark, so that the lip would have a permanently blue-black swollen appearance, as if the girl had a moustache like her hairy brothers. Girls' arms were also tattooed yearly from the elbow downwards so that, by the time they married, there were black crossed lines deep in the flesh as far as the knuckles. Apart from undergoing the rigours of these sinister processes, the life of Ainu women was dull, laborious and peaceful. From the soft hides of otter and deer they made jackets and leggings to combat the winter cold; where fishing was carried on, it was their duty to keep the village dogs away from the drying manure; where millet was grown, they ground it into coarse flour for their mushy puddings.

The one major excitement of the Ainu calendar was bear-hunting, principal activity for all able-bodied males. Isabella did not see this, but John Batchelor witnessed several hunts and describes what happened. In early spring the village men trooped off into the forest carrying hunting knives, spears, bows and arrows tipped with a dark red poisonous paste made from monkshood-root. Keen-eyed, with endless time, knowing the sort of places to look, they were sure, eventually, to come across a little discoloured patch in the snow under which snuggled a hibernating bear. Often, though harassed by dogs, spears and sticks and smoke from a fire lit above him, the torpid animal refused to leave his cosy hole. Some hunters believed, Batchelor explained, that bears though normally fierce, will not kill anything inside their own den. So relying on this, a particularly brave Ainu 'ties his head and face up leaving only his eyes exposed, hands his bow and arrows to his friends and, with his hunting knife firmly fixed in his girdle, makes a call on the bear in his home. The animal gets so angry and surprised at this that it unceremoniously seizes the intruder with its paws and hastily thrusts him behind its back. The Ainu now draws his knife and pricks the beast behind and this is said to make it take its departure.' Lumbering into the unwonted light, the bear was shot at with poisoned arrows, bitten by dogs, punctured by spears, knifed through the heart, his head and viscera given to his killer, his huge carcass dragged back to the village. Sometimes, of course, there was a funeral to hold instead of a feast – to bury the mauled remains of a hunter. But usually the men returned unscathed, washed down the bear's succulent flesh with *saké* and lily-bulb soup and stuck the bear's head on a pole near the chief's house, round which the glum people danced for joy at the bravery of both the bear and its killers. For the Ainu adored the bear – the courageous foe, giver of fur, fat and flesh – and sometimes they captured its cubs (it was rumoured that they were suckled by the Ainu women) and kept them in cages and fed them well. But when the captive bear was almost grown, they killed it with great brutality, praising it the while and praying that its noble soul would return to earth in the shape of an Ainu.

They apparently considered such a reincarnation an appropriate reward for nobility, though, in human terms, they had little enough. 'Poor benighted Ainu' the missionaries called them and Isabella, who did not set quite the same standards, also pitied them for their spiritual poverty; 'They have no history, their traditions are scarcely worth the name, they claim descent from the dog, their houses and persons swarm with vermin, they are sunk in grossest ignorance, they have no letters or any numbers above a thousand, they are clothed in the bark of trees and untanned skins of beasts, they worship the bear, the sun, the moon, fire, water and I know not what, they are uncivilisable and altogether irreclaimable savages.' And yet, like most people who stayed among them, she remembers with nostalgia the sweetness of their low voices, the simple warmth of their mild dark eyes, their sad, gentle smiles. 'I left the Ainu yesterday with real regret,' Isabella told her sister, 'though I must confess that sleeping in one's clothes and lack of ablutions are very fatiguing.'

A few days later the travellers returned to Hakodate, a town which the Ainu shunned, and where bears' legs were sold at the butchers for about three shillings each. It was civilisation, and Miss Bird dodged up a side alley in an attempt to avoid an encounter with the British Consul who was on his way to dine on a flagship in the harbour. He was dressed in his neatest suit, a nice clean white shirt, whereas she – 'in my old *betto*'s hat, my torn, green-paper waterproof and my riding skirt and boots not only splashed but caked with mud, had the general look of a person fresh from the wilds'.

But compared to the spacious freedoms of those wilds, nothing else in Japan had much attraction for Isabella. She had cantered over the wide plains and the desolate beaches where the Pacific rollers crashed mightily, she had seen the black cones of naked volcanoes rear above her and the lakes below them, ice-blue and gold in the empty dawns; she had drifted down the inland rivers where heavy walls of vegetation thrummed with birds and insects on either side; she had seen the Ainu, slept in their huts, tasted their food, liked them. 'Are you sorry it's the last morning?' asked Ito, as he woke her in Hakodate the day the steamer sailed. And she was indeed sorry, sorry to start 'dressing' again so that she could face people like the British Consul in his best suit, sorry to be back in the world of 'door-bells, "please mems" and bills'.

Ito continued to work as a guide and interpreter and, twenty years later, tourists record that they were shown round the Nikko temples by 'Miss Bird's companion in the wilderness' – so presumably he never stopped talking about her. Isabella left Japan just before Christmas; but she had not 'done' with the country entirely and had only just started her discovery of the 'real' Far East.

II

Each visitor and resident enjoyed his own Japan. Miss Bird's pungent descriptions of wild, desolate Yezo which were published in 1880 undoubtedly caused great surprise to many a western merchant who had no particular desire to travel beyond the twenty-four mile treaty limits. On the other hand, the jargon, the secret intrigues and machinations, the high points and hazards of a merchant's business day were almost as exotic to the uninitiated as the bear-worshipping rituals of the Ainu.

The merchants worked in *hongs*. *Hong* is a Chinese word for a 'foreign trading establishment' and during the seventies and eighties the leading *hongs* in Yokohama and Kobe were wealthy and formidable establishments indeed. To the passerby, a *hong* showed the outer walls of several sturdy godowns, propped up, usually, by *jinrikisha* coolies hopefully waiting for the odd 'guest' to emerge from the courtyard. Around the yard sprawled a veritable village – dim, stuffy offices, more warehouses, stables, outbuildings, kitchen and bathhouse for the staff, a western-style reception room for western visitors and a Japanese one for Japanese. Sacks of tea and bales of old brocades were dumped against the walls and piles of 'silk waste' were, at certain times of the year, laid out to dry. The 'waste' was so called because it came in broken lengths from punctured or deformed cocoons; but it was not wasted and was increasingly used in the manufacture of organzine and sprig-muslins.

The *hong*-yards throbbed with commercial activity. Porters staggered under cases of imports – catties of coral beads, 'high-class French soaps', Swiss cuckoo-clocks – and creaking handcarts left, piled with sacks of dried octopus, silk-floss, or a 'mixed bag' of temple-bells, bronze ornaments and religious figurines for the 'oriental shops' of Paris and London. In the offices, copy-clerks and money-counters made their numbers tally; grooms lathered their masters' horses in the stables for the next race meeting; cleaners scraped the dust about with whisk-brooms; packers roped up bales of grey shirtings, crates of dried mushrooms, deer-horn and ivory fans. Now and again the comprador (chief agent) emerged from his secluded, well-appointed office, a Chinaman invariably, 'a creature of imposing pretensions', remarked William Griffis, in whose deft yellow hands 'lay the deep things of finance'.

Because the Chinese could read and write both Japanese and, after a fashion, English, and had good heads for figures, they had early established themselves as reliable and indispensable middle men in the mercantile world. There were between five and six hundred British residents in Yokohama by 1880, about two hundred Americans, a hundred Germans, some Frenchmen, Dutchmen and Swiss – and at least a couple of thousand Chinese. As money-changers and compradors they were notorious for their merciless 'squeezing' of the Japanese merchants, but most were faithful to their foreign masters in their fashion and they exercised considerable behind-the-scenes power. The prices of yellow peas or kerosene, the exchange rates of the different national currencies, the relative qualities of silkworm-egg cards, narrow iron hoops, blue damasks, all came under their bland, keen scrutiny. A good comprador was a treasure and he knew it, he cut an imposing figure on the streets of his treaty port, as Isabella Bird noticed during her short time in Yokohama: 'He has a swinging gait and an air of complete self-complacency as though he belonged to a ruling race. He is tall and big and his many garments, with a handsome brocaded robe over all, his satin pantaloons of which not much is seen, tight at the ankles, and his high shoes whose black satin tops are slightly turned up at the toes, make him look even taller and bigger than he is. His head is mostly shaven, but the hair at the back is plaited with a quantity of black purse twisted into a queue which reaches to his knees, above which, set well back, he wears a stiff black satin skullcap. . . . His face is very yellow, his long dark eyes and eyebrows slope upwards to his temples, he has not the vestige of a beard and his skin is shiny. He is not unpleasing looking, but you feel that as a Celestial he looks down upon you.'

Most people in the stratified society of the nineteenth-century treaty ports had someone to look down upon – except, perhaps, a Japanese outcast living under a bridge who had to kick the dogs for comfort. The diplomats, on the whole, kept aloof from the merchants, though there was much less virulent hostility between the two groups than when the ports first opened; members of the leading mercantile firms, such as Jardine Matheson & Co., which had opened a branch in Yoko-hama as early as 1859, wielded political as well as commercial influence and had cemented friendships with several of the country's new leaders in business and government circles. Such 'old Japan hands' regarded with suspicion and some scorn the later, lightly-ballasted hopefuls who continued to bob in periodically from Shanghai and ports south with little ready cash and lots of bravado. Much deeper, apparently, was what Griffis termed the 'great gulf' between merchant and shop-keeper. 'Advertising, the use of a signboard and such-like improprieties,' he writes, 'are evidence of low caste and con-sign the offender to the outer darkness, far away from happy club-men and select visitors.' Griffis blames the rigidity of the social structure on the preponderance of class-conscious Englishmen in the port, particularly those who, 'removed from the higher social pressure which was above them and which kept them at their true level in England, find themselves with-out that social pressure in the East; and obeying "the law of pressures" are apt to become offensively vaporous in their pretensions'.

Grateful even to inhale the pretentious vapours of, say, the leading dignitaries in the local Chamber of Commerce, were the young clerks and juniors who performed the routine com-mercial chores in the trading firms and banks. In high summer, little was accomplished after the heavy noon tiffin, but as mail-day approached, quantities of long handwritten letters (often dictated by a senior partner) were wedged in the 'out' pigeonholes of the roll-top desks – for the main branch on the China coast mostly, and a few for the sedate, wood-panelled rooms of 'H.Q.' in Leadenhall or Lombard Street E.C.2. Some of the news was hopeful: 'I have shipped about a 1,000 piculs of seaweed to Shanghai. This is a trial and I hope if it turns out satisfactorily that it will lead to a large business later on'; some of it was discouraging: 'Mousselines are again lower and tea is dull. Stocks are not more than 4,000 piculs and very little coming in, according to native accounts, which, however, are not to be depended upon'; sometimes there was no news at all: 'I have very little to advise about the Market, for the past week has been quite a Blank owing to the Races'. When the ships – the *Flying Spur*, *Red Riding Hood*, the *Porpoise* – were loaded, Bills of Lading arrived on the roll-top desks announcing that the Master was about to sail and deliver his cuttlefish, copper ore, and *awabe* shells to ports north and south 'in good order and condition' – *if* he emerged unscathed from the many hazards of the voyage: 'Acts of God, Insurgents of Pirates, the Restraint of Princes and Rulers, Fire at Sea or on Shore, Accidents from Machinery, Boilers, Steam and other Perils and Accidents of the Seas and Navigation of whatever nature or kind.'

Incoming ships brought coded telegrams from distant bosses, 'Abdomen cornutia corporal' they explained, or 'Crombech injurieux hawthorn December', and equally colourful and esoteric messages about the price of Red and Blue Dragon Chops (types of yarn), Yellow Iron Mock Water Twists, Black or Pink Lion or Green Dog Yarns. Each oscillation in the price of silk deserved an explanatory paragraph, and then there were the various crises to be mulled over. Once, a whole cargo of imported rice was packed in rotten sacks which split in the slings while being unloaded and another rice cargo overheated in the hold because of insufficient ventilation and emerged looking yellowish-grey; bundles of nail-rods frequently went missing for mysterious reasons and once, in high summer, the tar on all the tarpaulins melted and 'penetrated hopelessly into the shirtings'. The import of syrup and guano to Japan was a shaky proposition: the syrup leaked out of its casing and the guano hung around on the quayside for an embarrassingly long time, until anyone who could bear to take it away could have it. Sugar too was risky. Cube sugar was a dead loss and 'White Sugar is used by the Japanese only for the outside of Cakes,' explained a clerk carefully, 'but Common Brown Sugar enters largely into consumption for sweetening generally, where colour is not the object'. He had, however, a thousand bags of the stuff 'unplaced' after a month and had to let them go for a song. 'Would there', he asked plaintively in a later missive, 'be any sale for sulphuric acid in South China, do you suppose?'

Another cause of mercantile uncertainty during the seventies was the fluctuations of the native currency. When the early traders had set up shop during the previous decade, they had found a bewildering wealth of coins and notes in use, very attractively designed, most of them, but of dubious value. There were the square silver *ichibu*, first cast in 1854, the little gold *nibukin*, some of which were hastily withdrawn as they contained a 'heavy substance' carefully gilded over, the cracked rusty coins of brass or iron known as *'cash'*, copper-coated coins mostly, some with a hole in the centre, so they could be strung like beads on loops of straw twine, lovely oval-shaped gold *cobangs* and, for the specially gullible, wads of colourful, tattered paper notes of which 1,694 varieties had been issued, sometimes without the reigning Shogun's knowledge, by landed noblemen during the Tokugawa period. In order to lubricate commercial transactions, the silver Mexican dollar, popularly called the 'Mex', was early introduced as an acceptable unit of currency between the Japanese and western traders. This trusty, but essentially alien unit was still the main basis for international calculations during the seventies and eighties, when it was worth just over two shillings, or fifty American cents.

After the Restoration, the government tried to improve

matters: *kinsatsu*, officially-backed paper money to replace all the 1,694 previous varieties was issued and a national mint was opened in Osaka, from which tumbled a promising shower of *rin*, *sen* and *yen*, all shiningly imprinted with rising suns, chrysanthemums and coiled dragons. The Mint was one of the sights of New Japan and many a visiting V.I.P. was guided over every orderly foot of its twenty acres while its magical processes were explained – the melting and the refining, the rolling, cutting, making of impressions, hardening, blanching, heating, boiling, weighing, storing and finally the stripping of each employee at the end of the day to make sure he was not secreting new-minted riches.

But Japan still lacked capital to finance its burgeoning ventures. During the seventies, banks were opened to stimulate the circulation of money and soon the national economy began, like those of its western mentors, to display the familiar signs of inflation and deflation. The early eighties were a time for belt-tightening; rice prices, both for White Rice and 'Hulled Rice at one Month's Sight', slumped – an ominous sign; the foreign press was loud with letters from business men complaining that the natives' lackadaisical attitudes were ruining them and that the native currency was not worth the paper it was printed on. The Japanese, concurred the *Mail's* reporter, 'are deficient in earnestness and unmarked by tenacity of purpose'. Worse yet, the vast majority of the ordinary people still insisted on eating seaweed and raw fish and living in almost empty, straw-matted rooms, and how could you expect to earn a living by selling modern, civilised appurtenances to the natives if they refused to learn the art of conspicuous consumption? 'It is to be sincerely hoped that no worse times are in store for this settlement than those through which it has just passed,' prayed the *Mail's* editor, at the beginning of 1883. 'Whether the last straw has still to be added or whether it has already been added to the burden of loss and misfortune is a question we almost fear to discuss. . . .'

In spite of Japanese intractability, many of the foreign

merchants made a comfortable living, especially if they had early established their interests in the silk or tea markets. The softly interwoven colours and textures of Japanese silk were widely admired in Europe and America and the trade expanded almost effortlessly, but the slightly acrid, thin taste of Japanese tea was harder to sell and was in constant demand only in America. May was the month of the first tea-picking, and if the crop looked like being a poor one, rumour said that wistaria and camellia leaves were gathered also to swell the harvest. Reed sun-hats and coloured kerchiefs bobbed brightly among the plantation terraces on the hillsides as the village women picked the youngest shoots from the dark bushes, and soon the dusty roads were clogged with hand-carts and pack-horses taking the rough upcountry leaf to Yokohama to be fired and exported.

Before the process became mechanised towards the end of the century, tea-firing provided sweated labour for thousands. The thousands, mostly women, came clattering into the settlement at dawn carrying lunch-boxes, small teapots and babies on their backs. The doors of the sheds were flung open by the foreman, fires were rekindled under the sunken iron pans that were filled and refilled every fifty minutes or so with the natural green leaf and, for the next thirteen hours, with only an occasional break the firers stirred and tossed the leaves around in the pans to dry. The tea was also 'polished' – a process of adding artificial colouring which made it more acceptable on the foreign markets, but which, in the view of at least one of the merchants concerned, was both insanitary and harmful to its true flavour. During this process, he explained, the leaves 'are changed into a dingy blue or greasy grey colour by means of ultramarine or indigo mingled with gypsum or soap-stone, and the whole mass is flavoured with the perspiration which drops abundantly into it from the filthy and often-times diseased work-people who, for hours together in a high temperature, turn the tea in the pans'. And certainly, as the sun waxed the air grew thick and hot with the aroma of indigo, charcoal and drying leaves, and the noise rose with the temperature – thudding feet of coolies, yelling of babies, shouting of foremen, chattering of women who, by all accounts, were very cheerful in spite of everything, rattling of carts, pots, stirring rods – 'and the overnote to the clamour, an uncanny thing too, is the soft rustle down of the tea itself, stacked in heaps, carried in baskets, dumped through chutes, rising and falling in the long troughs where it is polished . . . always this insistent whisper of moving dead leaves', of tea that 'continues to mutter unabashed till it is riddled down into the big, foil-lined boxes and lies at peace'. This last quotation is from Rudyard Kipling, who twice visited Japan on his later travels and who appreciated the country, in his humorous, slightly patronising, but always original fashion. And so here he found something fresh to say about tea-firing, a process which many visitors as well as Kipling described, though less vividly, as one of the most memorable, typical sights in both Yokohama and Kobe.

For in the matter of tea-exporting, as in several other ways, Kobe was second sister, a potential, sometimes actual rival to Yokohama, and a considerable amount of raillery and some animosity hummed between the two ports. Kobe was opened for trade nine years after Yokohama and its early foreign inhabitants, who determined to learn from the mistakes that citizens of the older town had made in matters of municipal organisation and the provision of amenities, proceeded to build a 'model settlement'. So Kobe-dwellers were soon rather smug, much given to pinpricking the duffers of Yokohama about their inability to catch their own thieves, light their own streets or even dispose of their own sewage decently. As early as 1873 the British Consul had given a full, proud description of Kobe's public works for the benefit of Sir Harry Parkes and the Yokohama press: 'The largest warehouses and stores built by foreigners in Japan have been erected at this port. The streets, which are regular, spacious and well-drained, have been macadamised, and large wells sunk to give a more abundant and more convenient supply of water for the extinguishing of fire and laying of dust when required. New municipal buildings are being erected in a central position, consisting of a municipal hall which will contain accommodation for the municipal superintendent and the foreign police, a prison and permanent sheds for fire engines. The streets have hither-to been lighted with kerosene, but arrangements for gas-lighting are well in hand.'

Settlers in Yokohama took scant pleasure in Kobe's successes, for their municipal affairs remained unsatisfactory and insolvent. Throughout the late seventies and early eighties the inadequacies of the police force continued to make local headlines, as did lack of space for the unloading and storing of goods and the shortage of water – for drinking, much less for extinguishing fires or laying dust. Water-carts trundled over the stony streets during the hottest months, leaving hope-ful sprinkles in their wake; but in Yokohama one had to pay individually for the service, and so careful were the con-tractors to damp only their customers' patches of territory that, on summer days, Main Street presented 'a checkered scene of wet and dry intervals'.

Yokohama's most cogent riposte to Kobe's immaculate order-liness was that the younger port had no problems because it did not have sufficient citizens to create them. And it was true that Kobe's commercial expansion was gradual at first; twelve years after its opening in 1868, there were no more than about two hundred and fifty western residents. A reporter from one of the Yokohama papers, mindful of his readers, laid it on with a trowel when he visited Kobe about that time: 'The streets', he explained, 'only require a few houses to become everything that can be desired... avenues are wide, well-drained and quiet, owing to the lack of inhabitants; wheeled vehicles run almost noiselessly as there are only two of them. ... The inhabitants seldom speak but eat a good deal and read newspapers ... the sale of a bale of shirtings is a thing to be talked of. Once sixteen bales were sold at one time by a single firm, but the house was ruined by the cost of entertaining to less fortunate foreigners which it was forced to give in con-sequence.' The reporter saw that, as had been foretold, the streets were now duly lighted by gas: 'there is an average', he adds, 'of two lamps to each inhabitant'.

But back in Yokohama the sarcasm wore thin, for the 'stygian darkness' of the settlement area so lamented several years before was still unrelieved.

Nevertheless, the settlers had one comfort: even if it was black outside, *they* could constellate sufficient stars among themselves to lighten the evenings indoors. 'Yokohama', explained the *Herald*, 'is a perfect whirl of excitement – a perfect vortex of dissipation – compared to Kobe.' The reporter is again being facetious, but certainly the sheer galaxy of entertainments which the thousand or so western residents in Yokohama managed to devise 'for each other's delectation' was astonishing. Between them they could muster every kind of talent – tenors, sopranos and basses, cellists and violinists, trumpeters, pianists and flautists, actors for farce and tragedy, dancers of Highland flings, singers of glees and arias, soliloquists, ventriloquists and mimics of all the funny dialects. It was no place for false modesty; you trod the boards and did your stuff and if you were good enough for the occasion, the audience paid generous tribute, and if you were not then the critics in the local press were often very rude.

The entertainment centre of Yokohama was the Gaiety Theatre which had opened in 1870 with a grand Christmas performance of *Aladdin or the Wonderful Scamp*, a title which set the tone for the ensuing succession of popular farces. There were 'sprightly' ones about *The Irish Compradore*, frothy ones about merry matrimonial misunderstandings like *Cool as a Cucumber* and *Should This Meet the Eye*, broad side-splitters such as *A Regular Fix* and *The Lion Slayer* for which the actors 'assumed an exquisite vulgarity which greatly tickled the audience'. The audiences happily multiplied, so that after only six years of operation, the management could afford to refit and redecorate the whole theatre. The proscenium, announced the *Herald*, 'has been entirely remodelled and massively gilt so that the scenes now appear set in a rich gold frame by which arrangement their effect is considerably heightened'. This beautiful frame did not, alas, lessen the pain of really excruciating acting and critics took particular delight in savaging the efforts of the poor young men, who, during the theatre's early years, played the female roles on the stage. There was faint hope for the actor who 'with experience and care might be able to correct her present imperfections and be a fair representative of the Fair'; but his colleague had a long way to go: 'She must first study her action and her poses as well as her voice and delivery and avoid the angularity and awkwardness which her nervousness rendered only too noticeable last night.' 'The acting of "Mrs Barker"', announced the *Mail* of the next production, 'had but one merit, that of being the worst possible. We say this to encourage "Mrs B.", because any step she may take must be upwards and her evident confidence that she has the inspiration in her, could she but make it available for the regeneration of the stage and of society, forbids our believing that she will be forever content with the first step on the ladder.'

It was perhaps performances like this that finally persuaded the amateurs to follow the example of similar groups in Shanghai, Nagasaki and Peking and put their daughters on the stage. After all, purrs the *Herald*, 'in this little outlandish place which has the enviable privilege of so much beauty, taste, refinement and, we are sure, dramatic talent, some ladies might surely be found to tread the boards?' In 1878 the refined Fair succumbed to these blandishments and two of their number appeared in that rollicking comedy, *To Oblige Benson*, which had been specially chosen so as not to overtax their capacities. The ladies were a triumph, so poised, so elegant and *feminine*, gushed the critics, their toilettes so dazzling – how richly they deserved the rain of bouquets, 'of almost Brobdingnagian proportions' that flooded the stage afterwards! Now that the ladies were indisputably present however, it was even more incumbent upon the Gaiety Group to be most cautious in its selection of plays. A performance, warned the *Herald*, must never be marred by 'the introduction of an implied indelicacy or a coarse expression; amateurs in particular must eschew anything that could possibly give offence to the most fastidious'.

If, as a result of this policy, the steady good clean fun of theatrical farce became a trifle boring, there were plenty of alternatives. Frequent musical evenings were held in the ball-room of the Grand Hotel, in the various public halls and the Gaiety itself, and a few selected and selective recitals were given in the drawing-room of the British Legation. It was there that John Black, editor of a local newspaper, 'sang the love-song of a giant "Oh ruddier than the Cherry" with admirable execution, but with almost too much refinement and delicacy' and there too Mr Townley, who was generally a little wobbly in his upper registers, 'sang his second song, "Love's Request" with more effect and spirit than his first' – even though the first was entitled 'Lo, it is the wife'. Mr Marshall's poignant renderings of 'O Life let us Cherish' and 'Hark, the Tower's deep-toned Bell' won much applause from the white hands of the ladies, and the evening was brought to a cheerful end with choruses of 'Come Jolly Comrades' and 'My Pretty Jane'. Compared to these exclusive private programmes the public concerts at the Gaiety were indiscriminate, gargantuan musical feasts. Fourteen pieces were once included in a programme, among them, complained the *Mail*, 'three entire Beethoven sona-tas, two entire trios by Hummel with every "repeat" religiously repeated, an overture by Weber and one by Beethoven, to say nothing of songs and minor pieces'. By a quarter before midnight, when the star performer rose to play his violin, most of the audience had gone home.

This medley of musical entertainment was frequently aug-mented when large ships of the various western fleets were in port. The permanently-stationed bands of the Tenth Regiment and the Royal Marines had sailed away with their regiments several years before, when it was realised that there was no longer any need to keep western troops stationed in Yokohama for the protection of settlers against Japanese reactionaries, but the bands from the visiting ships helped to fill the void.

The U.S.S. *Missouri* always sent ashore its popular troupe of Amateur Ethiopians, with the flute solo by Ginger Blue, 'Tilda Horne' sang by Sambo, a Clog Dance, Hornpipe and a grand 'march through Georgia by the whole company which was a very ludicrous performance'. The band of H.M.S. *Encounter* was positively eager to play at balls – particularly the Volunteer Fire Brigade's Fancy Dress Ball, which was always a bumper affair. On those sparkling nights, a Dresden-dainty shepherdess would foot a frilly cotillion with Mephistopheles; Aurora 'in a diaphanous robe of white relieved by a gauzy tissue of roseate hue' marvelled the *Mail*, floated, with Christopher Columbus, through a waltz; Old Mother Hubbard flirted with the King of Diamonds; phalanxes of Roman soldiers, Swedish peasants, pirates and *samurai* with cardboard swords battled for drinks round the bar, there were prizes for the wittiest, the prettiest and the silliest and the band blew itself dry.

The music-loving lads from the *Valiant* could usually be persuaded to mount the bandstand in the Public Gardens and swing through 'The Yellow-Haired Laddies', a couple of gay mazurkas and 'The Balmoral Lancers'; the Yokohama Glee-Singers jovially mustered with them for 'If Doughty Deeds' and 'Launching the Lifeboat'; sometimes, on week-end summer evenings, lanterns were strung along the paths and, when everyone felt a little replete, a little philosophical, a little melancholy, the plangent notes of Mr Marsh's solo violin playing Ernst's pathetic 'Elegy' whined from the bandstand towards the stars and they all dreamed of home.

For, in spite of all these jolly recreations, a sour undertone of boredom and inertia, a wistful, self-pitying sense of exile seemed often to sully the settlers' days. Home was a horribly long way away; official leave was infrequent, and many of the smaller merchants only went home when they could afford to take themselves. As Kipling remarked, one tends to see a country, even as charming a one as Japan, in a different light when there is no return half to the ticket, nor the money in the bank to buy one. Usually, people put the appropriate social smiles on, even if they were not feeling so cheerful, but one evening, the *Mail's* editor, returned perhaps from some particularly drab occasion, gave vent to a burst of honest spleen which roused considerable comment from his readers: 'We move in an eternal circle of similar dinners where a constant succession of similar dishes destroys the palate, while the everlasting outpouring of similar talk interlarded with more than twice told jokes and stories blunts our intellect with wearisome repetition. In public and in private we see the same faces day after day until beauty itself loses somewhat of its charm and even official dignity declines towards the commonplaces of ordinary men. In our theatre the same actors enact and re-enact the same pieces and the same lyres are twanged by the same kindly artists in the ears of unchanging audiences. So runs our life from year to year and every year is duller than the last, until at length we find ourselves metamorphosed into a callous race, almost denuded of nationality by the waves of eventless time and lulled into intellectual sleep by the absence of all healthy stimulus and mental exertion.'

That was gratitude for you! There were Mr Townley, Mr Marsh and all the pianists, trumpeters and gay hornpipers trying to divert everybody and then the *Mail* printed something like that. The trouble was that a sore point had been probed and many of the settlers nursed similar secret bellyaches; they *did* often feel callous, unrooted, dull, and, in a flood of responsive letters to the editor's tirade, they all indulged in an orgy of self-pity. Among the replies, came a gentle little missive from 'A Lady Exile', of particular interest because the wives of the settlement (and there were not yet very many of them) so seldom raised their voices. The majority of the committees, sports activities, clubs and meetings functioned without them; they were not of course expected to work for money; their homes were well-staffed with servants and they seldom dared to displace the Japanese cook in order, as the suddenly-sympathetic *Mail's* editor puts it, 'to perform those delicate culinary mysteries in which the female mind takes such delight'. There were few shops in which they could indulge their whims; they travelled little, for the gentlemen were seldom free to accompany them and in any case 'the bad conditions of the roads in winter and heat-relaxing effects of the summer prevent the ladies from continued exercise either by walking or riding'. In short, as 'Lady Exile' and editor agree, 'Climate and circumstances all combine to deprive women here of nearly everything which goes to give colour and variety to their lives elsewhere.'

Lacking so much, what did the women of the settlements do? Their names figure largely in the birth and death columns of the papers; they arranged cakes on plates for the sailors' Christmas tea at the Mission; those of missionary inclination held bible classes for young girls; in their most lavish hats they 'graced' the pews of the church every Sunday, the grandstand seats every Race Day. Those whose husbands or fathers had sufficient status in the community were frequently called upon to award prizes. And so, when the young males came sweating up to the dais, having 'hopped, stepped and jumped' the farthest, thrown the farthest hammer or cricket ball, caught the running bellringer or the greased pig, tugged the other team over the white line, paddled the swiftest canoe, won the Shanghai Stakes on 'Tallapoosa' or the Tokyo Plate on 'Kickapoo', the ladies were waiting to present their 'Purse' or the Celestial Cup and this they invariably did in a manner so gracious according to the *Herald* that the value of the prize was 'infinitely enhanced' as they 'addressed a few congratulatory words to each, to which the winners replied, more or less eloquently, according to their respective powers'.

But between these small hours of zest, what *longueurs* of trapped emptiness the women must have endured as they waited ... waited for husbands to return from late work at the office, from the Masonic lodge-meeting, the Rowing Club dinner, the land-renters committee, the Chamber of Commerce stag supper, waited for children to be brought in by the amah all scrubbed and ready to kiss good night, for the steamer to bring the latest news of sweet home, for the maid to announce lunch, for the sultry heat to end, when a lady's body, clamped in stays and long skirts, wilted and peevishly itched – waited, surely, for something to do. 'If pleasure be simply the absence of pain, it is a pleasant life,' murmured 'Lady Exile' to her readers. 'If virtue be the absence of temptation it is a distinctly virtuous one. But it is a negative and inconsistent state of being.' But pleasure is not simply the absence of pain; even the quiet ladies of the settlements knew better than that.

III

When the ladies and gentlemen of the settlements gathered to share that 'constant succession of similar dishes' and so fill the hours before the recital or the ball, between the afternoon ride and the evening committee meeting, one subject above all others could be counted upon to arouse a response from even the most somnolent, the most over-stuffed among them. The response ranged from sincere, often passionate support, through a distasteful shrug of the shoulders, to the most intemperate and blasphemous invective; the subject was 'the missionaries'.

William Griffis, arriving unsullied from the New England 'atmosphere and influences of the Sunday school, the church and various religious activities' records with shocked surprise that 'a newcomer to the ports is soon assured that missionaries as a class are "wife-beaters", "swearers", "liars", "cheats", "hypocrites", "defrauders", "speculators" etc etc. He is told that they occupy an abnormally low social plane, that they are held in contempt and open scorn by the merchants and by society generally. Certain newspapers even yet love nothing better than to catch any stray slander or gossip concerning a man from whom there is no danger of gunpowder or cowhide. Old files of some of the newspapers remind one of an entomological collection, in which the specimens are impaled on pins, or the storehouse of that celebrated New Zealand merchant who sold "canned missionaries". . . . The only act approaching to cannibalism is when the missionary is served up whole at the dinner-table and his reputation devoured.'

The path of the missionary in Japan had always been a thorny one. During the 1540s traders and missionaries from Portugal reached the shores of the unknown country and introduced to its people a variety of new commodities, firearms and Christianity – the usual sixteenth-century 'package deal'. They were followed some fifty years later by the Spanish, whose Franciscan and Dominican monks quarrelled bitterly with the Portuguese Jesuits. The Jesuits, who had, of course, been first on the scene, made the greatest impact and by 1581 it was reported that 150,000 Japanese had been converted to Christianity. During this period of Christian fervour, a party of young Japanese noblemen made a pilgrimage all the way to Rome to kiss the Pope's feet and many a Kwannon, Goddess of Mercy, was recast to make a Virgin Mary and many a bronze Buddhist bell, its boom slightly muffled, was used to call the new believers to Mass.

But within a few years Hideyoshi, Japan's strong ruler at the time, became increasingly alarmed at his subjects' transference of allegiance to a completely alien faith and he felt, not entirely wrongly, that it was endangering the political unity of the country which he had worked and fought to consolidate. In 1587 he ordered the first decree of banishment against the Jesuits, this was followed by other more stringent decrees, and Hideyoshi's successors, who at first encouraged foreign trade, soon came to share his belief that Christianity, of whatever particular colour, was too big a price to pay for either guns or butter. At the very beginning of the seventeenth century Dutch and British traders also arrived, but brought no missionaries with them. This was as well, for the Shogunate was becoming so suspicious of Christianity that, some years later, it ordered the deportation of all foreign priests, the demolition of all foreign churches and renunciation of the faith by all Japanese converts. Priests who evaded capture and natives who refused to recant were persecuted –

a persecution that culminated in the massacre of some thirty thousand Japanese Christians at Shimabara in 1638. By this time nearly all foreigners – except the few Dutch and a number of Chinese – had been forced to leave the country, the Kwannons were put back on the household god shelf and Japan's long period of isolation from the world began.

During that entire period and indeed until 1873, some twenty years after Commodore Perry's 'peaceful invasion', public noticeboards were placed permanently at crossroads, on mountain passes, by ferries and bridges, in every town and village which proclaimed that Christianity was a doctrine of sorcery, corruption and violence and that any discovered adherents of it would be put to death. It was hardly surprising that western missionaries who preached in Japan during the eighteen-seventies met with some fear and resistance from the ordinary people, whose first reaction to the mention of the word Christ was often the instinctive raising of a protective hand to the throat to indicate what a perilous, inadmissible word it was. However in 1872 several leading members of the Japanese government visited fifteen western countries in the hope of beginning preliminary negotiations to revise the foreign treaties, whose unequal terms they had been more or less forced to accept some fifteen years before. En route, they sent disturbing news back to the Emperor: Japan could not hope to gain the confidence and esteem of the world's industrialised and progressive nations until the country mended its 'pagan' ways. In short, no Christian government from Washington to St Petersburg was going to allow its nationals living in Japan to be subject to the laws of a country which openly advocated the persecution of Christians. So, the next year, the signs condemning the 'evil sect' were taken down; a number of amazingly faithful adherents who had secretly kept their Christian beliefs alive through two hostile centuries were, after an initial period of opposition, allowed to worship freely. The prohibition of Christianity was at an end; the few missionaries who had been tacitly allowed to preach within the foreign settlements were able to expand their fields of endeavour and there was room for many more to come and swell their ranks.

Early in 1872 the number of baptised native Protestants on the church books was ten, a ratio of four missionaries to every saved Japanese soul in the country. Two years later native baptisms still rated a paragraph in the local papers. *The Japan Herald*, for instance, noted that on Sunday, 15 November, the 'Reverend Wilton Hack baptised two Japanese in Hiroshima River. One of the converts is a *samurai* and he has declared his intention of boldly preaching the Gospel of Jesus Christ.' Five hundred townspeople, apparently, gathered on the river banks to watch this outlandish ritual. Up to the end of the decade only about four thousand Protestant converts were on the books, but then came the glorious days of the 1880s, 'harvest time' at last.

The first Protestant church for Japanese Christians was opened in Yokohama in 1872; congregations swelled and choirs of native children stumbled bravely through 'Onward Christian Soldiers'; the Bible was translated into Japanese and a copy presented, with due ceremony, to the Emperor, who promised to have a look at it; Japan's first 'Society for the Promotion of Charitable Objects' was formed. The latter was due to the initiative of eight Japanese gentlemen who, as they indicated in the Society's prospectus, had quickly learned what sweet haloes Christianity awards to those who loudly proclaim their shunning of the vices which do not tempt them and their giving to the poor of those things which they do not want. 'Did even those who, steeped in indolence and lust, wasting their money in idle pursuits, lulled into an evil dream by the beauty of women, knowing nothing of the priceless pleasures begotten by work and well-doing, did even these turn their eyes honestly inwards and reflect, they would see that the bestowal of one old coat on a beggar gives a finer satisfaction of well-doing to the donor as well as a thousand times more joy to the recipient than the lavishing of a hundred yen upon a dancing girl ...'

By the end of the decade a hundred thousand converts had

been counted and, as their numbers multiplied, so did the varieties of Christian sects competing with each other to gather them into their bright particular folds. The Baptists were there and the Presbyterians (both the ordinary ones and the 'Cumberland' ones); the Lutherans, Wesleyans and Anglicans along with the Roman Catholics (who had, in 1862, opened the first Christian church in the country for over two hundred years); the Plymouth Brethren were there and the churches of the Russian Orthodox, the Dutch Reformed, the Scandinavian Alliance; the American Evangelicals, the Methodists (British and Canadian) and their cousins the Episcopal Church South Methodists were in attendance; the Universalists and the Unitarians appeared ('to poison many minds here' snarled one Lutheran minister); and there were the Women's Union, the Deists, the Christian Church in Zion, the Society for the Propagation of the Gospel, the Seventh Day Adventists, the Church Missionary Society and the Hepzibah Faith Association.

The diversity and plurality of ecclesiastical endeavour inspired many a visiting church dignitary to begin his tour of the country – and later his book about the tour – with a few broadsides at some of his competitors in order to clear the field somewhat for himself and his flock. Thus Bishop Bickersteth of Exeter begins by asking which faith will ultimately win over the Japanese and decides that it will not be 'agnosticism with its heartless no-creed; not Deism with its icy distance between God and Man; not Roman superstition with its Mariolatry and priestcraft; not Plymouthism, that molluscous kind of Christianity; not the hideous nightmare of annihilation nor the baseless dream of Universalism – but the good old faith of the everlasting Gospel on Bible foundations and Apostolic lines'.

Undaunted by competition, hostility or apathy, hopeful sowers of all these conflicting seeds arrived by every boat, until by the late 1880s there were more than five hundred of the Protestant strain alone. Even then the missionaries who lived in the country at this crucial stage of its development exerted an influence on it that was greater than their actual numbers or the number of their converts would suggest. This was partly because the Japanese were still suffering from feelings of inferiority based on their recognition of the West's superior industrial power. In simple terms, they felt that, if western engineers and scientists could teach them technical equality, perhaps the preachers of the western gospel could teach them spiritual equality. This feeling did not last long, but while it did the Japanese were particularly receptive, if not to final conversion, then certainly to general Christian influence. And although the attitudes of some individual missionaries were almost incredibly bigoted and puritanical (especially by present-day standards), the influence thus exerted by the movement as a whole was, in some ways, beneficial. In the spheres of education and medicine, missionaries helped to spread new knowledge and new methods of practice; in the moral sphere they demonstrated the virtues of self-discipline, honesty and dedication to hard work, which were certainly useful attributes for the youth of Meiji Japan; in the intellectual sphere, expounders of the Christian faith encouraged a general reappraisal of spiritual and philosophical judgements.

The missionaries who came were detailed to spread the gospel in various ways. Groups of bachelors arrived, and they usually disappeared into the hinterlands with bundles of texts and bicycles. There were coveys of maiden ladies – the Misses Amelia Carpenter, Eliza Talcott, Dora Higgins, Clara Makepeace for example – who hoped to instruct their gentle Japanese sisters how to become Bible women. 'Grenon', a foppish and foolish young fellow who wrote a bunch of trivial letters about his experiences in Japan, remembers sharing the doldrums of the shipboard dining-table with one such: 'of the Missionary persuasion she was; arrayed in mouse-coloured silk that matched her mouse-coloured hair and formed a shade darker contrast to her faded complexion and mildly enthusiastic orbs'. The young lady also lisped and sometimes when 'Grenon' was being particularly boisterous, there issued from her lips 'a faint ripple of old-girlish laughter like a little pinched gasp'. These ladies were viewed with respect, tolerance or disdain by the settlers according to their views and many clustered in Tsukiji, the foreign concession in Tokyo which contained seven parsonages, a hospital and, as Miss Bird noted, 'a complete nest of Missionary Church edifices, a wonderful testimony to the shattered unity of the Christian Church'.

The commercial community's real spleen was reserved for the married clerics who shunned both the minor discomforts of Tsukiji and the rigours of the hinterlands and established themselves and their families in large comfortable houses in some of the treaty ports' choicest locations. From the secular point of view, these men of God were encroaching on others' preserves and, to put it bluntly, living far too luxuriantly in them. Thundered 'Proselyte' in the *Herald*, 'Missionaries are the best off members of the foreign community. They, one and all, have salaries from home, regularly paid and of no mean figure, a house and a travel allowance ... with ample leisure, duties but nominal and those of a nature more like recreation than work, these people have a wonderful advantage over the rest of us!' Another correspondent in similar vein wryly recalls that, as a child in Sunday school, he was taught a verse about the sad lot of evangelists labouring among the heathen:

> The poor missionaries live there in small sheds,
> Where leaky roofs let in the rain on their heads,
> The dreadful privations that they undergo,
> Are enough to fill all our bosoms with woe.

Following this piteous tale, came the appeal for the children to forgo their 'sweet-money' for the week and send it to the church instead. The writer makes a jaundiced survey of the typical missionary establishment in Yokohama – villa, servants, private *jinrikisha* – and concludes that if he'd known then what he knows now, he'd not have given up 'his pennyworth of hard-bake'!

These relatively superficial attacks on the missionaries' personal lives were, for most of them, mere pinpricks, trials to be borne by those who had been instructed not to court the approval of the ignorant; some of the allegations made, however, were of a more serious nature and engendered even greater heat in the local papers. The *Mail* accused missionary societies of publishing triumphant roll-calls of converts for home consumption but stated that 'the public is greatly deceived as to the amount of actual effect produced by missionary effort'. 'A few penitential tears from a peasant at a prayer-meeting', the editor pointed out, 'were not sufficient to make a true Christian.' In fact – and this was the *Mail*'s second point, endorsed and elaborated upon in many a reader's letter – missionaries overseas expended too much effort and money for too little result; why didn't some of them go home and 'deal first with the enormous amount of vice and ignorance there'? Edward House, editor of one of the *Mail*'s short-lived rivals, went even further. In his view, evangelical activity in Japan was downright harmful, it undermined the traditional culture of the country and offered nothing in return but a 'few petty and narrow-minded prejudices' on matters quite irrelevant to the ordinary native's way of life.

But the missionaries were not without their defenders. Professor William Griffis wrote 'Our missionaries, a noble body of cultivated gentlemen and ladies, with but few exceptions, have translated large portions of the Bible in scholarly and simple verse and thus have given to the Japanese the sum of religious knowledge and the mightiest moral force and motor of our civilisation.' And that other pedagogue, Arthur Maclay, complained in a letter home that far too many young bachelors 'pursued a life of licence and shame' in the treaty ports and that many more would be similarly tempted were it not for 'the presence of large numbers of missionaries'. Surely, he continued indignantly, it is extremely impertinent 'publicly to investigate their respective salaries, the houses they live in, the number of their servants, what society they keep and whether or not they are activated by mercenary motives'?

Impertinent or not, such investigations were conducted with considerable relish and, as there was no way of stopping them – particularly while there were too many local newspapers chasing too little hard news – missionaries might have been wiser to get on with their work and ignore their critics entirely. Some did; others, such as an American, the Rev. G. B. Peery of Yokohama's Lutheran Mission, picked up the gauntlet and proceeded to defend, at book-length and with a kind of gloomy fervour, the evangelist's way of life and its purpose.

Peery was a muscular Christian, a large-boned, narrow-lipped person, one imagines, with a sonorous voice that often trembled with righteous wrath and equally righteous self-pity. He lived, he tells us, in a 'nice roomy house' surrounded by lawns and flower-beds and containing 'all available pleasures and conveniences'. 'A beacon light shining in a dark place' it was, 'a little bit of Christiandom set down in the midst of heathendom'. No exotic taint of 'orientalism' was allowed to shadow the solid glow of its western furnishings, its 'civilised appointments'; he and his family kept this much inviolate from the 'subtle influence of heathenism which creeps in at every pore'.

Seated in his quiet, upholstered study overlooking Yokohama harbour, Peery commences his 'delicate task': in the interest of his fellow toilers, he will 'attempt to draw aside the veil and look at their private life – the holy of holies'. First and foremost – and the italics are Mr Peery's – 'a missionary *must be a married man*'. Married men 'enjoy better health and are better satisfied' with their lot and physical health was the second major prerequisite for the evangelist. Mission boards, he explained, have spent a deal too much money on those workers who allow themselves to fall ill and have to be sent home before their allotted span. No, to be effective a missionary must have an iron constitution and a perfectly fit spouse; he must be a steady man, neither 'a bundle of nerves who will wear himself out in a few months', nor 'a man of too much zeal' who will burn himself up with the stress of over-enthusiasm. A sensible missionary 'must exercise self-restraint, husbanding his strength for future tasks'. And here too a fit spouse was most important, for she helps him to relax with the children and provides 'loving ministrations in times of sickness and despondency'.

Even with these solaces, however, a missionary finds that 'the petty worries and trials that constantly meet him, the rivalries and quarrels which his converts bring to him to settle, the care of the churches...' are 'a constant strain on his vital force' and, in order to survive at all, he must have regular periods for 'rest and recreation'. And so Peery urges his fellow-labourers and himself to leave their fields of work 'for six weeks or two months each year and go to sanatoria in the mountains', where there 'is good accommodation and the hot weeks can be spent very pleasantly'. Then indeed it was a blessed time, when the tired, isolated missionary 'can enjoy the society of his own kind', when his 'wife can meet and chat with other housewives and his children can enjoy the rare pleasure of playing with other children white like themselves'. While the foreign pastor rests, the churches can be kept ticking over by Japanese helpers as, fortunately, 'the same need for a vacation does not exist in their case because they are accustomed to the climate and they work through their native tongue and among their own people'.

These mass summer vacations and conferences in the mountains were, perhaps, the most galling of all missionary habits in the eyes of other foreigners – of the tea merchants for instance, making their hot rounds of the firing-sheds, of the shipping clerks, sitting on their stools and thinking of bathing and beaches, of the doctors, consuls, bankers whose high white collars wilted damply as the sun rocketed to its zenith just above their heads on yet another cloudless day.

And so, in cool autumn, when Peery returned to his flock, he probably found that he was even less popular in the secular community and that some of his converts had, in his absence, quite got above themselves and were running the church in their own way. As for the unconverted, Peery despairingly concluded that he had to preach long and diligently to them on the subject of evil before they even understood what it was. 'I am forced to believe', he wrote, 'that the

Japanese are really without a sense of sin and have no word in their language to express the idea exactly.' So recalcitrant indeed were the artless natives that his harvest of souls was small. Thus, he was frequently denied even that one great compensation of the missionary's hard life which was, as he defined it, 'to watch the transforming power of the gospel in the heart of some poor heathen changing him from an idol-worshipping immoral creature to a pure, consistent Christian'.

The Rev. Mr Peery, while attempting to formulate and justify his conception of the missionary vocation, seems, in fact, to embody in his unhappy person the whole gamut of evangelical attitudes and practices that aroused the ire of his secular critics. But, of course, not all missionaries were so bigoted, miscast or impotent as he. There was, for example, the energetic Doctor Guido Verbeck, of the Dutch Reformed Church who came to Japan from New England in 1859, when Christian missionaries were forced to behave rather like members of a secret society. Over the years however, Verbeck like several of his pioneering compatriots attained a position of considerable prestige and influence in the country and William Griffis, who stayed in Verbeck's home when he first reached Tokyo, confessed that 'It impressed me mightily to see what a factotum Mr Verbeck is.' He records that a steady concourse of important people flowed through Verbeck's book-lined study: heads of new government departments seeking advice on educational structure, diplomats anxious to send the right envoys to Europe and America and doctors wondering which was the most suitable language to convey the subtleties of the new medical science. And Verbeck, in his turn, was granted frequent audiences with the Emperor and was appointed principal of one of Tokyo's earliest colleges called 'The First Middle School of the First Grand Educational District'. A few days before the ban on Christianity was removed in 1873, it was Guido Verbeck who smartly confronted His Excellency, the grand new Minister of Religious Affairs with 'A Rough Sketch of Laws and Regulations for the Better Control of Church Affairs in Japan'. In short, as William Griffis put it, Verbeck was an intelligent and dedicated man who rose early and 'wrought much before breakfast'.

And for missionaries like Verbeck who were truly concerned in the welfare of the country and the problems of Christian unity, there was much to be done. As an educator, he gave guidance and encouragement to earnest young teachers – which was how Griffis met him – and tried to dissuade the Japanese from hiring those 'graduates of the dry-goods counter, the forecastle, the camp and the shambles', who drifted by in search of teaching sinecures. As a preacher, he undertook several mission tours with marathon programmes of lectures. In one such, he wrote to a friend, 'Mr Hayashi gave a spirited address on "The Superiority of Christian Ethics"; Mr Miura lectured on "The Person and Character of Christ"; and finally I treated of "The Survival of the Fittest from a Christian Point of View"' – the latter sermon of particular relevance and comfort, no doubt, to those of the audience still remaining. Wearied at last, the good doctor returned to his family hearth and 'refreshed his soul with the music of the harmonium'.

As well as teacher and preacher, Verbeck was an able administrator and tried to co-ordinate and unify the large numbers of educational establishments for Christian converts that were founded in Tokyo during the eighties and nineties. Some of the new colleges were excellent and several of their graduates became famous for their academic or political abilities as well as for their Christianity; missionaries also pioneered education for girls and young women, though they, according to Peery at least, were 'taught all kinds of abstract sciences and advanced ideas that can be of no possible use to them afterwards'. But the quality of the mission schools varied considerably, as Verbeck realised, and some were run by unqualified teachers in ill-equipped buildings where youngsters sat for hours uncomprehendingly chanting the catechism.

The school 'for little maidens' that Mrs Clara Mason started in the gatehouse at the bottom of her garden was probably of this kind. Mr Mason had founded the first Baptist Chapel in Tokyo in 1876 and, as one of his first converts admiringly noted, 'his taking pains in sowing the seed was great'; Clara, his wife, was similarly energetic and addicted to teaching hymn-tunes, visiting the sick (it was she who rescued Sam Patch from hospital) and composing verses. This latter addiction struck her the moment she left San Francisco and sailed into the sunrise towards Japan with,

> Oh rays of light from out the East,
> I hear a voice of wailing.
> Come Holy Spirit breathe on me,
> Thy comfort never failing!

Knowledge, like poetry, was 'borne in upon' Mrs Mason and the sum of it was that the teachings of Christ happily allied to the technology of the West formed an invincible combination: 'Science also is undermining and divine fires of religious thought are consuming the ancient Japanese systems of idolatry. From Yokohama to Tokyo the steam cars go whirling through rice-fields past heathen temples. The telegraph flashes its electric words along the wires, the idols sit silent within their gilded shrines and must soon lose power to hold the worship of a progressive people. And these marvels of force are teaching the Japanese the power of the one Lord who maketh the clouds his chariots and his ministers a flaming fire.'

Mr Mason, unfortunately, was perhaps one of those ministers whom Peery chided for burning themselves up in an excess of zeal, for, in spite of several vacations in the mountains he soon, in his wife's words, 'went up the shining way to be forever with his Lord'. And so Mrs Mason had to leave their task unfinished, sad in the knowledge that 'not only are there in Japan 35 millions of people yet untaught, but connected with that country geographically are the kingdoms of Korea and China. Korea has eight millions of natives yet unreached and beyond is China with its four hundred millions of people . . .' Of boundless ambition is the real missionary spirit, restlessly seeking the soul in the next village, the next country, while forever wondering if the one under instruction is finally and safely gathered in!

The urge for expansion meant that every corner of the Sunrise Kingdom must somehow receive the Christian message. Plans were in progress to launch a Gospel Ship that would 'carry the glad tidings southward to the islanders of the Inland Sea'; the fields of the north came under the care of John Batchelor of the Church Missionary Society, who bicycled gamely over the mountain passes wearing, in summer, 'knickerbockers, a négligée shirt and a bowl-shaped wicker hat' and carrying, always, bundles of texts strapped to the front wheel. Many a night Batchelor spent in the draughty Ainu huts, where, as has been said, he discovered that the people were by no means epicures and where plagues of flies and fleas 'grew fat by feeding on the poor missionary'. Undaunted, though thinner, Batchelor spent hours trying to persuade the local headmen to cleave to the One God instead of believing in the Ainu's various deities – gods of the forest and of the streams, the pair of sea-gods named the Rough Uncle and the Uncle of Peace (the latter was made much of at fishing stations) and the happy multitudes of godlings who dangled their divine toes along the shores of the milky river-in-the-sky on a bright night and angled for starfish.

A wooden-framed New England-looking church was opened in Hakodate in 1878; Miss Tapson and Miss Jex-Blake, female helpers whom, the clergyman explained, 'the Lord has greatly blessed and given many souls', ran a home for Ainu girls where writing, cooking and needlework were taught in addition to 'the Gospel of our Salvation'. In spite of setbacks – the first man to be baptised in the new church became a 'backslider' and 'Satan got him at last' – the faith flourished; two Japanese clergymen were ordained and a hospital for sick Ainu was opened in Sapporo. At a triumphant C.M.S. conference in Osaka, Mr Batchelor proudly announced that Yezo could now muster two thousand converts and an encouraging number of these were Ainu, who had, presumably, learned to roll all their gods and godlings into One.

Among those who listened with intense concentration and enthusiasm to Mr Batchelor's glad tidings of, as she puts it, 'the bright itinerating work going on in snowy Hokkaido' was Miss Amy Carmichael from Westmorland who went to Japan in 1892. It was Amy's 'first missioning' and she embarked upon it as a very intelligent, attractive, energetic twenty-four-year-old, positively glowing, as Bishop Fox wrote in a preface to her published letters, with 'a holy vivacity'. Concentrated in her resilient physique, her fervent, lively, resilient mind was all the best and worst of the proselytising Christian spirit of the nineteenth century. The best was her joyous sense of dedication, her lack of hypocrisy, her honest and fearless determination that utterly discounted those trivialities of daily life which so upset some of her colleagues. She was not one to whine about overwork or poor living conditions; more weighty matters than these demanded her complete participation – conflicts, no less, with the devil himself. For in Japan, as throughout heathendom, 'Satan has fowls always on the wing and the sun of scorn shrivels many a quick-sprung seed'. And, oh so vast was that Heathendom – a piteous 'open sore' teeming with two hundred and fifty million unredeemed souls drifting towards damnation and only she and a few other brave evangelists there to stem the flood. Such solemn and holy work it was, lovely terrible work, its most discouraging times suddenly radiant with hope, 'a sweet love-note from the Lord'; its successful moments pure glorious Victory, 'a literal lighting-up of Truth'. For perhaps the least attractive of Amy Carmichael's qualities was that she was possessed of a completely unshakeable, unquestioning, merciless conviction that she and her fellow Christians had an absolute monopoly on eternity, heaven and all its rewards.

The Church Missionary Society seems to have organised its evangelical activity along guerrilla-warfare lines and Amy Carmichael must have been one of its most tireless campaigners. By the time she arrived in Matsue, principal town in one of Japan's western provinces, four churches and several missionary outposts had already been established. These were her headquarters and from them she embarked on several 'missioning tours' accompanied by a fellow worker, a native convert as interpreter, and armed with parcels of pamphlets containing texts with pretty pictures and excerpts from the New Testament in Japanese.

She loved the warm colour of the countryside, its villages 'rich in fair things, fern-balls hung from cottage eaves, large pots of spring chrysanthemums, purple or white iris', its fields glowing with 'yellow lilies which turn to terracotta in old age, azaleas pink and crimson and sweet-scented creamy blossom like bramble'. For Amy, the beauty of the land and the people was not simply of itself, but was also a bountiful, poignant parable of Faith. Children, flying kites so high that the strings hummed in the wind, reminded her that she must keep her soul equally taut and high if she was to 'play God's music aright'; the first firefly she ever saw was 'as His Firefly carrying the lamp He has lighted over the edge of homeliness far away through the dark'; the farmer, sowing rice, was as the biblical sower, 'He walked up and down the flooded field, throwing his seed upon the water and it was muddy and uninteresting enough. The seed was the worthwhile thing.'

And she too had seeds, the 'little leaflet seeds' in 'His seed-basket' which she lugged for miles under the burning suns of August, and everywhere promiscuously distributed. She squelched through paddies and tucked the pamphlets slyly and hopefully in the peasants' lunch-boxes, she waylaid mothers with babies on their backs and presented each infant with 'a little prayer-package'; she cornered a fisherman on his way to market – though she admitted he was less concerned with her message than with keeping the tentacles of his cuttlefish inside his wicker trap; she sang hymns to the women who sat along the sea-shore picking whelks out of their shells with long bamboo needles; to the policeman, 'in tights, whites and gloves all complete' who showed her the way, she gave an especially flowery text. No one anywhere was safe from her ministrations. With the waitress at a wayside inn she had, through her interpreter, a long discussion about Sin; the ferryman who rowed her across a frigid lake one golden dawn was regaled with the strains of "'Tis Jesus in the morning, 'tis Jesus all the day'; and on one occasion she even invaded a local shrine and presented to flabbergasted robed acolytes waiting to attend their service, a selection of translations from the Gospel According to St Luke.

After the day's labour in the field, the missionaries put up at the village inn and usually held an evening meeting there. Amy describes several of these – the low, lantern-lit room often crowded with curious villagers who smoked, chatted, undressed their babies, slapped at mosquitoes, occasionally urinated while the sermon and the prayers went on. The big attractions were Amy's own turn – the playing of a small harp and the singing of solo hymns – and Question Time, 'a sort of weeding-out time it is', to uproot all the poor people's doubts and false beliefs. During harvest, when the peasants were very busy, the meetings did not begin until about ten and continued until midnight, after which a few of the more inquiring still lingered among the strangers, hoping, perhaps, to receive some more reading matter. It was from among these that Miss Carmichael often culled her prizes, her triumphs, her 'possible Pauls to be', her converts snatched from the dark shadows of Satan's very citadel.

And having secured her souls, she watched over them, exulted when they burnt their 'idols from the heathen god-shelf', prayed that they 'be no lukewarm half-hearted believers, but real red-hot blazing firebrands – fired with the fire of the Holy Ghost'. She cosseted them, craved more, counted them, as lesser women finger the pearls on a necklace, and each morning she asked the Lord 'what was in His heart for the place' that day and sometimes the answer was two souls, sometimes four, sometimes even eight. And then she and her helpers went forth, perhaps 'becoming fools for Christ's sake and holding an Open Air' of hymns and prayers when the spirit moved them, paying supportive visits to the homes of the converted, 'Jesus homes,' she called them, 'scattered here and there like stars in the darkness', and sometimes attending upon the dying, whose needs were so very, very urgent.

Once, Miss Carmichael relates how, in a mood of purely medieval ecstasy, she exorcised 'the evil fox-spirit' from an old man dying of fever. The Japanese peasantry had an awed respect for foxes, who, they believed, could enter a person's body either through the breast or the space between the flesh and any one finger-nail. Once inside, the fox harangued and bullied his 'host' causing him to act madly and violently – this, said the villagers, was the trouble with the delirious old man. Miss Carmichael seems to have half-believed in – not the fox-spirit exactly – but in the presence of an evil possession against which she had to battle. And a touchingly anachronistic scene it must have been – the aged man screaming and burbling in the small room, the lamp wavering in the hand of his trembling wife and the tense stranger-woman, with her eyes cast up to God, wrestling alone with the Prince of Darkness whose shadow was cast, not only upon that fevered brow, but upon the whole land, 'staining the new-born bud, leaving its mark on the frond, evil, evil everywhere, marring all things'. That particular struggle she won, though, she writes, 'all the glory went straight to God'.

But 'Evil' was not always conquerable; it continued, for instance, to goad her in the form of 'Buddhist agitation'. Occasionally, stones were thrown at the missionaries as they left their meetings, village boys gathered to jeer 'Yasu, yasu' ('Jesus, Jesus') outside their bedroom windows, doors slammed in their faces. Nevertheless, considering the dogged effrontery with which they pursued their 'missioning' practices, it shows some forbearance on the part of the Japanese that neither she nor any of her colleagues were ever really physically hurt by the agitators. Not that Miss Carmichael would have been deterred by a stone or two hitting its mark; she would have accepted the pain as a blessed sign of martyrdom, a sharp proof that she was at last making an impact. For, much more distressing to Amy's ravenous spirit than active opposition, was what she called 'the lack of soul-hunger' among so many Japanese – it was 'evil' in the shape of indifference that almost defeated her. At such times, watching the rows of unlighted, unresponsive faces, she longed 'to shake them, to clap one's hands, anything to make them come alive'. There was no sitting on grey fences in her spiritual arena: 'Either one must be intensely a believer or a black Nothing.'

At these times of near-failure, Amy's thoughts naturally turned to her fellow Christians back home, who were 'holding the guide-lines' and to whom her *Letters from Sunrise Land* were written. Sometimes she pleads for the support of 'ever so many prayer-telegrams' from them; at others, she prods angrily at those who were content to hold 'nice little meetings' safe at home, to partake of tea and cakes and read the news from afar. 'And what,' she asks with all the ferocious scorn of the youthfully self-righteous, 'and what will you wish *you* had done when the King comes?'

Eventually, the long days of pamphlet-lugging, the late night meetings to which she gave all her zeal, every time, and, most of all, perhaps, the stolid disinterest of the peasantry, sapped her fires. Amy followed the example of so many of her fellow-workers, had something approaching a nervous breakdown and was sent away on leave.

She went to Colombo first and then to India – where she found her spiritual home. For India, with its less subtle alliances of good and evil, its more frenetic and passionate obsessions with the religious spirit, was much better suited to her vehement temperament and singleness of mind. Apart from one brief sojourn in England, she remained there for the rest of her life and died there fifty-five years later. She became co-founder and moving inspiration of the Dohnavur Fellowship mission in South India, whose workers tried to rescue from a life of confinement and prostitution the children sold to the Hindu temples. So utterly dedicated was she to her new task, that she probably more or less forgot Japan or, if she remembered the land at all, it was with both nostalgia and dismay – nostalgia for the loveliness of its quiet countryside and for the youthful delight she had taken in it, dismay at the face of beauteous, polite indifference that it had turned to her.

And this indifference, sometimes amounting to hostility towards Christianity, slowly gained ground, led, of course, by Shintoists and followers of Confucius and Buddha. Members of these traditional faiths attacked upstart Christianity on the grounds of its cruelty and 'robbery of other countries', and produced in support of their argument harrowing details of the wars of the Crusaders, the struggles of the Reformation, the Spanish Inquisition. Worse than this, a missionary living in Tokyo wrote indignantly, was that Buddhists were not merely 'uniting the people' against Christian converts, but were 'determined to outdo them in works of charity and progress. Thus we have societies of Buddhist Endeavour, Young Men's Buddhist Associations and the employment of women in the service of the Buddhist religion on the lines of our Bible women.' In 1890, a celebrated Japanese professor, who was also a devout Christian, hesitated to bow before the imperial portrait on the occasion of the Emperor's birthday. He was dismissed from his post and the incident became a rallying point for anti-Christian agitators, who accused the professor and his fellow-believers of disloyalty to the Emperor – and so to the nation and the nation's ancestors.

And indeed, one of the impediments to the spread of Christianity during the last years of the century was a resurgence of extreme patriotism. In the middle of the 1890s, the Japanese fought and won with ridiculous ease a war against that too-near giant, China; they now fully appreciated the power of the tools the West had brought and they began to use this power, not, as Mrs Mason rosily foretold, 'in the service of the Christian God', but to forge their own national road to glory. Another harmful influence, from the Christian point of view, was the spread of scientific agnosticism. Japanese intellectuals who readily absorbed the works of Darwin, Herbert Spencer and Hegel for example, soon understood that, if Buddhism did not have all the answers, neither, necessarily, did Christianity. And as for the ordinary people, most of them, as Miss Carmichael had discovered, did not concern themselves overmuch with such matters. As Basil Chamberlain put it (and his remarks are nearly always to the point) 'the Japanese mind is too essentially unspeculative for the fine distinctions of the theologians to have any charm for it, much less for it to seek to split new hairs for itself'. And, when it came to everyday morality, it was painfully evident that some of the western traders could, whatever their professed beliefs, behave in quite as greedily materialistic a manner as any 'heathen' shopkeeper – so what was there to chose between them? The pendulum swung almost as far away from Christianity as it had swung towards it earlier. The 'harvest' was never to be so rich and full again, and those earlier missionaries who had prophesied that the whole nation would be safely gathered into the Christian fold by the end of the century, were sadly disillusioned.

IV

The most popular kind of missionary with the Japanese – and with the foreigner as soon as he fell ill – was the medical missionary. There was a great variety of diseases to catch and, with disturbing frequency, to die from in nineteenth-century Japan. The Japanese had for many years taken a keen interest in western medical techniques, but only a minority knew enough to practise them and foreign doctors were often importuned by students seeking to acquire their mysterious secrets. Doctor Henry Faulds, the medical missionary in Tokyo, remembers that, a few days after his arrival, he was awakened at day-break by some young doctors' apprentices tapping gently at his bedroom window and greeting him with a deferential *ohayo* ('good morning') and a plea for lessons in anatomy. And not only students; the sick too scented him out from afar. His waiting-room soon overflowed and in his small garden behind it, withered old men, women with drowsy smallpoxed babies would wait all day to see him, comparing their symptoms, listening to the frogs in the nearby canal and clutching, like talismans, their dispensary tickets, bottles for medicine and deep pink shells in which to carry away the soothing occidental ointments. On his trips to the interior, Faulds was, in his own words, perpetually haunted 'by the pitifully monotonous little groups of blear-eyed, crippled and occasionally leprous humanity who dog the steps of the medical missionary'.

During one of his journeys, to the home of a rich, dying silk-grower, Faulds aroused the extreme choler of the family's normal doctor, a stubborn, fiery man with a neat beard and a short sword in his brocade belt which, Faulds thought, he perhaps used when all else failed. Certainly the old gentleman was a traditionalist and vehemently maintained that his remedies – the hair-like acupuncture needles of gold, silver or steel, *do-sha* powder (the main ingredient of which was quartz sand) and his special musk-pills, 'guaranteed to cure anything from a bedsore to the bites of venomous reptiles' – were vastly more effective than anything inside the foreigner's little black bag. That particular silk-grower was apparently beyond all aid, eastern or western, so the case was not proven; but generally, people were losing faith in the old-fashioned cure-alls, and the dignified black-robed doctors who used to perambulate the streets followed by a retainer reverently carrying their medicaments in an oblong ivory box became an increasingly rare sight.

One of Tokyo's British doctors, Theobald Purcell, took a professional interest in the contents of these boxes and records that they usually contained supplies of clove pills, black-ball pills, 'Thousand Year Life Pills' and Rhinoceros Pills, the latter 'a certain cure for tightness of the chest, pain, gnashing of teeth, depression of the spirits... These pills (ahem) are best taken by dissolving in *saké*!' As a last resort, the doctor also carried some coloured pictures of the Goddess of Mercy which were to be dissolved in water and drunk down rapidly. 'If this is unsuccessful,' Purcell concludes, 'the patient is beyond recall and preparations may be made for the funeral.' New, western-style pick-me-ups were now swallowed instead of the goddess's portrait and these were advertised by their Japanese manufacturers in one of the English language newspapers – much to the amusement of its readers. The most frequently quoted advertisement was for *Nindoshu* 'an intoxicant liquol made from alcohol mixed with other things and flavoured with honeysuckles flower. It has a very sweet taste and is somewhat strong, it resembles whisky and is good for anyone. It has an effect of exciting the mind and promoting the health of withered persons. It has obtained a high reputation in the International Exhibition of Paris. Ladies and gentlemen we wish you would take a cup of it and know what we say is true.'

But neither *Nindoshu* nor Rhinoceros Pills nor, indeed, many of the western medicines, could do much to prevent the raging epidemics of typhoid, smallpox and cholera which felled hundreds of Japanese every few years and caused the deaths of many foreigners. A hospital for foreigners had been established in Yokohama early in the seventies, but at the first serious outbreak of smallpox its resources had proved inadequate. In the past the Japanese had taken smallpox almost as lightly as westerners take chickenpox. For them, it was something most children got sooner or later and when they did, their mothers simply put a red cloth or cap on their heads or a piece of red paper above the door to warn the unwary and just hoped that the child would recover – which it usually did. But now, according to the Japanese, foreigners had brought a new and virulently dangerous strain of the disease into the country; according to foreigners, Japan itself was at fault, for, wrote a *Mail* journalist, both cholera and smallpox tend 'to be generated in the atmosphere here'. At any rate, there was an epidemic, hundreds of natives succumbed; seventy-four foreigners were admitted to the hospital of whom nineteen died. And what with them and the numbers of whaling men brought down from the north with winter frost-bite and the numbers of stokers stricken with 'heat apoplexy' in the summer and the usual quotas of sailors ridden with scurvy or typhus from the rat-infested holds and the undefined, intermittent fevers which carried off a few residents each year, the hospital could not cope; it was badly in debt, there was no isolation ward and hardly enough bandages left in the store.

When the Hospital Committee (one of whose members was Mr W. H. Smith) examined the hospital's financial affairs, it was clear to them that the principal source of trouble was 'Charity Patients'. Inmates received treatment and attention strictly according to the fee they could afford: there were first-class patients, second-, third- and fourth-class patients and then the despised 'Charities', who had to be kept alive for nothing. According to the *Mail*, these men were a set of worthless vagabonds, 'revolvers' was the American name for them, because they revolved in and out of any institutions kind enough to take them and made 'a mere trade of their miseries'. Word had presumably got around that the foreigners' hospital in Yokohama was good for a clean bed and at least two meals a day and as a result bundles of shabby old tramps rolled in from Nagasaki, Hong Kong, Shanghai and conveniently fell ill – or became iller than when they arrived – and there they were, penniless, dirty, jobless and sick and what was to be done with them? One member of the committee felt it was incumbent upon the hospital to take them in, 'thus relieving the community from perpetual applications for relief and from the sight of miserable objects; and saving the lives of men who would otherwise have died in the streets'. However, as another member pointed out, even their deaths cost money – ten or so died regularly each month and the hospital had to pay funeral expenses. So it was decided that, in future, all expenses for 'Charities' must be met by the consul of the man's nationality in the town from whence he came and that, as this was frequently a cumbersome process, doctors should aim to get a man back on his feet long enough to propel him on to some ship going southwards – to Hong Kong perhaps, or Shanghai.

As charity patients were usually elderly and were not admitted to the hospital until they were nearing their last miserable gasp, their high rate of mortality was to be expected, but records show that even first- and second-class people among the foreign communities were prone to die fairly early in life from unnatural causes. Death by accidental drowning in the settlement canals, the harbour or while out duck-shooting, was fairly frequent, and several ferries or steamers with foreigners aboard blew up or capsized. Several young men broke their necks when horse-racing; several young wives died in childbirth. The number of bizarre accidents was also high: two settlers were suffocated by fumes from the charcoal stoves which were heating the bath-water; two others drank rubbing alcohol instead of gin; a young lady was killed when her *jinrikisha* ran over a cliff edge; every summer one or two marines from visiting ships died of sunstroke while on parade. Several men were shot in hunting accidents, and one or two accidentally shot themselves while cleaning their guns.

In addition, there was what a local moralist termed 'the usual crop of midsummer suicides'. These, he said, were the result of 'drinking, gambling, dissipation, intrigue with women, principally at country resorts, getting into the hands of Chinese and Japanese servants and money-lenders, consequent loss of self-respect, sympathy with swindlers big and small, a growing desire to be considered above the necessity of honest work...'.

What, then, with the hazards of incurable frustration and failure, the recurrence of fevers and epidemics, the unpredictable and frequent disasters, life in Japan was generally rather more precarious than life in, say, Somerset and this sense of precariousness was exemplified – vigorously, brutally, terrifyingly exemplified – in that Japanese speciality, the earthquake. An earthquake, like conscience, makes cowards of us all; as Kipling put it, the bravest man 'when he hears the roof beam crack and strain above him scuttles about like a rabbit in a stoppered warren'. 'There is something viciously unmitigated about them' wrote a recently-jolted resident. 'In most catastrophes one can usually fix upon some point beyond which lies safety', but the earthquake offers no havens, it is chaos incarnate. The dragon of the world, say the Japanese, uncoils itself and the moon and sun turn blood-red, evil wisps of steam exude from marshes and mines, clouds cluster ominously close to the ground's surface and in the distant mountains pheasants scream the first warning.

But by then it is already too late. There you are, innocently sitting down to dinner when ... well, this is how some who suffered the experience described it: there is a noise as of 'cavalry thundering down a hill', the floor 'seems to heave a sigh', the walls begin to shift and groan as if you were aboard a gale-tossed ship, the dinner plates clatter together 'like a lot of frightened turtles', the lamps swing the shadows about, china dogs slide comically along shelves, clocks stop, carpets ripple and fold, windows fly open or in or off and a monstrous hand 'grabs the house by the roof-pole and shakes it furiously'. And your heart beats against your front teeth and you sweat and you are in what Kipling calls 'the stage of "only let me get into the open and I'll reform"'. And so you rush into the open and find confusion confounded: 'pebbles grate in the garden paths, tall evergreens snap their tops like switches, bells ring ...' And if you are on a train, the rails writhe like serpents under the wheels, and if you are on a bridge, the supports crack and gape and the river rides up to meet you and if you are in bed, your sheets slither away and your empty boots on the floor start to play 'toccatas stately on the clavicord' and if you are in the wrong place at the wrong crashing, crumbling star-struck second, you are killed.

And after the quake there is silence. Then from the shattered towns goes up the communal wail of despair, children shriek, dogs yell, horses snort, mothers call and sob. A wicked wind whips up the dust that clogs and clouds the upturned streets, paddy fields float into sudden fissures of mud and stone, telegraph wires, that stretched and snapped like elastic, coil dangerously along the pavements, flames flicker madly away from overturned oil-stoves or paper lanterns to wreak more damage and pain among the already-suffering. The unluckiest are buried under debris in the jostled earth, the injured join the queues outside improvised hospital tents, the unscathed hurry to each other for comfort and swap survivor stories –

'If I had been in the bedroom the wardrobe would have fallen right on top of me ... if I had not stopped to tie my shoe-lace, I would have been going through the front door when the chimney fell down.'

One of the few westerners on record as having received a certain satisfaction out of an earthquake was Nurse Grace, incorruptible dispenser of medicines at one of the Protestant missions. Nurse Grace wore rimless spectacles, her hair was scraped in a bun beneath a white cap, a large chain of medicine-cupboard keys jangled in her starched apron pocket. Called to help the citizens of Osaka recover from a particularly terrible quake, she was most impressed to note that 'the houses of the faithful were left standing when all around was in ruins,' and she was 'bound to acknowledge that God took care of His Own'. Though savage maelstroms of thunder, earth tremor and fire continued to ravage the city for two or three days, Nurse Grace remained relatively tranquil in the know-ledge 'that it must all be to teach the heathen that above all He is God'.

But Nurse Grace's enjoyment of earthquakes was, at best, negative and laced with trepidation – she admits to twice seeking shelter under her bed, presumably in fear of a divine mistake. The only foreigner who seems to have positively enjoyed these disquieting phenomena was Professor John Milne, and he could never have enough of them. A number of leading representatives of various western sciences and technologies had by now appeared in Tokyo to elucidate their doctrines to the natives and among them, Milne was the first to realise that the city, which stood, as one resident complained, 'over a kind of Seismic Junction on the world's surface' needed an Earthquake Expert, and a Seismological Society, which he helped to form in 1880. The society's aims were to record the motion and frequency of earth tremors, explore the possibility of making alarm-devices and, later perhaps, to 'investigate the morality of earthquake-ridden countries'. For these un-settling occurrences may well, suggested the *Mail*, produce a permanent sense of mental insecurity, so that 'drinking, gambling and other vices might consequently be characteristic of the residents of Japan' and even 'imbecility be particularly prevalent'.

This latter, potentially fruitful, area for study was never developed, but more tangible measurements accumulated apace. Within ten years the society published fourteen volumes of transactions in which, explained Basil Chamberlain, could be found every possible variation on the themes of 'seismometers and seismographs, earthquake maps and earthquake catalogues, seismic surveys and microseisms, earth tremors, earth pulsations and general earth physics'. For light relief the society also printed searingly vivid illustrated accounts of earthquakes that had devastated Japan in the past. As Chamberlain remarked, for long-term residents, 'truly these are gruesome books'. To accumulate his ghastly array of evidence, Milne 'contrived such a number of instruments of various kinds that', confessed an admiring assistant, 'it is almost hopeless to enumerate them'. There were conical pendulums, pendulums with their bobs suspended over smoked glass, buoys attached to wires and floating in water, Double Brackets, Rolling Spheres and the Professor's favourite seismograph which recorded the severity of vibrations by the tracks of a magnetic needle on a revolving cylinder. With the aid of these devices, Milne was eventually able to analyse the earthquake into its component waves – the direct, the transverse and the vertical – and to discover that the area around Yokohama was one of the flimsiest, quakiest, wobbliest layers of the earth's crust.

On the occasion of all major manifestations, 'Earthquake Milne', as he was popularly called, hurried to the scene, dropped his special plumb-line into the new fissures to see how deep they were, measured their lengths with rods and chains and recorded eyewitness accounts from trembling survivors. But even in Japan the earth did not erupt with sufficient frequency to keep all Milne's instruments fully occupied, so he and his assistant devised a way of making their own private quakes by dropping a one-ton iron ball from heights of up to thirty-five feet and measuring the resulting vibrations. The Professor was also an expert on earthquake precautions: (buy a solid oak dining-table and get underneath it) – observation instruments for amateurs: (take a tub of molasses or water rubbed with chalk on the inside). He also recommended that houses should have steep roofs, trenches dug round them to absorb vibrations and handfuls of large round shot should be piled between the corner posts of the house and its foundations.

Milne was, of course, correct in his contention that an increasing amount of injury and damage was being caused by earthquakes because of the Japanese adoption of 'foreign-style' architecture – so called, explained a local wit, because it was foreign to all known styles of architecture. The varieties of western-inspired imitations, all plentifully smeared with pink and white stucco, were scornfully defined by Chamberlain: there was the 'rabbit-warren style,' the 'cruet-stand style', of which the Yokohama Custom House was a good example, and the 'bathing-machine style', the prize in this class going to the new Houses of Parliament. Chamberlain might also have added the 'pastry-cook style', described by another member of the Japan Society as being responsible for the concoction of edifices that were like 'sugared cakes with layers of white plaster hiding a framework of unseasoned and disjointed wood'. Not only was the timber unsuitable, but the bricks were as porous as sponges, the lime between them was too soluble and the stucco, prone to crack at any time, needed only a slight tremor to make it crumble into powder.

Architects might, then, have been well advised to at least consider Milne's ideas on the construction of earthquake-proof buildings, but there is no evidence that they did so and, as not even the most complex of his theories or his instruments could be relied upon to prevent even the simplest of earthquakes, most people tended to lose interest in the Professor's work after a while. Milne persevered however, and sought to arouse greater enthusiasm for his favourite phenomena by suggesting ways in which they might be of practical use.

Advised the Professor, in one of the papers he read to the Japan Society, 'When a shock is felt, especially in those districts where shocks are rare, the first thing which ought to be done is to draw out your watch quickly and then glance first at the second hand, then at the minutes and then at the hours. After this, at the first opportunity, a visit ought to be paid to the nearest telegraph station and ask the clerk in charge to be kind enough to compare your watch with the twelve o'clock signal from Tokyo.... Certainly those who live in remote localities might use them [earthquakes] by subsequently comparing their observations with newspaper reports or the letters of their friends as a means of obtaining a very close approximation to Tokyo meantime and thus furnishing themselves with the means of giving their clocks and watches a new starting point.'

In the interests of his chosen field, Milne also inveigled practically every foreigner in Tokyo to go and admire his laboratory crammed with instruments and his 'baby seismometer, a sweet thing that stands on the mantel', explained one irreverent lady visitor. 'Can always tell by looking at it in the morning how many earthquakes occurred during the night and whether any chimneys down or not. Professor says thing no family subject to seisms should be without.... Very interesting. See pamphlet.'

So much for earthquakes and their experts. There were also typhoons and their experts, volcanoes and their experts and diligent investigators into the strata of the country's mineral mines, the formation of its fossils, the varieties of its seaweed and glass-sponges, the sulphur-content of its healing springs and the temperatures of its bath-water. The Japanese had never imagined that so much could be said and written on so many incredible subjects. The eighties were a heyday for the experts – in travelling, spreading the gospel, ministering to the sick, describing the land and its characteristics – soon, the amateurs were to arrive in ever-larger flocks, the people who visited Japan simply for fun.

Part Three

1889–1895

Of diplomats, butterflies and things
that were done for the fun of it

'Tokyo – this flowery, stinking, adorable city', wrote Reginald
Farrer, the well-known botanist and traveller who adored
the place so much that he impulsively rented a home there
and stayed for months. Several tourists with sufficient time and
money did the same, and what fun they had fitting themselves into the jack-in-the-box Japanese rooms, making friends
with their quaint servants, learning a few words of the
language, buying curios and, above all, exploring and re-
exploring those bustling, blustering, hullaballooing Tokyo
streets.

In springtime the streets blossomed like their names –
Wild Cherry, Plum Orchard, Willow Branch, Flower River
and Hill-Facing Pine – and, when the rains came, melted
into mires: 'water-pipes sink', wrote the writer Lafcadio
Hearn, one of the city's most celebrated foreign residents,
'water-pipe-holes drown spreeing men and swallow up play-
ful children; frogs sing amazing songs'. Over the frogs stepped
the kite and balloon sellers, their airy toys streaming behind
them in the breeze, and the sellers of poison for the new crop
of rats. Treacherous, ragged men these, who carried a long
banner proclaiming the fatal efficacy of their wares: sure
death for all rodents, also useful for cats and dogs if necessary.

Sunnier days brought out the aged flute players who wore
large, wastepaper basket-shaped hats over their heads, and
the toy-pedlars who tempted children with flamboyant trays
of painted butterflies, bunches of tiny bells, puppet-sized
priests – pull a string and they clap their hands in prayer –
plaster kittens, gourds of emerald and violet, and little wooden
gods of longevity, their heads so elongated with age that a

barber would need a step-ladder to shave the top of them. Temptation-merchants too were the makers of coloured sugar candies who set up targets behind their stalls and invited youngsters to aim at them through blowpipes. The nearer to the bull's-eye, the more sweets you got; but if you missed completely he sometimes let you have another go. Some children, who had no money for such luxuries and no parents to give them any, kept themselves alive by street-tumbling. Wizened, india-rubber, dirty little creatures they were, who grinned hopefully and 'made wheels of themselves with arms and legs as spokes' as soon as they saw a rich foreigner. They worked in groups, doubling down, leaping up, over and under each other like a nest of brown eels while the oldest boy beat a drum to draw the crowds.

Darker, chillier days were high-season for the noodle vendor, who carried two large wooden cabinets slung across his shoulders and clanged a bell as he came. When hailed, he put down the cabinets, plonked a board across them for a table, scooped a dollop of noodles into a wire basket, dipped the lot in hot water, bounced them and tossed them, slithered them into a bowl, added (on request) a sliver of seaweed or a boiled onion top, ladled fish soup and soy sauce over it all – and there was a good hot supper. And if that did not fill you up, the next man might be hawking buckwheat cakes, crystallised oranges, boiled red beans, amber syrup, rice dumplings, greasy wildhog steaks or wedges of white bean-curd. In midwinter these goodies were supplemented by the New Year specialities: roast chestnuts, pickled lotus root and decorations of lobsters surmounted by fern leaves. Cold weather comfort for children came with the itinerant 'cookshop man', whose brand of do-it-yourself cookery was performed over a charcoal brazier with the aid of a big copper plate and a tub full of sweet, runny paste. For his *rin*, the child received a dab of the paste on a saucer which he poured on to the plate and, with his chubby fingers, made into any shape he liked – a monkey, a mushroom, a heron or a tortoise. Then his creation was heated hard over the fire, scraped off the plate and he could eat first whichever bit he chose – leg of heron, tortoise head or dangling monkey's tail.

For those who ate too many monkeys' tails or indulged in a surfeit of New Year lobsters, *Senkintan* or 'Thousand Gold Medicine' could be highly recommended. This precious remedy came in the unpromising shape of brown caked squares and was sold by men who walked the streets in red tights carrying umbrellas plastered with slogans. *Senkintan* sellers were celebrated for their loud chant – a sort of musical commercial – which informed passers-by that their product was guaranteed to cure inflation of the belly through indigestion, worms and fevers; it would also help to strengthen the spleen and ward off the direst effects of earthquakes. An English doctor analysed *Senkintan* and solemnly informed members of the Japan Society that it contained mainly peppermint, camphor, catechu and a bit of silver leaf; but never mind, everyone liked the song and it sold well. And in the evenings, for those who still ached, there came, tapping and feeling the dark, the blind *ammas*, the masseurs whose long-short-short wailing note on their bamboo whistles was one of Japan's most characteristic and well-remembered sounds. The profession of masseur was reserved for the blind who promised, as they kneaded the tired flesh, to 'smooth the weary pain of the day away' – and who must have done so, for most people, however poor, paid a couple of *rin* for a massage two or three times a week.

Down the dim side-alleys, away from the bells of food-hawkers, the masseur's plaintive call, the caterwauling of the medicine-men, flitted sly bird-catchers carrying long bamboo poles smeared with bird-lime who whistled soft bird-notes to attract their prey. They reckoned to pop at least sixty victims a day into their reed bags and sell them to the man at the corner stall whose speciality was sparrow-on-a-spit. Other sleazy denizens of the back ways were the ragpickers, whose mildewed straw sandals scuffed over the stones from dawn until midnight. Their faces were muffled in dirty cloth up to the eyes – eyes bloodshot and sickened from continual probing of the foulest corners of the city, its cesspools, refuse pails, garbage pits and cinder heaps. They stuffed their booty – scraps of material, wisps of straw, wastepaper both clean and soiled – in tattered sacks which they took to the junk shop for pulping and reselling to the neighbouring mill. 'An unwholesome bird of prey' was a ragpicker, commented Theobald Purcell, who wrote a series of bright sketches on the people of the Tokyo streets, 'as he slinks along, the very dogs seem to shun him'. And with good cause apparently, for one of a ragpicker's side-lines was the sale of tough canine skins to the local drum-maker.

And sometimes, padding almost as quietly as bird-catcher and ragpicker, came the fortune-teller, with a mirror in one hand and a bundle of thin divining sticks in the other. A crafty old bird of prey he was too, with his collected scraps of raggedy histories, flighty dreams and fears, some of them soiled, some unsullied. Twisting his sticks and watching the eager face of his customer in the mirror, he pulped together his snippety bits of knowledge, his straws of wisdom to make a fortune, a personally-tailored, wondrous fortune, usually – sweethearts for the lonely, children for the barren, health for the aged, wealth for the impoverished.

But fortunes are arbitrary: less than a mile from the lowliest, saddest ragpicker in the filthiest back-alley lived the public people at the opposite end of the social scale – the aristocrats in their new western-style mansions, the Imperial Family in its moated palace, the foreign diplomats in their legations.

From the roof of the biggest legation of them all – a thick, square-towered, square-chimneyed building, with a wide gravel drive that curved impressively away behind high, wrought-iron entrance gates – fluttered the British flag. On 1 May 1889 all the flags were, presumably, out, the antimacassars in the drawing-rooms were all very clean, the furniture was redolent with wax polish, the chandeliers all sparkled, for Mr Hugh Fraser, the new British Minister, and his wife were arriving to take up residence.

Mrs Hugh Fraser, who recorded in her *Letters from Home to Home* just what it was like to be the Minister's wife in

Tokyo at the time, already had considerable experience of far-flung places and interesting people. She was born Miss Mary Crawford, third daughter of Thomas Crawford, an American sculptor in the classical tradition who designed part of Washington's Capitol; her younger brother was Francis Marion Crawford, the cosmopolitan novelist. Her childhood had been spent at the Villa Negroni in Rome, where the family lived the gracious, fortunate life of rich, cultured expatriates. Her handsome, gay father taught her to walk by rolling oranges ahead of her down a long avenue of cypress trees in the villa grounds; she could always see the oranges in her mind's eye – they were as big as pumpkins.

After her father's early death, Mary, her sisters and brother were taken by their mother to live in the Villa Odescalchi, quite near the Brownings. Mary used to play with their petted only son, Penry, who, she said, 'was always beautifully dressed, with long chestnut curls'; and once, reluctantly, she was taken to visit the formidable Mrs Browning, who reclined on a sofa in a shaded room, her 'great cavernous eyes glowering out under two big bushes of black ringlets'. Practically every eminent American who toured Europe during the 1860s seems to have been a weekend guest at Odescalchi. Bayard Taylor went, James Russell Lowell, General Grant, Augustus Hare and the ageing Henry Wadsworth Longfellow who read Tasso aloud to them all in sonorous, still-vibrant tones.

In 1874 there was a strawberries-and-cream and champagne wedding between Mary Crawford and Hugh Fraser, a secretary at the British Embassy in Rome, and almost immediately the couple were whipped away to Pekin for four years. Mrs Fraser long remembered with some dismay the severe, desolate winters, the fly-ridden, stifling summers, the interminable, insulated joyless rounds of the inter-legation parties in the Chinese capital and she was most relieved when Hugh's next post was Vienna. There, too, the diplomatic mill ground relentlessly on; during her first ball Mrs Fraser was introduced to her future social companions – roomful after roomful of 'gorgeously bedecked dowagers with historical names who gazed at me sadly over breastplates of diamonds'. Ball followed ball, most splendid of them being the court ones in the Hofburg Castle, for which the ladies of the British Embassy with 'our men in cocked hats and gold lace' formed in procession up the wide stairs past lines of liveried flunkeys to be presented to Elizabeth of Austria. The Empress had, apparently, but two questions to ask of foreign wives: had they children? did they ride? If the answers were affirmative, conversation might continue; if not, it ended there. Nevertheless Mrs Fraser enjoyed her two years in Vienna as she did their next assignment – in Chile; when she arrived in Tokyo she was prepared, indeed eager, to enjoy Japan also, which she did. She was then a discerning, witty, cultivated woman of thirty-eight years, and a marvellous letter-writer.

Looking out from the upstairs veranda of the Legation over the unknown oriental city, its network of swarming streets, its temples, stone walls and arched wooden bridges, the Minister's wife felt 'at the heart of things'. To her left, across the banks of the moat, was the Emperor's new palace, its imperial life shielded from the common gaze by impenetrable foliage, ancient pines, and it was here that her official duties began a few days later, with a visit to the Empress. To reach the royal presence, one was conducted through corridors panelled with orange and cedar wood, along galleries glowing with designs of golden rabbits, flowing seas of ivory, emerald birds, and across 'enclosed courts full of fruit blossoms and palm trees and the play of fountains in the sun'. The Empress herself, seen at length after the 'three regulation curtseys', was a 'pale calm little lady' with very tiny, very white hands and a voice so soft that, Mrs Fraser admits, 'even in that hushed atmosphere I could hardly catch its tones'. Luckily, the royal welcome was translated for her by one of the attendant retinue of fragile ladies-in-waiting who were all, like their sovereign mistress, attired in rather old-fashioned European-style gowns of pale blue, mauve or grey satin.

Following the first Imperial Audience came the introductory round of official dinners. Inscrutable Japanese ministers resplendent in gold braid, silently ate their *pâté de foie gras* on either side of her; they seldom admitted knowledge of any European language so that ponderous comments on the weather or the table-decorations were channelled through an interpreter – which made them sound much sillier. There were garden parties too, in the grounds of noblemen's villas sweeping down to the sea edge, and guests sipped champagne and ate cherry-ices under the cryptomerias. Conversation was again low-toned and intermittent, but the feasting went on and on, 'We are expected to eat as if it were eight in the evening instead of four in the afternoon,' Mary Fraser protested.

She performed her social rituals without real complaint however, sometimes with vague pleasure, but they rarely involved her. Her joys were less calculable – junks on the water at dawn, the cook's two-year-old son, fire-flies, the cry of the woman selling millet cakes outside the Legation gate each evening. The cook's son, her 'adopted godson' is 'so fat and round that he never remembers where to find his feet and is always rolling over the mats in search of them'. When his 'godmother' approaches, the child is told to prostrate himself respectfully and 'the little bullet head goes down on his fat hands with great readiness; but it is a terrible business to get it up again'. Then there are the gardener's three children who run across the great lawns at twilight to receive from her hands a pink cake each 'and one for baby brother'. Mary Fraser was amused to discover later that these pink trophies were 'considered too fine to eat and have been put in state in a niche of honour, beside those which I gave them last week!'

As for the fire-flies, their green-gold stars winked at her from tiny cages piled on a fair-stall during one of her first unofficial explorations of the city's back streets. She stood before the stall for a while and then told her interpreter that she must have all the fire-flies out of all the cages. A crowd gathered 'to watch this foreign woman spending her money in this mad way', and the insects were piled into one large cage made of horsehair and carried to the Legation. Late that night, when her husband slept, Mary crept outside into the balmy spring darkness, opened the cage and set every fire-fly free. 'This way and that they flew, their radiant lamps glowing and paling like jewels seen through water, some clinging to my hair and my hands as if afraid to plunge into the garden's unknown ways. I felt like a white witch who had called the stars down to play with her.' And then, in case this all seems a trifle stagey, she adds that some of the staff apparently shared her vision, for suddenly, she 'became aware of a string of dark figures hurrying across the shadowed lawns in a terrified rush for the servants' quarters and I noticed next day that I was approached with awe amounting to panic'.

She too craved freedom from cages, particularly from the grandiose, airless cage of the Legation in midsummer. Wanly, 'seeking for something to breathe' she drifts through the high empty corridors; the large-leaved potted plants limply wilt against each florid pillar; the sun, beating against the blinds of split bamboo which are all drawn down, filters through as a greenish humid twilight and the blinds themselves emit a smell of hot rank grass; dust from the thick carpets, the plush chairs, hangs in the weary air. Tip, the dachshund, 'popularly known as the Brown Ambassador', 'lies on his back between door and window with ears all over the place and fat brown satin paws turned up in the hope of catching a stray breeze and showing it the way to his nose'. The Emperor's favourite dog, she recalls, has a servant to sit 'beside it all day, fan the flies away and pop bits of ice in its mouth' and she wishes some kind fairy would do the same for her.

Once again the real contentment seems to exist behind the official scenery – in the farther courtyard where the servants spend their leisurely after-lunch hours. There, the pastry-boy is arranging camellias in a vase, grooms are smoking, amahs are drinking tea, the cookboys are cleaning salads and sprinkling each other with wet lettuce leaves, the maids are spreading out the vast ambassadorial tablecloths to bleach and stiffen in the sun. Mary Fraser, herself too awe-inspiring to visit the courtyard except on special tours of inspection, used often to sit at an upper window and peer secretly down to watch, from a distance, the 'many-sided, brightly-coloured life' below.

Like other embassy wives, missionaries and school-teachers, Mrs Fraser was not called upon to endure the entirety of Tokyo's enervating summer doldrums. In late July, trunks, hampers, hat-boxes, wicker baskets were filled and the Minister's wife was 'comfortably packed in my Hong Kong chair', swung high on the shoulders of four coolies and borne away to the cool distant mountains. Their summer house, her 'Palace of Peace', was a two-storey wooden structure on a secluded hillside at Karuizawa. Its rooms were divided by curtains of mosquito netting, its cupboards, tables, beds were made by a local carpenter from beech wood and bamboo. Consuls in white tropical suits snoozed or read old copies of *The Illustrated London News* there, servants glided in with trays of iced lemonade, visiting ladies carefully arranged their lawn skirts as they sank into low rattan chairs and the Minister's favourite labradors padded quiet as lions along the verandas.

These particular verandas were perfect patterns for the 'veranda life' that so many Far East hands of those days remembered with nostalgia. They were deep wooden galleries that completely surrounded each floor, the highest one fitted with glass panels so that Mrs Fraser could sit and watch the pine trees in the rain. Their branches scraped against the veranda rails in a high wind and on moonlit nights cast shadows over a lawn that sloped to a pond, a stream, two bow-bent bridges. The Minister, his wife, and visiting members of the Legation staff with their wives spent their quietest after-dinner hours there. Time for brandy and cigars, to watch the spindly ghost-moths bashing against the screens as they tried to reach the pools of lamplight in the dining-room behind, to listen to the frogs under the bridges dozily creaking. Conversation meandered, died undemandingly away. They talked about the latest exploit of the pastryboy who, on his last day off, had dressed himself in a white drill suit with pith helmet to match and gone riding with the cook, similarly attired; they debated the composition of the new Diet and which members of the cabinet were being the most intransigent over the endless problem of revising the foreign trade treaties; they praised again and again the thick sweet perfume that poured from the sheaves of wild lilies which the gardener arranged every day in tall jars around the doorways.

It was on the very first of the many happy veranda evenings that the Frasers saw, to their surprise, a lantern bobbing towards them over the bridge. 'The lantern-bearer paused, then found courage to approach and a gorgeous person in white uniform, white gloves and a good deal of gold about him slowly loomed on our astonished sight and stopped on the veranda step with a military bow. This was our special policeman under whose charge we are to be for the summer. He held out a piece of paper towards us, exclaiming, "My card!" Then he looked at H—. "You Minister?" he inquired; and when H— nodded he proceeded to explain that he would guard us with vigilance and zeal. The English was very queer and ground out a word at a time; but he would not be helped and was rather offended when Mr G— [one of the Legation Secretaries] addressed him in fluent Japanese. His parting salutation was original: "Please! Receive! Sleep!" ' The policeman, who wore his spotless gloves on all occasions, became one of Mrs Fraser's favourite people and took his duties with extreme seriousness. Late one night, when a terrible typhoon was raging, she saw him on his beat round the house, wind tearing through his oilskins, as he checked that all the shutters were secured.

It was always too soon that they had to leave the Palace of Peace and tread again the stately measures of the capital's diplomatic round. Its rhythms were seasonal, disrupted, sometimes, by momentous public events or the arrival of especially distinguished visitors. Foremost among the latter were Their Royal Highnesses the Duke and Duchess of Connaught whose entourage for their visit in 1890 was so extensive that Mrs Fraser found it simpler to move out of the Legation and give it over to them completely. They arrived

during cherry-blossom time and Mrs Fraser had the whole
residence filled with branches so that 'every place was a
bower'. The Duchess said that 'her blossom-bedroom was the
prettiest she had ever slept in'. The visit was an unofficial one
and the party travelled everywhere quite casually in *jinrikishas* – which greatly outraged the Legation's coachmen. The
Duchess was, apparently, straightforward and easy to please,
a 'daintily neat and trim' person, Mrs Fraser decided, 'and
when she clicks her little heels together and bows straight
from the waist, one is irresistibly reminded of a smart German
officer'. So it was with appropriate exhaustiveness and energy
that the royal party whisked round Japan. As Mrs Fraser
wearily concluded the day before they left, 'Everything in
fact, that could be "done" from Tokyo has been done
thoroughly.'

And the Minister's wife was entitled to her weariness. For,
from the late eighties onwards, ever larger flocks of foreign
visitors teemed into the Japanese capital, many of them lured
thither by the pretty dream-pictures of a cherry-blossom and
kimono world which had, by that time, proliferated over the
tea-cups, glove-boxes and biscuit-tins of Europe and America.
On the same popular level, Gilbert and Sullivan's opera, *The
Mikado*, first performed in London in 1885, delighted huge
audiences and further encouraged the belief that Japan was a
fascinating and charming fairy-tale land. Among the discrimi-
nating, there was an increasing vogue for Japanese pottery,
screens, scroll-paintings and woodblock prints which clearly
manifested the sensitivity and sophistication of the country's
artists. The drama, literature and music of Japan had not then,
and never has, aroused very widespread popular interest
abroad, but the Japanese stimulated the enthusiasm and appreciation of many in the western art world by sending examples of their visual arts as cultural emissaries to the foreign
capitals.

As a result of all this, a general attitude of benevolent
interest and curiosity about Japan and its people was engendered in the West. And so, in addition to royalty with its

retinues, official visitors and collectors and connoisseurs of art, strings of globe-trotters came eagerly prancing through the Legation halls. There were bishops and their elder daughters, journalists and admirals, judges and their families from China, business executives and linguists, young lords and their eligible sisters, retired colonels with wives, young bachelors from Oxford finding their feet, maiden ladies of good family, political academics and junketing M.P.s studying The Far East Question; all with letters of introduction to the Minister, all wanting passports for the interior, all aiming to climb Mount Fuji, tour the Nikko temples, watch a tea ceremony – 'do' Japan.

II

They came in large floating hotels that trundled across the Pacific or up from Hong Kong. They usually came in spring and early summer, so that the sky was blue and the sun hammered on the awnings that flapped above the promenade decks and made bright lozenge-shaped patches of light where it thrust through the loosely-laced joins of the canvas. Ladies moved their deck-chairs to keep out of the little treacherous glares; their husbands and fathers, less cautious, sometimes stood openly against the breeze and became pink-cheeked. Stewardesses, condescending creatures in 'gorgeous maroon satin and velvet' brought beef tea, and pigtailed Chinese stewards slipped by with gin fizzes. If the wind got up and the ship began to buck, ladies retired to their cabins with sal volatile; the numberless Chinese who were always travelling steerage in either direction and who cooked their two-month-old duck eggs, peas and salt fish on a humble patch of lower deck, threw handfuls of white joss-paper towards the waves in prayer for better weather; but the ship's officers in their gold braid, with their stomachs still and confident, stayed at the rails and watched the ladies vanishing and the joss-papers churning down-water in the wake, and smiled to themselves.

And when at length they sailed, safe and well again, into the harbour roadsteads of Japan the travellers all said to each other, as the anchors rattled down, that the junks scudding over the water looked just like white butterflies and the ladies quickly averted their eyes from the near-nudity of the boatmen. And those who were Yokohama-bound were shepherded into small boats, 'a delicious and curious moment', wrote one traveller, 'this first sense of being freed from the big prison of the ship; of not understanding a word of what one hears and yet of getting at the meaning through every sense; of being close to the top of the waves on which we dance instead of looking down on them from the tall ship's sides; of seeing the small limbs of the rowing boys burning yellow in the sun and noticing how they recall the dolls of their own country in the expression of their eyes; of the first sensation of feeling, while lying flat on the bottom of the boat, at the level of our faces tossing skyblue water dotted with innumerable orange copies of the sun. Then subtle influences of odour, a sense of something very foreign, of the presence of another race came up with the smell of the boat.'

Deposited safely on the quayside, with their leather portmanteaux and wooden trunks, they all said to each other that the quaint little ladies in their kimonos who were hurrying past looked exactly like the ones they had left on the tea-caddies at home. And then they all took their first hilarious *jinrikisha* rides to their foreign-style hotels – establishments which, by this time, offered something for everybody. If you wanted your name to appear in the local papers' gossip columns, you went to Yokohama's Grand Hotel, which 'Caters for First Class Travel Only' or the Oriental Palace with two ballrooms and Private Parlours for entertaining. Those with fewer aspirations went, perhaps, to the Club Hotel 'with a Bar and five-table Billiard Room fitted up in a Superior Manner' or the Windsor, with its 'extensive veranda 12 feet wide, not only making a grand promenade in all weathers but giving that airiness to all parts of the house so desirable to guests'. For the lower orders there was Carey's, run by the jovial mulatto Bill Carey himself – whalers and engineers went there, tea merchants whose ships had not yet come home and writers like Rudyard Kipling, in search of local colour. The Takuradzuka Hotel at Kobe was the place if you still felt a trifle peaky after the voyage: its air was 'universally recommended by the Medical Faculty for its bracing nature' and its famous 'HOT IRON BATHS are much sought after for their health-giving qualities'.

Usually, for the first few days, the globe-trotters were content to canter round the well-trodden tourist tracks. From Loxton's Livery Stable they could hire 'Buggies, Sociables, Wagonettes, Barouches, Landaus, Broughams, Dog Carts or Gigs' for the first euphoric ride round Yokohama Bay; they had their photographs taken at Farzuri's who kept 'special dresses for ladies and gentlemen and *jinrikishas* etc for taking portraits and groups in costume'; they went to see 'Daiboots' (the Daibutsu or Great Buddha at Kamakura) and gasped up at his unseeing eyes and snaily hair; they called at the Foreigner's Cemetery on the way back, where, the guidebook told them, lay several victims of the two-sworded warriors – murderous cowardly reactionaries of the 1860s, who 'always struck from behind' and thus held unfair advantage over 'the unwary foreigner who, on account of his training and belief that brave enemies always come in front, was helpless before his butcher in the rear'. They visited various temples, again consulted the guidebook and found that 'The Buddhists worship Buddha and a host of minor deified men and pray to a vast number of saints.' And they all went into stitches at the 'Japlish' signs above some of the stores: 'The Time Piece Snop'; the polyglot chemist's 'Patent Apotheik Seiseisha Compagnie' and the 'draper, milliner and ladies outfatter' where they sold 'the ribbons, the laces, the veils and the feelings'.

Most of the globe-trotters did this sort of thing; one of the more celebrated among them however, declined. Landing at

Yokohama, Rudyard Kipling went straight along to the house of the French Consul, whom he knew, walked out into the garden, sat down and looked around: 'Half a dozen blue black pines are standing akimbo against a real sky', he explained, ' – not a fog blur, nor a cloud bank nor a grey dish-clout wrapped round the sun – but a blue sky. A cherry-tree on a slope below them throws up a wave of blossom that breaks all creamy white against their feet and a clump of willows trail their palest green shoots in front of all. The sun sends for an ambassador through the azalea bushes a lordly swallow-tailed butterfly and his squire, very like the fluttering "chalk-blue" of the English downs. The warmth of the East, that goes through, not over, the lazy body, added to the light of the East – the splendid lavish light that clears but does not bewilder the eye. Then the new leaves of the spring wink like fat emeralds and the loaded branches of cherry blossom grow transparent and glow as a hand glows held up against flame. Little warm sighs come up from the moist warm earth, and the fallen petals stir on the ground, turn over and go to sleep again. . . .'

Part, at least, of Kipling had come home; he did not perhaps, need to go farther than that. But most globe-trotters were very much abroad, and when you are abroad you keep moving to see as much as possible, so, following their acclimatisation period, they all got ready for the big Excursion into the Interior to discover the elusive 'real Japan' that still lurked secretly behind the westernised façades of the treaty ports.

The kind of tour you took depended on what sort of person you were, and, in case of doubt, the 1888 *Handy Guide to Japan* conveniently defined the categories: firstly, there were the well-trodden little trips 'for delicate persons and those who dislike accommodation at Inns kept in pure Japanese style'; the second category of more exotic explorations was for 'Lovers of the Curious and Picturesque in robust health'; and lastly there were the really testing safaris for those 'desirous of avoiding the beaten track'. The most authoritative Japanese handbook of the period, produced by a Lieutenant Hawes and

that erudite diplomat, Ernest Satow, when the latter was a
secretary at the British Legation, presumed a considerable
degree of masculine stalwartness in all its readers. For a trip
of up to two weeks in the interior travellers are advised to
equip themselves with, at least, the following:

'One light flannel coat and with pockets to button up, 1
pair light flannel trousers and 1 pr. knickerbockers (ditto); two
flannel shirts with breast-pockets, three pairs each of Merino
singlets, Merino socks and stockings, two prs. loose flannel
pyjamas and jackets and Japanese loose gowns and sashes,
lots of pocket handkerchiefs, a portable dressing case and looking glass, a plaid shawl or rug, a pair of slippers, three sheets
and an air pillow, two towels and soap and stout walking
shoes and white canvas shoes and strong umbrella and two
white covers for it and patent grease for the boots and a travelling thermometer and Persian insect powder and a supply of
carbolic acid.'

And, if one still felt insufficiently furnished for all possible
contingencies of the Japanese climate, one could, on Yokohama's Main Street, buy a couple of 'Ellwood's Patent Air-
Chamber CORK AND FELT HATS, that are manufactured WITH
INDIA-RUBBER and are perfectly free from the dangerous and
objectionable qualities of all articles of clothing made of that
material when used in tropical climates . . .'

Perspiration, about which Mr Ellwood is presumably talking, was a problem. And washing, Satow and Hawkes explain,
unfortunately 'could not be done properly in the interior'.
They therefore advise their pilgrims to send ahead further
supplies of knickerbockers and shirts in order to avoid an
excess of luggage. Curiously enough, 'pyjamas with short
gaiters are strongly recommended for walking' and those who
feel this to be a trifle négligé even for oriental village life,
can relieve the 'loose appearance by having a jacket made to
button down the front and collar a little higher than usual'.
For walking, even in pyjamas and gaiters, a gentleman must
have the right food. Care should be taken to employ a servant
capable of baking bread and supplies of flour for this pur-

pose could be sent in advance with the spare socks etc.; 'ovens could be improvised'. Liebig's Extract of Meat and Epps' Cocoa were as indispensable as they had ever been, but to encumber oneself with cases of beer and wine was a foolish extravagance – 'Preston's Lemonade with a very small quantity of sherry will be found an excellent drink' after presumably, a hard day's footslogging.

Some intrepid travellers scorned all these crutches of western civilisation; some of them regretted it. 'For breakfast,' explained young George Pearson, 'going native' somewhere in the interior with a stronger-stomached friend, 'we had one bowl of warm salt water with a fish's eye and tail (extreme tip) and three shreds of green ginger floating in it.' On a nearby plate sat 'a section of something brown, with little holes in it, like a magnified piece of colt's-foot rock, very soft, very cold, very nasty'. Another bowl offered what were 'said to be salted plums but which looked and tasted like balls of pink blotting paper that had been lying for some months in bad red cabbage pickle'. The cabbage motif was continued at the next meal, when he was faced with 'a little pyramid of singularly offensive vegetable matter like cold boiled turnip tops or neglected saeurkraut' and a heap of snails in a lacquer dish which looked like tanned periwinkles and tasted like india-rubber. Tea seldom brought much in the way of treats. 'Do you remember', asked Sara Duncan, gayest and funniest of the female globe-trotters, 'how, when you were very small and blew soap-bubbles out of a clay pipe, you sometimes made a mistake and blew bubbles in? The pink cakes of Japan revive many such gustatory memories.'

And so, suffering from what Miss Duncan terms 'a vagrant and uncared-for gastronomic feeling', to bed. But before this came the washing problem. The inns provided large wooden-sided box-like baths which were full of water, steam – and other guests. 'It was a novel position truly,' remarked a travelling professor, 'to be jammed in this Tartarean hole between two flabby middle-aged women.' So sometimes, mindful of foreigners' delicate susceptibilities, single tubs were provided for them, small steaming ones, in an open room, 'without even so much as a native newspaper between oneself and the public' groaned Pearson. Towels were useless as shields, they came handkerchief-size and one rub 'reduced them to the consistency of a damp cobweb'. Innocent pretty Japanese maids, landladies, other less inhibited guests of both sexes, popped gaily in and out, uttered no warning, doors would not lock, worried young men helplessly flapped nightshirts at them, improvised screens with overcoats hung across lines of string, kept guard for each other, boiled themselves alive (afraid to come out), stayed dirty for days – anything 'to preserve the proprieties'.

And then at last, still damp, pink, shaken, to bed. Inns still specialised in fleas. *Wetmore's Guide to Japan* advised 'Buy an ounce of powdered camphor at a native drug store to take with you. At bedtime sprinkle the camphor abundantly under and upon the bed and on the floor for a foot or so around the bedding.' After this and a flying leap over the camphor to the three quilts on the floor and after deciding which of these was to lie on and which under, 'sound sleep', concludes Mr Wetmore, 'is warranted'.

But this depended, in fact, on the extent of one's exhaustion. The walls of Japanese inns were, literally, paper-thin. It was all rather like open-plan living – and not everyone liked it. Lewis Wingfield (the traveller who had climbed Mount Asama with a battalion of *jinrikishas*) certainly did not. He recalled with extreme clarity each particular sound of the medley that buffeted across him as he lay, courting sleep, in his Osaka hotel. 'Each new arrival required, in the first instance, a bath, and here, as everywhere else, there was an inner yard reserved for the purpose of ablution. Splash-splash-a-palm-clap-towels!' Then after the masters were satisfied came the turn of the 'ricksha men, who had well earned their washing – and how they enjoyed the luxury! With what untiring energy did they apply themselves to the creaking well-windlass and draw up pailful after pailful; and then what a showering and a sloshing with a crowing *obbligato* of delight. Eventually

... the travellers disposed themselves to sleep – at last! A murmuring, a snoring, conversation in low tones, varied by rippling laughter. Too-too-too! A trumpet! Good heavens, what could be the matter? Absolutely a trumpeter [the hotel's night-watchman] was perambulating the corridors, opening each partition as he went – too-too-too – then to the next. My partition worked stiffly. He knocked it out of its groove. It fell inward on the floor. Too-too-too! A grumble and a grunt and after some fumbling the screen was replaced. Too-too-too! Good night!'

And then good morning. A bright blue morning very often. Time to jump into the *jinrikisha*, clamber on to the saddle, grease the walking boots, forget to grumble – for around them lay the lovely Japanese countryside. Early spring, when a few globe-trotters began their travels, brought the periods of 'The Awakening Insect' and 'The Seed Rain', two of the twenty-four divisions of the old solar year; by the time of May's 'Little Plenty' plenty of foreigners were about, each one discovering his own 'real Japan'. It was the beginning of the mysterious silk season and among the mulberry bushes flitted hawk moths, Indian Moon moths and spotted crimson butterflies. Mulberry leaves were precious now – food for the silk worms that lay on the shelves in the farmhouses munching and crunching their lives away and making a sound exactly like a heavy fall of rain. Great care had to be taken at this stage, each separate leaf must be wiped dry of any moisture, minced very finely for the youngest worms, left whole for the oldest. For about forty days the worms, if they had been properly treated, 'moulted' four times, ate voraciously between moults and gradually lightened in colour, then, replete and lethargic, they fastened silken guy-lines to a twig and wound themselves to sleep inside their precious cocoons. June came while they slept, the period of 'Transplanting the Rice' and the peasants knee-deep in the paddy-mud often unbent their backs to smile their wrinkled peasant-smiles as the globe-trotters rode by. Fields of rape-seed flower flared sulphur-yellow along the valleys and wild lilies and roses grew over the verges. The first cocoons had already been laid out in the sun on trays along the roadside. This killed the pupae, and was administered to all but a few that were kept for seed, in order to prevent the emergence of the moth, as the cocoon was best kept unbroken for reeling.

July was time for 'The Little Heat and Great Heat' and tourists were glad to rest awhile at the tree-shaded shrines. The stone courtyards and their statues were rough with creamy-grey and purple lichens, dragonflies vibrated their electric-blue bodies above the lotus leaves in the pools and goldfish flickered under them, waiting to be fed by the robed acolytes. Along the open roads again only the birds were really active. Snowy egrets poked their beaks into the paddies searching for worms, green pigeons with amber eyes picked, unlawfully, at sweet potatoes and a few painted snipe squawked in the trees – stupid unwary birds foreign sportsmen called them, hardly worth the powder and shot – dry to the taste, perhaps because they fed on rice and beetles.

The thatched wayside cottages were wide open to catch any breeze that blew, and heaps of cocoons tumbled over the mats like snowdrifts. It was time for grandmothers and other elderly relatives to begin to reel the silk. They sat among the drifts, drawing the slender threads off the cocoons, along a trough of hot water and on to a hand reel. It was exacting work and the old people were as careful as they could be, but even so this 'country silk' was much criticised when it reached the markets. Indeed, according to one member of Yokohama's Chamber of Commerce, its faults were legion: the ends were too fine or too thick, or it was 'soon-run-down-ended'; it was sticky; it was double-ended or flat-ended; it contained 'slubs, gouts or dirt'. Its stickiness was caused by over-heating the water, but the rest of its deficiencies were 'simply due to the idleness of the reeler'. Had the speaker but considered the number of times that granny had to stop to collect the eggs or the children, shred the luncheon lily bulbs, wave and smile at the globe-trotters who stopped to watch her work, he would surely have realised that a few slubs and flat ends were inevitable and not the result of mere idleness. But such excuses would not do; as a modern economist put it, 'Under the stimulus of foreign demand, cocoon-raising was improved and the reeling process began to be taken out of the peasant household to be organised in workshops and factories employing mechanical power.' Large government filatures were established in some areas and women employed in them earned such good wages that their menfolk complained because there was no one left at home to do the housework. Each year, merchants, both Japanese and western, prayed that the silk harvests of France and Italy would be poor so that prices of oriental silk would rocket. Sometimes they did and all the East was happy, but sometimes there was a slump and once, in the early days, the Japanese merchants burned thousands of their silkworm egg cards in order to keep up export prices. 'We'll burn half our imports next year,' warned the foreigners, only half-joking, 'to keep up the price of the remainder.'

But back in the slow rhythms of the August countryside it was just too hot to bother about exports or imports, gouts or ends too soon run down; the aged reelers dozed among their cocoons, great leaves of melon and gourd wilted against the barn walls; the remaining globe-trotters joined the missionaries and the embassy-wives in the mountains. Unfortunately, when it came to mountains, August, hot or not, was the time to climb Fujiyama. Everyone knows now and knew then about Fuji. It is a volcano, symmetrical, extinct. Tradition says it uprose suddenly into the world on a certain June night in the year 286 B.C.; certainly it has been there for as long as any chronicler remembers, holy glorious symbol of the nation. Fortunate globe-trotters who happened to arrive on a very clear day saw it floating fifty miles away over the plains as they came into Yokohama harbour. To many it was like a vision, a lonely and majestic god suspended in the pale blue and they at once understood why it was sacred. It is a peerless mountain, honourable Lord and Master of the land, sweetly shaped, say the Japanese, like a half-open inverted fan – an image, remarked Lafcadio Hearn, 'made wonderfully exact by the fine streaks that spread downward from the notched top like shadows of fan-ribs'.

The fan of Fuji is variously described as being gold, black, silver, red, purple or white according to the time of day and the season when the beholder saw it. It was always a versatile mountain, as Miss Charlotte Lorrimer, globe-trotter, explained: 'She [Fuji] poses there against the sky, a wonderful carved cameo drawing her mists around to adorn her; she drapes them about her waist, or her beautiful sloping shoulders, floats them across her bosom or throws them scarf-wise over her lovely head. Never for an hour is she content with one kind of garment. Everlastingly, continually, she rearranges her draperies, squandering filmy folds, velvety soft, with reckless prodigality – alluring, calling, beckoning, disdaining her lover the Sun' . . . So continual and agitated a mating display on the part of any mountain might render the ascent of it a hazardous enterprise; nevertheless every summer, when 'her summit' was free of snow, thousands of pilgrims took the risk and climbed Mount Fuji. Not attempting to compete with their hostess in terms of sartorial virtuosity, they traditionally wore plain white cloaks, white leggings, straw hats and sandals and carried hand-bells. And of course, some of the hardier and more enterprising foreigners, seeing this, donned their toughest climbing boots, their pith helmets and went up also. In 1874 Messrs Steward, Poate and Christison had measured Fuji's height using one of Eckhold's patent omnimeters and had decided that it was 12,365 feet above the level of the ordinary spring tides; Mr Rhymer Jones had descended into its crater and found it to be five hundred feet deep. Later estimates vary by a hundred feet or so, but clearly it was not an easy ascent and both pilgrims and globe-trotters took it in stages.

The first stage was to take a pack-horse or a *jinrikisha* up the sloping plains as far as the 'Horse-Turn-Back Station'; there, the climber bought a thick pilgrim's staff – which was the only aid to locomotion allowed from that point up – and had it stamped with the Fuji crest. Ten stations were placed at intervals along the normal route of ascent, little huts, half-buried in the volcano's side and crammed with pilgrims, their spare shoes, food, fleas and charcoal smoke from the open fire. When the traveller was quite exhausted he forced his way into one of these, staked his claim to a square of matting, dined ravenously on rice and seaweed (tinned meat and biscuits for the globe-trotters), then tucked himself into a cold achy ball on the floor and fell asleep. Dawn was a miracle, the vision become volcano. 'The tremendous naked black reality – always becoming more sharply, more grimly, more atrociously defined,' wrote Lafcadio Hearn. 'A black lighthouse springing towards the sky,' decided another climber, Herbage Edwards, 'delicate as Giotto's lily tower; slender in its grace and fragile.' '. . . a line', adds Hearn, 'that now shows no curve whatever but shoots down below the clouds and up to the gods know where, straight as a tightened bowstring.'

But as the sun grew hotter it was less joyous crawling like a fly up the side of a lily tower, lighthouse, bowstring. Cinder-dust buried itself in skin, hair and eyes, muscles trembled with fatigue and heads and hearts thrummed dizzily. Western women sometimes linked themselves with rope to one coolie who pulled them forward, another coolie pushed them from behind and a third hovered near to carry bags and provide extra ballast. The coolies always received orders to get their 'fares' to the top, even if they had to carry them pick-a-back. The top – as the morning dragged on that was all anyone thought about. 'We're going to the top, to the top, to the top,' chanted the lines of skinny pilgrims as they tinkled their bells and hurried skywards past the panting foreigners.

The top, at last, was a soft ash-flaked rim of crater, an icy well called the Spring of God, two shaven-headed priests who took the staff from your sweaty hands and burned another vermilion crest into the wood – symbol of conquest. Often, the top was above the clouds which, wrote Edwards, 'herded as a fold of sheep along the mountain sides below', huddling up, gathering, falling back. And when the clouds parted, as they did with any luck, came the view – the land wide and empty below. 'Rivers appear as sun gleams on spider threads,' said Hearn, 'and fishing sails are white dust clinging to the grey-blue glass of the sea.' It was an appropriate setting in which to think about Life. 'After feasting our eyes on such views as language is too poor to describe, we sat down on the side of the crater and gave ourselves to half an hour's meditation on the use of mountains in general and this one in particular,' a lady climber records in her journal. Fuji's particular function, she decided, was 'to fulfil the thirst of the human heart for the beauty of God's work, to startle its lethargy into deep and pure thoughts...' 'What words can describe the beauty and grandeur of this lonely and symmetrical mountain?' she inquires. 'What speculations tell from whence it has arisen?'

Even Sir Edwin Arnold, who gamely clambered to Fuji's summit, did not attempt to define its origins, but he felt his language was adequate to describe the vista below. So he sat down right there, on the dusty crater's rim, wrapped a rug round his legs and began:

> On top of Fuji San
> Now we lie; and half Japan
> Like a map immense unrolled
> Spreads beneath us, green and gold.
> Southwards – pale and bright – the sea
> Shines from distant Masaki
> Round Atami's broken coast
> Till its silvery gleam is lost
> Mingled with the silvery sky
> Far away towards Narumi...

Probably, before Sir Edwin had completed his survey, a chilly wind had sprung up, as it often did about midday, and shepherded the clouds back across the view. Unless you wanted to spend another night in one of those abominable huts, it was time to go. The descent was a painful, but rapid, half-controlled slide down steep heaps of cinder, a forward-sloping trek over thorn bushes and tree-roots back to the first station. 'There are two kinds of fools,' says an old Japanese proverb, 'those who never climb Mount Fuji and those who climb it twice.' Everyone who climbed it once agreed with at least the second half of that dictum.

Most of the sights were seen by now; it was autumn, time to plunder the curio shops of what Kipling termed their 'mauve, magenta and blue vitriol things', to rummage hungrily among silks, vases, *netsuké*, scrolls and teacups. So loaded down with rather indiscriminate purchases were some of the departing globe-trotters that a resident, Osman Edwards, composed a little rhyme about them, to be sung derisively to the tune of 'Yankee Doodle Dandy':

> Doodle San will leave Japan
> with several tons of cargo,
> Folks will stare when all his ware
> Is poured into Chicago.
> There's silks, cut velvet, old brocade
> And everything that's *joto* [first-class]
> And ancient bronzes newly made
> By dealers in Kyoto . . .

And so, innocently clutching their new-old statues of the Goddess of Mercy, their temple bells and painted frogs whose tongues came out, the globe-trotters departed for another year. A few were glad to go. Lewis Wingfield for instance, who wearily dismissed his numerous retinue of *jinrikisha* runners, cooks and porters and sadly purchased a few of the only decent bronzes left in the country, now that the 'hordes of Cook's Tour people' had descended like locusts on the scene. 'A foreigner', he sighed, 'grows very tired of Japan and its numerous discomforts after the novelty of strange dress and custom has worn off. He becomes weary of constantly putting on and off his shoes, of sitting on the floor and sweltering in a vapour bath or shivering in draughts. He resents the constant noise, the frequent dripping of rain, gets sick unto death of the wrinkled visage of the unintelligent peasant.'

But Wingfield's was very much a minority view. Most visitors enjoyed Japan enormously, they were sorry to leave

171

and they wanted to preserve their joy by writing about it afterwards. At least, as they all explain in their prefaces, it was not so much that they wanted to write, but that they were cajoled, nay coerced, into the author's role. 'No wish for publicity nor the faintest claim to novelty has prompted the publication of my four months' experience,' protested Arthur Crowe, who took to *The Highways and Byeways of Japan*, but his friends insisted on it. 'During my leisure hours while a sojourner in the land of the gods,' says Arthur Maclay, 'I carefully reduced to writing my observations and experiences.' These 'wayside jottings' accumulated in a manner quite surprising to himself and lo, when he submitted his work to 'several impartial readers' he was most strongly urged to publish it. 'Bowing to their judgment in the matter, I now submit my *Budget of Letters* from Japan . . .' Let Mrs Catherine Bond, another visitor who was erroneously persuaded to, as she puts it, 'launch my frail barque on the oceans of literature', say the last word for the globe-trotters, when, back in humdrum home, they started to unpack: 'We rejoice for a time to say goodbye to our guidebooks and all the impedimenta of travelling, but we fear we shall often hear the East a-calling and when the days are dark and cloudy and the east winds blow, we may set sail again over silvery seas, if not in reality, in imagination, and hear the temple bells and other soothing and dreamy sounds.'

III

And while home-returned globe-trotters cocked their ears wistfully eastward, Mrs Hugh Fraser, wife of the British Minister in Tokyo, prepared for another autumn, 'time of maples, chrysanthemums, Imperial Garden parties and the beginning of our queer little gay season'. The most sensational event of that 1890 season, from a national point of view, was the opening of the new Diet, to house the first Japanese assembly of elected representatives. This event had been foreshadowed in Japan's new constitution which had been promulgated in February of the previous year. It was a document which, though containing the appropriate genuflexions in the direction of western democratic procedures, was very much concerned to perpetuate the power of the ruling oligarchy and the Emperor – perhaps the shades of 'oriental despots' still stalked. Still, it was enthusiastically accepted by the people and (with less enthusiasm) by the main political parties, as Kipling, who was there at the time, rather patronisingly recorded, 'The new Constitution has a pale grey cover with a chrysanthemum at the back and a Japanese told me then, "Now we have Constitution as other countries and *so* it is all right".'

The elections, held in the July before the Diet Opening in November were also all right, in so far as they were orderly and well-managed – though they were hardly democratic. Franchise was granted only to males over twenty-five years of age who fulfilled certain taxpaying and residential qualifications, which meant, in effect, that about one citizen in every hundred could vote. The Diet's Opening too was all right – magnificent in fact – but the new body's subsequent career was somewhat turbulent. The Lower House was dissolved and the Diet building itself accidentally destroyed by fire during its first year; for several years after that, Prime Ministers resigned and cabinets fell with alarming frequency; and – in the traditional Japanese fashion of veiling from the public gaze those who actually manipulate the strings – most of the real power still lay with the oligarchy of so-called Elder Statesmen, the veteran aristocrats and ex-clan leaders who had controlled so many of the country's fortunes during the previous two decades. Seven Diets came and went in the first four years of constitutional government and the political lives of their members were frequently stormy, waspish and short. But in 1890 all seemed set fair. The Emperor, arrayed as any European monarch, rode to the Diet in a State Carriage of glass and gold, flanked by plume-hatted, gorgeously-uniformed outriders, followed by a body of mounted Life Guards and the coaches of the Cabinet Ministers. In his opening speech, he announced that, 'All institutions relating to internal administration' have, 'during the twenty years since Our Accession to the Throne been brought to a state approaching completeness and regular arrangement' and that, 'Our Relations with all the Treaty Powers are on a footing of constantly growing amity and intimacy.'

Mrs Fraser was not able to attend the Opening, at which the only females present were members of the Imperial Household, but, the following month, she made her own personal contribution towards the growth of amity and intimacy between Japanese and foreigner by the holding of a very special Christmas party. This was for the children of the two hundred employees on the Legation staff; it was her favourite event of the year and she prepared for it with more enthusiasm than for any of the court balls. Under her instruction, the mast-high Christmas tree became a fantasy of pink and white balls, shells made from rice paste, oranges, silver hairpins, paper roses and long glass chopsticks that shone like icicles in the lamplight. On the appointed afternoon, the children, all in their loveliest native costumes, were marshalled in procession into the Legation hall, 'till they stood, a delighted wide-eyed crowd round the beautiful shining thing, the first Christmas tree any of them had ever seen. It was worth all the trouble to see the gasp of surprise and delight, the evident fear that the whole thing might be unreal and suddenly fade away.' Then for each child a present, one for the 'Minister's second cook's girl', one for the 'student interpreter's teacher's girl' and for the 'Vice-Consul's *jinrikisha*-man's boy', who was brought to the party by the 'Vice-Consul's *jinrikisha*-man's grandmother'. The plunder was bounteous and the children dropped it into the voluminous sleeves of their kimonos, 'so as to leave hands free for anything else that the lady of the house might think fit to bestow'. One little lady, O'Haru San, aged three, got so over-loaded with goodies and toys that they kept rolling out of

Watching a naval display from the Azuma Bridge, 1888

Picture of a non-event — artist's impression of the Emperor welcoming the Czarevich. Because of the attack made on him, the Czarevich never actually reached Tokyo

IV. THE GLOBE-TROTTER AT KAMAKURA

Air : "*Yankee Doodle.*"

Doodle *San* will leave Japan
    With several tons of cargo ;
Folk will stare, when all his ware
    Is poured into Chicago.

    There's silk, cut velvet, old brocade,
        And everything, that's "*jōto*,"
    And ancient bronzes, newly made
        For dealers in Kyoto.

        His tones entice with accent nice :
            "*Ikoorah !*" and "*Ikutsu ?*"
        A million dollars is the price
            For mammoth *Daibutsu*.

            Doodle *san* will leave Japan,
                A happier man, though poorer :
            Unpurchased yet, the god, you bet,
                Will stay at Kamakura.

*A 'Residential Rhyme' by Osman Edwards, satirizing the acquisitive
instincts of the globe-trotter*

Lafcadio Hearn

Ernest Satow: from a Spy cartoon

A pilgrim ready for the ascent of Fujiyama

The Yoshiwara — outside a third-class brothel at night, with the prostitutes behind bars. Better-class establishments were conducted in a less crude manner.

A bored butterfly, waiting to play the 'Butterfly Game'

Above: '*The cleanest and most ingenious soldier in the world*': *makeshift bathing arrangements for the Japanese forces besieging Port Arthur as photographed for* The Illustrated London News

Opposite, above: *Balloon's-eye view of Port Arthur and the Tiger's Tail*

Opposite, below: *Villiers' view of Port Arthur as seen from the vicinity of 203 Metre Hill*

The annihilation of the Russian fleet at Tsushima: '. . . one hour sufficed to turn our squadron into a floating caravan of death'

Admiral Togo, the 'Nelson of Japan', directing naval operations from the bridge of his flagship during the Battle of Tsushima

her sleeves, to the great delight of the Brown Ambassador Dachshund, Tip, who pounced on them like lightning, and was also convicted of nibbling at cakes on the lower branches of the tree.

Impressed to help Mrs Fraser on such occasions were 'two somewhat antagonistic volunteers' as she terms them: the 'intensely Anglican severe-looking ascetic', Bishop Bickersteth and Sir Edwin Arnold, now safely descended from Mount Fuji and still 'basking in Buddhistic calms'. Sir Edwin, author of the highly successful poem 'The Light of Asia', former editor of *The Daily Telegraph* and now, in his late fifties, touring the world as a roving correspondent, was quite bowled over by Japan. He originally came with his daughter for a few weeks, but he stayed for almost two years, rented a Japanese house and wrote *Japonica*, a fulsome hymn of praise to the dainty ways of old Japan and to, above all, the bewitching Japanese woman, with her 'soft, symmetrical brown little palms and neat, close, roseate finger-tips and delicate supple wrists', 'emerging dewy and blooming' from a bath-house perhaps, or tripping towards him in her snow-white socks that 'are divided into a private room for the great toe and a parlour for the little toes'. The most interesting thing Sir Edwin did while in Japan is not mentioned in his published letters or his book – though one might hazard the possibility from them – he met a Japanese lady called Tama Kurokawa, married her and took her back to England with him as the third Lady Arnold.

Permanent, 'respectable' and bindingly legal liaisons between western male and Japanese female were not frequent, and Sir Edwin, had he so chosen, could perhaps have made an interesting and novel contribution to the theme. The few foreigners who married Japanese women in this way were usually professional men, such as linguists, teachers, journalists or doctors, who settled in the country for many years, often for the rest of their lives. The women they married were the refined and cloistered daughters of the middle and upper middle classes who took little part in their husbands' social or professional life – whether the husband was foreign or

Japanese. They were content to be the *okusama* (the lady in the house), confined to a domestic routine with the children.

For a few women of this class then, the coming of westernisation to their country meant that they had to adopt an entirely new and unprecedented role – as respectable wives of foreigners – but even the many who were not so drastically affected, found that they had to change the patterns of their quiet lives. Nevertheless, they accepted change obediently, as they always had accepted without question whatever measures their lords and masters – their menfolk – might care to impose upon them. And how was it, wondered some western men enviously, that the Japanese male had been able to fashion for his convenience and delight this docile and gracious female creature who sweetly and willingly complied with his every command? Well, the process of training was a traditional one and it began early. Basic and compulsory reading for young girls of good family was a large, grim treatise, written, of course, by a man, which explored with considerable thoroughness the subject of *The Whole Duty of Women*. This was divided into sections entitled, for example, 'Women's Great Learning', defining the moral obligations of the female, 'Women's Small Learning', an introduction to the weighty subject of moral obligation, 'Women's Household Instruction', a summary of duties relating to the reception of one's husband's guests etc., 'Moral Lessons', in paragraphs, and 'The Lady's Letter Writer'. Often appended to these were twenty-four stories about 'The Twenty-Four Paragons of Filial Piety in China', which were to instruct both boys and girls in their prime duty of subordinating their own interests in the cause of their parents' welfare. Professor Chamberlain, in his invaluable *Things Japanese*, amusingly enumerates the self-abnegatory exploits of some of the Paragons: one, 'though of tender years and having a delicate skin, insisted on sleeping uncovered at night in order that the mosquitoes should fasten on him alone and allow his parents to slumber undisturbed'; another, burdened 'with a cruel stepmother who was very fond of fish ... lay down naked on the surface of a lake. The warmth of his body melted the ice at which two carp came up to breathe. These he caught and set before his stepmother', who, it seems, was not even grateful. Drollest of all, as Chamberlain says, was the story of Roraishi, a paragon who, though aged seventy, 'used to dress in baby's clothes and sprawl about upon the floor' in order to delude his ninety-year-old parents into the belief that they were still young!

Most males did not carry matters to Roraishi's extremes, they accepted man's estate and with it their period of subjugation was over; for women it had but begun. Once married, a female must obey her husband as absolutely as she formerly submitted to her parents; if widowed, she must yield to the rule to her eldest son; even the contingency of sonlessness was provided for – in such a case a widow must render obedience to the eldest male member of her husband's family. A woman, explained the Treatise, must be ever industrious, 'in the morning she must rise early and at night go late to rest. Instead of sleeping in the middle of the day, she must be intent on the duties of her household and must not weary of weaving, sewing and spinning.' Complete tolerance of her husband's shortcomings (if, indeed, he had any) well became her, as did staid temperance (she must not, for example, drink overmuch tea or wine or feed her eyes and ears with theatrical performances, ditties or ballads), chastity was of course a prime requirement, as was mercy and a quiet serenity. If she were not quiet her husband could divorce her for, as the Treatise expressed it, 'talking and prattling disrespectfully so as to disturb the harmony of kinsmen and bring trouble on the household'. He could also divorce her for barrenness, lewdness (which term included the writing of a letter to another man), jealousy, thieving, or disobedience to her parents-in-law. It was almost unheard-of for wives to divorce their husbands.

In view of the Japanese women's traditional posture of subservience and tractability, it was not surprising that their menfolk regarded with awe and some horror the behaviour of the increasing numbers of western women in their country. Foreign women themselves were still shackled by the repressive conventions of patriarchal authority, but with their small freedoms – to receive a reasonable amount of education, to become missionaries, teachers or nurses, to attend many social functions with their husbands – they seemed dangerously uncaged and foot-loose as birds of the air to the Japanese male. As William Griffis wrote, describing the attitude to female emancipation in the seventies, 'Such ideas, they imagine, will subvert all domestic peace and will be the ruin of society and the nation. For the state of things to be "as if a hen were to crow in the morning" seems that point in the sea of troubles beyond which the imagination of man (in Japan) utterly fails to go.' If the imagination of the ordinary male will not go, then it must be pushed, and during the seventies and eighties some enlightened intellectuals, Christian missionaries and a few determined Japanese women themselves pushed. Mission boarding schools for girls were opened and some day schools, both public and private, for the education of girls up to the age of fourteen; the legal system was somewhat revised to give women more rights at law; ladies began to accompany their husbands to some of the social functions attended by foreign couples.

This latter duty, which the wives obediently performed, was not, at first, a pleasurable one for most of them. They were unversed in the art of holding vivacious and trivial conversations with chance male acquaintances – behaviour which, in the old days, would presumably have been termed 'lewd' – and their efforts to deal graciously with cocktail glasses, canapés, forks and napkins all at once probably caused them at least as much social discomfort as the foreigners' early fumblings with chopsticks. Worse yet however – when their menfolk wore swallow-tails and top hats, they had to be laced into inflexible, cumbersome, heavy-skirted garments. Lewis Wingfield describes, with patronising sympathy, the result, as it appeared upon the wife of a leading Japanese politician: 'She had a fearsome bonnet of velvet and bugles which would persist in tumbling backwards, though sternly tied under the chin, and a wrinkled European gown decorated with uncanny furbelows ... When she got up a spasm of pain crossed her face at the torture of high-heeled narrow shoes.' It was a comfort to observe, Wingfield concluded, 'that her gloves, poor dear, were at least three sizes too large'.

In 1888 gowns from Berlin had been ordered for all the ladies of the court and along with the gowns came stays, feather boas, those painful shoes and tippets in various shades of vibrant blue, brick red and bottle green. Court procedure was, as always, imitated, and the imitation was encouraged by an official circular which recommended that 'the ladies of Japan adopt European dress for social occasions at which foreigners are present'.

And so, obedient as always, but uneasy, the women of Japan's upper classes in their European gowns, twirled under the chandeliers of the Deer Cry Pavilion in the arms of be-ribboned, bewhiskered western diplomats while the band played Viennese waltzes. The late eighties were the years of the Pavilion's greatest popularity and the leading members of Tokyo's native and international society flocked there. In its high cold halls, charity bazaars, meetings of newly-formed cultural societies and concerts of western music were held; in the games-rooms players shuffled cards, rolled dice, clicked billiard-balls. The place was a hectic glittering temple dedi-cated to the pursuit of that social intercourse between Japanese and foreigner which the Minister of Foreign Affairs had so fervently advocated at its opening. In 1887 a grand mas-querade ball was held there for foreign representatives, distinguished visitors and leading members of the government. The then Prime Minister, Count Ito, appeared as a Venetian nobleman, the Director of the Legislative Bureau went as a mendicant Buddhist monk; there were people of all nationali-ties disguised as beetles and fairy-queens, pirates, butterflies and hobgoblins and exactly what went wrong is not on record – but something did, for there was an orgy of ribaldry, bawdy and ridicule.

It was the last gala masquerade to take place at the Pavilion and after it the fancy dresses were stowed away. Within a few years, the popularity of the club declined; no specific accusations were made against it, but people just did not go there much any more. In 1893 the building suffered extensive damage in an earthquake and repairs needed were too expensive to carry out on the appropriately lavish scale. Accordingly, a number of aristocratic members of long standing enlarged a pretty little Japanese-style pavilion in the grounds and frequented that instead. This building was equipped with matted rooms, sliding paper screens and serving maids to bring *saké*, fish and rice to members and visitors alike. It seemed to satisfy everyone quite well.

In fact, these native gentry had decided, politely but firmly, that the violins and the *canapés*, the chandeliers and the potted palms were not their idea of comfort and joy. Moreover, they saw that, however internationally acceptable the modern Japanese lady appeared in her gowns and furbelows, she represented a disastrous aesthetic decline from the flowing, free lines and subtle colourings of the traditional kimono, the dainty flat pattens, the glossy-black uncovered hair.

Unfortunately, some Japanese husbands felt that way about it too. They, perhaps, were frequently among those who left their diligent, uncomplaining wives in their new western-style drawing-rooms and slipped away to the traditional oriental courtesies and rituals of another world, that lay but a mile or so from the legations and the international ball-rooms – the secret and cruel world of the Yoshiwara. The Yoshiwara was the Entertainment Quarter, the Nightless City, the 'Place of Reeds' literally, because it was built near a marsh and frogs added their mocking commentaries to the gaudy chorus of its pleasures. The area was enclosed within high wooden fences and on one side of its main entrance-way there stood a neat police-box, on the other a famous, aged willow-tree, 'The Willow of Welcome'. The main street was wide with flower-gardens blooming along its centre, and on either edge stood a series of stone and brick buildings with bell-towers, balustraded verandas and pillared doorways, that looked more like municipal government offices than what they were – the House of the Three Sea-Shores, the House of the Well of the Long-Blooming Flowers or the Abode of the Dragon Cape. And inside these pretentious edifices lived, not tax inspectors and filing clerks, but the gilded, fragile women – Jewel River and Miss Moonlit Foam, The Honourable Brilliance and Young Bamboo.

When the westerners arrived at its gates with their fine, contemptuous denunciations, their disgust, both real and feigned, their pity for the caged girls and their secret indulgences, the Yoshiwara was already about two hundred and fifty years old. Its ways were esoteric, harsh and subtle, perfected by the same race of men who, for centuries, cultivated the beautiful distortions and rigid postures of the miniature *bonzai* tree. Among the small number of foreigners to understand its devious charms was Mr De Becker, an 'English Student of Sociology', he calls himself, whose sociological explorations enabled him to write one of the few printable histories of the Yoshiwara's 'Life For Pleasure'.

An *habitué*, De Becker explained, went first to his favourite 'introducing tea-house' just inside one of the main gates, where he was provided with tea, sweetmeats and a young female attendant who asked which particular courtesan in which particular house had taken his fancy. The attendant then acted as servant and guide for the night's festivities. Lighting her moony-white lantern, on which was emblazoned the name of her employer's tea-house, she led her client to the brothel of his choice and there negotiated prices on his behalf with the madame – the *obasan* (auntie!); later, she sat by her client's side to replenish his *saké*-cup, pass the raw fish while he dined with his chosen. Sometimes, they would all visit a neighbouring house of joy together and then she would trip ahead, carrying the courtesan's *samisen*, the client's night attire, two flowery oiled-paper umbrellas to shield them from the elements. When all the bottles were empty and all the songs sung, it was she who led the man to the sleeping-apartment, arranged his wooden head-rest, kindled a dim night-rush, secured the shutters and withdrew with an unheeded bow when the courtesan arrived, her silken skirts rustling.

And the next morning, it was the little attendant who presented the gentleman with his bill – a beautiful bill to behold, delicately inscribed in great detail on a long roll of thin white paper. But the size of it often stunned a man out of his hangover, because it usually included, in addition to the expected charges for the courtesan herself, the attendant's services, the food and the wine, a miscellany of vague 'extras' towards the wages of the brothel's unseen functionaries – 'the shopmen, the inside men, the upper storey men, the overseers, the nightwatchmen, the bathroom men and the downstairs men' are in Mr De Becker's list; and this on top of occasional tips to the tea-girl, the chap who fetched the extra plate of fried eels and an appreciatory present to kind 'Auntie' herself! In fact, to frequent the real Yoshiwara in proper style was always an expensive occupation; as an old Japanese proverb remarked, 'The tears of the *Oiran* cause the roof of one's house to leak.'

Oiran were top of the Yoshiwara hierarchy, women who bestowed their favours seldom and with discrimination. They stirred the most hearts with the melancholy sweetness of their singing, their dances were sinuous poems of motion, their robes were of the most ravishing brocades, they presented to their admirers the most exquisite, the most expressionless pearl-white faces. Sometimes, at dusk as the moon was rising and the *samisen* twanged their first notes behind the lighted shutters, an *oiran* would emerge from her secluded domain. A tiara of long gilded combs she wore, a gown of silver and gold, her face was a mask of thick powder, her lips vermilion. She balanced on black lacquer pattens a foot high so that she could only just manage to carefully raise and swing around one foot slightly forward in front of the other – 'figure-of-eight' walking, the Japanese called it. Flunkeys heralded her coming with muted drums and a lantern dancing high on a pole; other handmaids followed – a parasol-carrier, a chaperon, girls to support her heavy train. People quietened as she passed, stared up into the almost-hidden, polished-black eyes set in the rigid, disdainful face; the drum beat soft and slow; crystallised, encrusted with beauty, she tottered laboriously towards her secret assignation.

But the lesser blossoms of the Yoshiwara, the courtesans of the second and third class, appeared regularly and with less ceremony. As one young (male) poet expressed it, 'On a calm spring evening, when the women of the quarter enter their cages it seems as if flowers were being scattered in the Yoshiwara by the bell announcing nightfall.' The 'cages' referred to were the brothels' 'show-rooms' which faced on to most of the side streets. Their front walls were slatted with wooden bars through which passers-by peered to select, or merely appraise, the women seated in the room behind. Like the *oiran*, these courtesans appeared totally detached, their fixed gaze, noted Reginald Farrer, who went to see, was 'of hopeless calm', their eyes glazed 'with an immovable and strenuous indifference'. The wide sashes of their kimono, tied in front to denote their profession, were 'cataracts of gold and silver' that tumbled down gowns of emerald, amethyst or dark blue. Only in the cheapest of the brothel show-rooms were the women at all active; in these some played a *samisen*, others made paper frogs or butterflies to throw at spectators, a few dangled come-hither branches of cherry-blossom through the bars at a likely customer.

This brazen, humiliating display of 'women for sale' was one that few foreigners could stomach, and the Japanese government was soon informed that all 'civilised' Christian nations would severely censure the country for permitting it. As early as 1872 therefore, the Ministry of Justice, in a fine flow of brand-new moral fervour, ordered the liberation of all courtesans. Proud headlines announced the edict, 'The Caged Birds return to the Sky. Geisha and Harlot released by Order'. 'Prostitutes and singing-girls have lost the rights of human beings,' the Judicial Department suddenly discovered. 'They may be likened to cattle. There is no sense for human beings to endeavour to exact repayment from cattle! Therefore no payment shall be demanded from prostitutes or singing-girls for any moneys lent or debts due.' This latter referred to the contracts which many hard-up fathers had made with brothel-keepers whereby, for an advance sum of money, they had sold their daughters into prostitution for a fixed number of years – usually three in the first instance. Thus the girls were twice-caged – behind their bars each evening, and, as they represented the surety on capital investment and were not always eager for the life, they were imprisoned for years inside the Yoshiwara area itself. Occasionally, on production of a special pass signed by her brothel-keeper and the police at the gate, a girl might be allowed out for a few days' holiday, usually on compassionate grounds, such as for 'visiting the graves of their mothers or fathers, nursing their grandfathers, fathers, mothers, uncles, aunts or brothers' (grandmothers or sisters did not apparently rate high enough).

All this, of course, had been supposed to end in 1872; but in fact it did not. The girls failed to enjoy their uncaged freedom when they got it, people said; there was no other work for them to do; their fathers still could not afford to keep them. So the fences went back around the brilliant birds and the Yoshiwara continued to exist well into the twentieth century, with a few minor changes in deference to western Christian opinion. Some of the brothels started to call themselves 'houses with rooms to let' and a few closed their cages and displayed highly-coloured photographs of their girls round their doorways instead, which was a boon to Japanese photographers, of whom there was already a surplus. Women wishing to work in the Yoshiwara (as some did) had now to apply first to the normal registry of employment offices where all 'persons seeking situations' were interviewed; the medical regulations to control the spread of venereal disease were carefully enforced. For a few years, in the early nineties, a craze for 'westernisation' swept through the Yoshiwara. Prostitutes in black stockings clambered into high foreign beds; their clients dined on beef-steak and beer; under harsh electric lights the caged women, in thick Victorian gowns, prowled among plush-velveteen arm-chairs and gilt mirrors.

But the Yoshiwara was one of the few places in the eastern capital where such westernisation did not, could not succeed. The quarter was fashioned for the pleasure of Japanese men, some of whom were single, but many of whom wanted to add the exciting spice of music, sex and wine to the staple diet of marriage and family life. Such men might be straight and brisk inside pinstripe suits, starched shirts and spats during official functions and office hours, but off-duty they liked their sharp edges blurred – with lantern and kimono, quiet straw mats, the moony *samisen*. This traditional, inviolate quality also meant that western men did not, on the whole, enjoy the Yoshiwara. The sailors stayed with the bar-girls in the treaty ports, really interested young bachelors usually wanted a temporary substitute for a marriage-relationship, not a supplement to it. And so, to accommodate their special needs, the Japanese, ever-inventive, came up with what might be described as the Butterfly Game.

It was an easy game really. A westerner needed no more than a little money and an introduction to a Japanese 'go-between' who took him along to a certain tea-house where numbers of pretty girls tripped gaily about. And eventually (there was no hurry) he chose the one who most appealed to him and said he would marry her. The marriage – a perfectly legal union, signed and sealed in the nearby police office – was arranged by the go-between, a quite indispensable person who could usually suggest a house to rent also. Here, the foreigner could install the girl and live with her just as long as he wanted – during a five-year tour of duty perhaps, or for a couple of years, or until he got bored or a baby was due, whatever was the most convenient. And when he went away the marriage just dissolved itself; the girl returned to her family or the tea-house, or, in some cases, she then married a man of her own race and lived happily ever after.

Temporary liaisons such as these were common in all the treaty ports and were described, often fictionally disguised, in a number of romantic, sad, sentimental, contemptuous, gay little tales that make up a sort of Madame Butterfly syndrome.

As early as 1860 when Bishop George Smith of Hong Kong visited Yokohama, he expressed his outrage at the number of foreign bachelors in the port who had native 'wives'. In those early days, local Japanese customs officials often acted as go-betweens and the Bishop was almost as scandalised by this implied approval of authority as he was by the practice itself. As more foreign bachelors – junior clerks, shopkeepers, commercial agents, young engineers and military men – came to the treaty ports, so the procedure became more organised. The owners of some bars and tea-houses, a few strategically-placed flower-sellers, bath-house keepers and even laundrymen took over the role of procurers and certain houses were rented again and again for these brief partnerships. The women, who were invariably the daughters of working-class families, stayed inside the home, as most Japanese women did anyway; they were not accepted in the wider social life of the foreign community but mixed almost exclusively with their own relatives (who usually accepted the situation) and with other couples on the same footing. Nevertheless, the practice was tacitly allowed as a convenient solution in a society where there were not enough unmarried western women to go round and where pressures of convention and finance often prevented a young man from making a 'respectable' marriage until he had attained a sufficiently high economic and social status.

Long before Madame Butterfly was created, Nagasaki was the most notorious for this particular business, its girls were supposed to be the prettiest and the easiest to live with; arrangements were cheap and made with a minimum of fuss. Nagasaki had always been an easy-come-easy-go sort of place. It was one of the first three ports in the country opened for foreign trade and was soon famed for the rowdiness of its gay quarter and its amiable desire to keep visiting sailors happy. Very soon, however, Yokohama and Kobe between them lured away much of its export trade and Nagasaki could not be bothered to keep abreast in the commercial rat race. 'The principal productions of Nagasaki', wrote a disdainful journalist who visited it early in the eighties, 'are tobacco, *jinrikishas*, desponding commission agents, unripe plums, ships' chandlers, tomatoes, bow-legged Custom House officials, bankrupts, water melons, intoxicated sailors, tortoise-shell bracelets, mosquitoes, grog-shops and stagnation. The prevalent epidemics are dysentery and insolvency.' 'Nagasaki', opined another, equally unimpressed reporter four years later, 'has rather the look of never having been thoroughly vitalised ... and money here is scarce as angels' visits.'

The vitalisation was to come, but not for a few years yet. At this period the fairytale-pretty port remained a backwater and its inhabitants continued to pursue a number of safe, regular trading activities which kept them from going quite on the rocks. Crates of brown, sun-dried fish always stood and stank along the Bund awaiting export to Shanghai, together with the occasional bales of goose quills and peony bark recently arrived from Korea. On even the doziest afternoon, grimy women and young girls carrying baskets of coal swung on poles across their shoulders, shuffled along between the moored junks in the water and the coaling-sheds. Dingy-red canal-boats, merchant-vessels and globe-trotters' steamers called to fuel up with this locally-mined coal as did Russian convict ships whose blind black hulks were skulking quietly north to Vladivostok and beyond. No one left these clandestine vessels and only a few merchants with passes were allowed on board; chains could be heard clanking below decks, it was said, and occasionally a whey-faced prisoner might appear at a narrow opening and gaze at the sparkling sun and sea of the lovely harbour. Naval vessels of the various western powers also called there, sometimes just to stoke up, sometimes for several months – for a long hot summer, perhaps, long enough to take a wife.

'I shall at once marry,' announced M. Pierre Loti, young French naval officer and author, to his tall friend Yves, as they stood on the bridge of their warship and looked towards unknown, exotic Nagasaki. M. Loti had already written about his love affairs in Turkey and Tahiti, and now, for his Japanese period, he decided that, 'I shall chose a little yellow-skinned woman with black hair and cat's eyes. She must be pretty. Not much bigger than a doll. You, [Yves] shall have a room in our house – a little paper house in the midst of green gardens, prettily shaded. We shall live among flowers, everything around us shall blossom and each morning our dwelling shall be filled with nosegays, nosegays such as you never dreamt of.'

It was not to turn out quite like that and Loti did not really expect it to. He found a woman of course, a contemptuous amber-skinned tea-house girl called 'Madame Chrysanthemum' with 'dainty paws' for him to clasp and gilded ornaments swinging in her glossy hair. And he married her by signing a hieroglyphic sheet of rice-paper in the police office one bright midday. They went to live in a little house on the hill, a straw-wood-paper house with a veranda overlooking the harbour, a pair of screens and a Buddha sitting on a golden lotus in the corner. And they made love at night under a dark blue mosquito net with powder-white moths fluttering over them and mice scurrying along the beams above and owls hooting from the distant bamboo thickets.

Loti seems to have slept badly. 'Our wooden house, with its thin old walls vibrates at night like a great dry fiddle,' he complained, awakened, as every irritated night, by the sharp snap, snap, snap of Chrysanthemum's tiny pipe-bowl against her porcelain smoking-box. His wife's inappropriate habit of smoking in the early hours was only one of her many short-comings: she was also 'meaninglessly withdrawn', given to fits of dreary sulks and childish, listless yawns; she was a finicky eater of too many sugar plums; she shovelled rice down the very back of her throat with chopsticks and her laughter was mirthless. He would have preferred to discard her affection as well as her body at the end of the summer and was offended when she chose to remain the 'doll on the shelf' which was his way of describing her.

The only feeling they shared for each other was contempt. Hers for him was prudently veiled, he hardly recognised it as such, though it clearly emerges from his descriptions of her behaviour; his for her was open and cruel. He describes with disdainful amusement the few personal tatty 'gewgaws' she brought to her temporary home – photographs of her family, faded letters from a real sweetheart, all stored in a hideous English biscuit-tin; her displays of kittenish coquetry are but grotesque parodies of other ardent adult passions he had known. The whole country was something of a parody in fact, a droll, outlandish frivolous place and, above all, little. 'Oh little, finical, affected Japan,' he drawls wearily, and one can see him elegantly disposing his tall, white-suited body in a wicker chair and languidly lifting another cup of *saké* towards his droopy moustache.

For, liking neither his wife nor the country, Loti's recourse was a self-conscious abandonment to as many light-hearted amusements as he could afford. The couple's best times were spent in crowds, when, on warm summer evenings, the town was a riot of coloured lanterns and fluttering streamers and in the temple courtyards the priests' 'long crystal trumpets keep up their gobble' to celebrate midsummer festivals. Then, Loti and his Chrysanthemum, and four other French officers who had been similarly fitted up with flower-titled wives, made merry procession through the streets. The women trotted ahead, pigeon-toed, their long kimono sleeves swinging, looped sashes 'gleaming at their waists'. 'Our little dancing-dogs,' the officers called them, as they leered and followed. They bought presents for each other at the jingling fair-booths: magic fans with sliding pictures of demons, creamy-puff rice waffles, bloated cardboard masks, bunches of purple ribbons, water ices that 'taste like scented frost'. And then they went on to 'The Beckoning Kitten', 'The Golden Camellia' or 'The Sandal-wood Box' where the girls were sliding their feet to the tune of the plucked *samisen* and the mats were littered with young men, empty *saké* bottles, crumbs, beans and broken chopsticks.

But to Loti it was all essentially dismal and unsatisfactory. Stripped of her kimono, he found Chrysanthemum to be, as all Japanese women in his eyes, 'but a diminutive yellow being with crooked legs and flat unshapely bust; she has no longer a remnant of her artificial little charms which have completely disappeared in company with her costume'. Darkness did not, then, bring him joy, but fell upon the town like 'a sombre shadow, strange, weird, a breath of antiquity, of savagery, of something indefinable which casts a gloom of sadness'. Sadness crawled too whenever rain fell and, under Chrysanthemum's listless fingers, the *samisen* whimpered in the chill empty air. It was an emptiness that often appalled Loti – the almost-unfurnished rooms, the faded walls decorated only with a couple of grey storks haughtily raising their legs to scratch themselves. 'Oh those eternal storks! How sick one gets of them at the end of a month in Japan,' he moans. He also despised his landlady, Madame Prune, whose 'empty prayers' droned up every morning from the room below and sounded 'like the bleating of an old nanny-goat in a delirium'. Empty too were the shallow courtesies of the local lantern-seller and the linnet-light laughter of Chrysanthemum's friends. Hollowest of all was the empty failure of his 'marriage' to this child-woman, this weird, unhuman, utterly alien creature, as she seemed to him one hot siesta-time, when he returned home unexpectedly and found her 'sleeping flat on her face upon the mats, her high headdress and tortoiseshell pins standing out boldly from the rest of her horizontal figure. The train of her dress prolonged her delicate little body, like the tail of a bird; her arms were stretched crosswise, the sleeves spread out like wings – and her long guitar lay beside her. She looked like a dead fairy, or still more did she resemble some great blue dragonfly which, having alighted on that spot, some unkind hand had pinned to the floor.'

Poor flighty Chrysanthemum, she might have been happier in the Yoshiwara where, at least, one was not expected to play let's-pretend-we're-happily-married games with moody foreign gentlemen who knew they were going away in the autumn. And thus, when autumn came, Loti threw his Chrysanthemum a parting shower of silver dollars and then, later, discovered her singing as she rang them vigorously against her ear with a small mallet to test their validity, competent and purposeful 'as an old money-changer'. It was her newly-acquired knowledge of the niceties of western-style hypocrisy that made her blush when she saw he had caught her at this little task; to Loti the scene was a final proof that her brain and heart was as empty of feeling as he had always suspected. Remembering it, he left Japan feeling cleansed and guiltless, with no regrets for his melancholy, fly-by-night dragonfly bride.

Dragonflies or butterflies, shimmering bright little women all with flowing silk arm-wings, flitting over the mats bringing sweetmeats to the 'augustly shining ones'. Some men loved it, they reclined in their basket chairs and purred with pleasure. Clive Holland describes such a liaison in his best-selling novel *My Japanese Wife*. 'My *musmé* is a butterfly from a Far Eastern land, with Dresden-china tinted cheeks and tiny ways, playing at life, as it always seems to me, with the dainty grace of Japan, that idealised doll's house land!' And he describes the enchantment of a first encounter... 'It was one night at the Tea House of the Peach Grove ... where I was fated to meet and be enslaved by the charms of Hyacinth.' A hyacinth this time, but also addicted to sugar plums which disappeared 'in vast quantities into her rosebud mouth' and to pleading with beguiling *moués* when she wanted her lord to tie her sash or buy her a box of fondants. But, as Holland is at pains to point out, his hero is no heartless Latin lecher, *he* is not going to abandon his 'scrap of daintily dressed femininity', his 'little figure off a tea-caddy' when *he* leaves Japan. No indeed, Mr Holland's fictional creation was a virtuous knight, one of Queen Victoria's own gentlemen, who would carry his faithful Hyacinth home with him like a trophy. '*Musmé*,' he tells her, 'you and I will conquer London together, you with your dainty grace and piquante face' and I, 'with my wealth and family name'. On what Holland based his novel is unknown, but it caught to perfection the mood of the time, ran into twenty-one editions and sold by the thousand.

The Butterfly Story, it seemed, was one that everybody wanted to be told. John Luther Long, an American author, realised this when he wrote the short story about the winsome, humorous, pathetic 'Mrs Benjameen Frangaleen Pikkerton' herself; David Bellasco realised it when he produced the play of Long's tale at London's Duke of York's Theatre, and Giacomo Puccini realised it when, after seeing the Belasco production, he wrote the-opera-of-the-play-of-the-story. The opera's first performance was given at La Scala in 1904 and was a disastrous flop; the following year Puccini produced a revised version which was performed first in Milan and then at Covent Garden, where it was an immediate and brilliant success. But Puccini's *Madama Butterfly*, who became the legendary figure of the devoted and tragic oriental woman faithfully waiting with cherry blossoms and lanterns for her heartless western lover, bore scant resemblance to the cute child-bride of Luther Long's version and less still to the average port-girl of Nagasaki.

Why was the legend so popular, one wonders in retrospect? Certainly, as a story simply, it had little new to offer – the orientals were poor and vulnerable and they lost; the golden-haired barbarians were allowed to sail away almost unscathed. Still, in spite of its sentimentality and its distance from the rather sordid truth, the story of Madame Butterfly made its point: it was not the light-living, amiable, frivolous, simple Japanese women, but the ruthless, sophisticated, selfish western men who committed the worst moral sin; the Japanese were not pretty playthings to be petted, admired, laughed at and left at will, like dolls, dragonflies or elves – they were people who got hurt, made jokes, felt love. Perhaps the worst fault of the Japanese was that some of them have always helped to sustain the westerners' illusions. Some forty years after the Madame Butterfly syndrome had reached its climax, the Japanese opened the Nagasaki residence of a former prosperous English merchant, Mr T. B. Glover, as a museum; to draw the crowds, they called it 'Madame Butterfly's House'. It would have amused Madame Butterfly, had she ever existed; it might even have amused Mr Glover – a hospitable and courtly gentleman, apparently, who lived in the country for nearly fifty years and had great sympathy with and understanding of Japan, at both its best and worst.

Mrs Hugh Fraser, as her letters from home to home clearly demonstrate, always looked upon the Japanese as fully adult people. She might smile at them of course, as she often smiled at the foibles of humankind, but her tone is not patronising, she does not deal in stereotypes. To her, the pretty young woman of Japan was no china doll, no picture off a fan, but a complex, vital person, 'of so many attractive contradictions, with her warm heart, her quick brain and her terribly narrow experience; with her submissions and self-effacements which have become second nature and her brave revolts when first nature takes the upper hand again and courage is too strong for custom'. She is referring, of course, to the women she met socially – the daughters of aristocrats and professors, the wives of aspiring politicians – and she watches sympathetically as these women try to gain for themselves a little room to manoeuvre, a little guidance as to how they should behave in the wider world outside the home.

Doyenne of these *fin-de-siècle* ladies during part of Mrs Fraser's stay in the capital was tiny twenty-two-year-old Countess Kuroda, wife of the Prime Minister. She 'has lovely diamonds and always appears in white satin with snowy plumes in her dark hair. She can talk a little English and is intensely polite about everything European, as all the little ladies are.' 'But,' Mrs Fraser concludes, 'I fancy in their hearts they put us down as big clumsy creatures with loud voices and no manners.' White satin, often brocaded with gold, was favoured attire for wives in society and their husbands soon learned to tread courteously in its wake as the shimmering skirts swished through the doors of ballrooms and legation reception halls. It was rumoured however that the strange western custom of 'ladies first' obtained only as long as the satin was actually on parade; returned to their own matted rooms, clad in their off-duty native dress, the man again went first, his wife, however publicly emancipated, privately trotted behind her lord.

This resistance to fundamental change was most deeply-rooted among many older members of the aristocracy, who had small stakes in the promises of the future and lost most when they lost the past. A group of these blue-blooded reactionaries clustered together for comfort at the court of the Empress Dowager, a dignified elderly lady who lived in seclusion and whose Grand Master of Ceremonies, recorded Mrs Fraser, wore 'an habitual expression of disapproving reserve and patient deprecation against the admission of *stultus vulgus*, the profane foreigner'. Once a year this grande dame emerged from her cocoon and enacted one honourable ritual as a reminder to the young of how gracious the world was before the flood: she and her courtiers went mushroom-hunting.

Mushroom-hunting, as Mrs Fraser's interpreter explained to her, was a 'kind of artistic sport' and traditional dress for male mushroom hunters included tight fitting bright green leggings and silk jackets; for women, white silk gaiters with underskirts of purple or scarlet silk and a white kerchief pinned atop the head to prevent pine boughs from disarranging the hair. The most succulent mushrooms in the land were grown in a certain wood near Kyoto and on a clear day in the appropriate season, the hunters gathered there and they all trooped off among the trees – the men leading (of course), then the women and servants carrying boxes of rice and gourds of *saké*. It was a proper occasion for punning, wit and laughter, a few quotations from the ancient classics perhaps, a plaintive love-song as they trod the woodland paths. In a clearing, the servants prepared for the feast while the hunters dispersed to seek their quarry. 'The dainty things grow quite hidden under a carpet of pine needles,' Mrs Fraser explained, 'so these have to be pushed aside in the search and then the strong sweet odour of the brown earth comes floating up in the warm air.' When the bamboo baskets were piled high the hunters returned to the

clearing, 'and those who have gathered much are congratu-
lated, while those who have made a poor harvest traditionally apologise in mock humility for their stupidity and awkwardness, which render them unworthy to be members of
such a distinguished party'. Then the spoils were roasted
over a fire of cones, flavoured with soy sauce, cuddled in a nest
of rice – and how deliciously succulent they tasted, there in
the crisp autumn sunlight, under the pines, washed down with
saké, so fresh, sweet-smelling and full of sap!

Rituals such as these were leisurely, picturesque anachron-
isms and were doomed to wither now that many of the
younger élite were taking an active part in government and
could not afford the time to put on green leggings and go a-
mushrooming when the fancy took them. Nevertheless, by the
late eighties, it was not only ageing noblemen who were concerned to see so many of their country's unique cultural patterns apparently being discarded. A growing number of educated men began to feel that indiscriminate westernisation
had gone too far. It had even seriously been proposed that
English should be adopted as the official language and that
Japanese men should marry western women in order to improve the racial stock! In 1890, reflecting a changing mood, the
Emperor issued the Imperial Rescript on Education – a
moral exhortation to his people, which, though couched in
very elevated language that did not dot the 'i's', emphasised
that the nation would do well to preserve unsullied its own
moral code and customs in matters relating to, for example,
the worship of ancestors, loyalty to superiors and filial piety.
The old, well-tried virtues, in fact, were sacrosanct; the new
ones – equality, personal liberty, conjugal love – were
secondary to these.

At this time it was principally an emotional reaction; political and social development within the country still sought to
emulate the West; 'Japan', wrote Rudyard Kipling, 'is studded, as a bower-bird's run is studded with shells and shining
pebbles, with plagiarisms from half the world.' A rather unkind comment perhaps, but not wholly inaccurate. The

Japanese navy, which, like the army, grew considerably in size and efficiency at this period, was after the British style, down to the last bit of gold braid, as was the Japanese Foreign Office, its rooms furnished with ottomans and aspidistras; the police force and prison system were principally à la française; much of the lower-school educational system had been worked out by American professors; Germany ruled the higher academic groves and the medical schools.

The influence of Germany was at its peak during the later eighties and early nineties in both the military and political spheres; its strongest advocate in the Cabinet was Count Ito who had, in 1882, visited Europe to make a comparison of its various constitutional systems and had been much impressed by Prussian ideas and institutions. On his return Ito is said to haved aped Chancellor Bismarck even to the extent of smoking cigars in a similar way, and he imported numerous German teachers and also introduced a new peerage structure based on the Prussian model. Mrs Fraser, who generally admired the Japanese politicians she knew, did not at all like Count Ito, though she had to admit the political astuteness of one who fully understood 'the wisdom of inactivity when other people are doing dangerous work or seem on the point of making fools of themselves'.

Another Japanese admirer of things Teutonic was Viscount Aoki. He was married to a German lady and a picture of his long, humourless face with rimless spectacles and a wispy beard makes him look very like a German professor of moral philosophy. Aoki became Foreign Minister during one of the many Cabinet upheavals and, one day soon afterwards, Mrs Fraser watched him drive up to the Legation 'in a victoria with the hood raised and inside the hood on either side hung a heavy revolver in a leather pocket with a heavy chain fastening it to a ring in the carriage frame'. The revolvers, she added, were very much loaded and their protective powers were supplemented by three detectives and a policeman on the victoria's box. 'The effect is that of a condemned criminal or a dangerous lunatic out with his keepers.' But the Viscount was no lunatic; his predecessor at the Foreign Ministry, Count Okuma, had been badly wounded a few months before when a bomb was thrown into his carriage by a young *soshi*. The *soshi* were a band of zealously chauvinistic fanatics who believed that their government was making far too many concessions to the western powers with regard to the revision of trade tariffs fixed by the existing foreign treaties and over the question of extraterritoriality.

Extraterritoriality was as knotty and unaccommodating a matter as it sounds, and it had ruined a great many tempers, caused a great many resignations and inspired more than one assassination attempt during the previous fifteen years. Sir Harry Parkes had started to tangle unsuccessfully with it a few years after the Emperor's Restoration and by the time Mr Hugh Fraser entered the same ring, the subject had already 'been on the Chancery table for fourteen years'. The extraterritoriality system existed in all the treaty ports in China and Japan, and it meant that foreigners living in those ports were not subject to the laws of the land, but came under the jurisdiction of their own national consular courts. In return for this concession, aliens living in Japan were forbidden to remain for more than three months outside the area of the treaty limits, nor were they allowed to trade outside these limits or earn money unless given special dispensation or on government service. Most Japanese felt that extraterritoriality was an affront to their new sense of modern nationhood because it implied that their legal system was not refined or enlightened enough to deal fairly with the offending foreigner. Not surprisingly many foreign settlers preferred extraterritoriality, and they believed – and probably helped to foster – the wildest rumours about the excessive brutality of Japanese police and the squalor of their prisons. Some of them, judging by the correspondence columns in the newspapers, had fully convinced themselves that, if extraterritoriality ended, they would at once run the risk of being arrested, marched off to jail and tortured most hideously and that, in general terms, such a measure would but add catastrophe to present adversity.

The *Mail's* editor commented sarcastically, 'If a heap of stones is badly located we are reminded that, were we not exempt from Japanese jurisdiction, every road round the settlement would be thickly strewn with boulders. If a *jin-rikisha* coolie is insolent, we are told that, could he but get the treaties revised, he would make our lives a burden to us. If a scavenger is unpunctual, we are warned that the satisfaction of his political aspirations would impel him to devote his days to carrying buckets of night-soil to and fro before our houses.' In short, he concluded, 'Extraterritoriality is a good old fossil which has survived the disappearance of the stratum it belonged to.' A minority of foreign merchants agreed with this view and chafed under restrictions which confined trading to certain specified areas; but a minority of Japanese, to be contrariwise, feared that, if westerners were allowed to trade freely, yet more of their nation's wealth would flow into foreign hands and a crude kind of modernism would everywhere triumph – so they wanted the extraterritoriality system to remain.

Drafts and redrafts of new treaties, memorandums and notes of approval and disapproval, apology and compromise on the subject shunted back and forth for years between the main agencies concerned – the Japanese Foreign Ministry and the Legations of the major powers. And each time these negotiations reached a certain notorious article of each new proposal (the one about the admission of foreign judges to courts trying foreigners for criminal offences) there was deadlock. The ministers of the great powers would not yield and the Japanese Cabinet resigned and remade itself yet again. 'No sooner', said Mrs Fraser, 'have I learnt which peer holds which portfolio than they all – excuse the simile – seem to toss them into the air and catch who catch them can in the fall.' It was a most tangled and frustrating labyrinth: 'The newcomer who wishes to make himself agreeable is advised not to touch upon the extraterritoriality controversy,' said Basil Chamberlain. 'All residents are utterly sick and weary of it.'

So, probably, were the ministers concerned, more especially because, each time some new compromise seemed on the point of agreement, the *soshi* again brandished their sword-sticks and threatened to kill all those involved. Mr Fraser had one or two unpleasantly close shaves with them, stones were sometimes hurled at foreigners' carriages in Tokyo and several other Japanese ministers were obliged to travel, like Aoki, with an armed escort. Fortunately, the simmering xenophobia of the late eighties and nineties did not erupt into the series of violent, sometimes fatal attacks on westerners that had occurred almost thirty years before, but one assassination attempt of great consequence *was* made. The incident was a hair-raising one because, in spite of all precautions, it almost succeeded, because, had it done so, the result might have been truly calamitous for the nation and because it did, in any case, throw a menacing shadow forward to the bloodier fracas that lay ahead.

'Very great preparations are being made for this royal visit,' Mary Fraser wrote home in May 1891. 'The apartments in the Palace by the Sea have all been furnished and decorated anew; there are to be triumphal arches and illuminations and Court Balls; and the Emperor intends to lavish honours – and fun – on his guest. The "S——s" at the Russian Legation have transformed their somewhat dingy house into a bower of floral beauty; I have just been going over it and rather envied the Grand Duke the two thousand pots of lilies in bloom which are to line the great staircase.' The Czarevitch himself was coming to the capital and all Japan's forebodings about Russia's encroachment into Manchuria and Korea were to be dissolved in lanterns and flowers of welcome. The Russian bear might be lumbering too close for comfort, but surely he could be tamed?

Unhappily, the period of enthusiastic amity which marked the Czarevitch's arrival in Japan was brief; in her next letter Mrs Fraser recorded that 'a most terrible blow fell on this un-fortunate country on May 11th' and she goes on to describe her personal involvement in what occurred. On that sunny afternoon the Minister's wife was returning from a drive in the suburbs when she was met by a friend who urged her to go immediately to the Russian Legation where the dire news of an attack on the Czarevitch had just been received. At the Legation she found the Russian Minister's wife and daughter pacing the decorated rooms and weeping with rage and sorrow as they read telegrams giving details of the disaster. The Prince's party, which had been due to reach Tokyo the next day, had been on a sightseeing excursion to Lake Biwa near Kyoto. After a pleasant lunch by the lake, they all bowled back towards Kyoto in *jinrikishas* – the Czarevitch himself fifth in the line with the Chief of Police and two inspectors ahead of him. Not that, as Mrs Fraser remarked, anyone dreamed their services, or those of the police lining the roadside, would be needed, for 'it is the boast of new Japan that a foreigner can travel from end to end of the Empire without receiving the slightest molestation; and this foreigner was the beloved Emperor's guest!'

However, among the rows of vigilant policemen stood ex-sergeant-major Tsuda Sanzo, an ageing, reactionary warrior and, it turned out, a secret fanatic. As the Prince's *jinrikisha* drew level with him, he lifted his ancient war-sword and aimed two heavy blows at the young man's head. One of the Prince's runners dropped the shafts and hurled himself at Sanzo, the other grabbed at his weapon; the Czarevitch, blinded with his own blood that poured from a gash in his skull, staggered helplessly into the arms of the local Governor who had been travelling just behind him. The assassin was pinned to the ground and beaten with sticks, the Prince was carried into the nearest house, officials shouted contradictory orders, spectators screamed and tried to run away; there was total confusion.

The Prince's wound was, fortunately, not serious, though, naturally, the royal tour was at once abandoned; several days after the attack, the young man, his pallid face swathed in bandages, sailed back to Russia, without ever seeing the lily-lined staircase of the Tokyo Legation. But the national pride of the Japanese was less easily cured. As Mrs Fraser wrote, 'So much was expected and hoped from this visit in the way of friendship with the great European powers. It was to have been Japan's first step in the Social Polity of the world.'

Baulked of this, the people expressed their humiliation and grief in a great flood of atonement towards the wounded Czarevitch. A friend of Mrs Fraser's who visited the Prince's ship before it sailed told her that, 'it seemed like to sink with gifts; the decks, the saloons, the passages were encumbered and still they came and came and came . . . Rich people gave out of their riches and objects of unexampled beauty and rarity were brought out from the treasure houses to the boy who lay healing his wound in Kobe harbour. The poor sent most touching gifts – rice and *shoyu*, the fish and barley-flour which would have fed the little family for a year; poor old peasants walked for miles with tiny offerings of eggs. The merchants sent silks and porcelain, lacquer and bronze, crapes and ivory; telegrams poured in expressing intense sympathy and more intense indignation at the outrage. In the first twenty-four hours after the occurrence so many thousands were sent that it was impossible to deliver them . . .'

But although the Prince, according to Mrs Fraser, behaved with calm forbearance during his ordeal and had fully understood that his assailant was a solitary madman, yet the silks and the eggs could not quite mend matters; a chance had been lost, the visit was not repeated, peace was that much more remote. The only people who profited from the affair were the two *jinrikisha* runners who had probably saved the royal visitor's life. They were showered with decorations and money both by the Emperor and by the Russian government and their subsequent behaviour furnished a neat and still-remembered morality tale for Japanese children on the theme of proceeding wisely from rags to riches. One of the coolies bought a nice little house, gave gifts of money to all his friends and relations and put aside a tidy sum for his old age; but of the other, wrote an amused reporter, 'the sudden fortune that befell him simply widened the circle of his mischief' – he revelled, in short, caroused, junketed and banqueted, painted the town red, swung high, too high, fell into debt, forfeited his pension rights and ended back in rags, too weak and ill after his wild indulgences even to pull a decent *jinrikisha* any more.

The fate of the runners was, clearly, a side-issue; what worried the government was that this much-publicised assassination attempt would revive old memories of the Japanese as a bunch of savage warriors who brutally cut down 'barbarian invaders' with their ancient swords – and that was not the image which the country wished to present to the civilised world of the 1890s. And it was indeed true that the Czarevitch's attacker was himself an anachronism; the time for such reactionary, insular violence was over; the violence that lay ahead would be outward-looking, solidly nationalistic, aimed at the forging of Japan's glorious future rather than the protecting of its cloistered past.

Three years later, on the occasion of his silver wedding banquet, the Emperor felt that national solidarity was now so firmly based that he could invite to the celebration not only his followers, friends and members of the legations, but his former enemies, warriors who had taken active part against him at the time of the Imperial Restoration. 'Old pretenders to the throne,' Mrs Fraser called them, 'old leaders of rebellions; fierce fighters, the story of whose feuds would make one's blood run cold but for the hot white fire of heroism that lights them up. Strange it was indeed to sit opposite these men here in the Palace; to watch the calm dark faces veiled by the mantle of cold suavity more impenetrable than an iron mask; to listen to the quiet small talk of an official feast; to watch the decorations rise and fall on breasts that were heaving to madness with the lust of war or the pride of race or the desire for revenge only a few years ago!' Now that violence at least was tamed, those schisms healed. Eight hundred important guests from every part of the Empire, representatives of all the old clan-factions, filled the banqueting halls; there were footmen in liveries of crimson and gold to bring gleaming platters of silver, goblets of wine, caskets of bonbons; the Meiji Emperor, with his tiny, diamond-encrusted Empress beside him, was the man to whom 'all glasses were lifted with a gesture of devout, passionate loyalty' as his health was drunk. 'I do not believe', Mrs Fraser concluded from that scene, 'that there is a man of any party in Japan who would not be glad and proud to lay down his life for his Emperor. If war should come, Japan's armies will gather themselves from every home in the Empire.'

It was the April of 1894 and one of Mary Fraser's last important public occasions in Japan, for, quite suddenly, two months later, after a brief illness, her fifty-seven-year-old husband died. The dear 'H—' of her letters, the busy Envoy Extraordinary, remains a shadowy figure, wrestling with dispatches in his Tokyo office during hot summer afternoons, waltzing reluctantly with countesses, battling over the same terms of the trade treaties with each new Foreign Minister. 'His abnormally retiring disposition narrowed the circle of his appreciators and impaired the public's estimate of his capacity,' judged *The Japan Mail* in its obituary. 'But by all who served with him or under him he was loved and respected.' The funeral was immense; there were not enough carriages for the mourners or the flowers; the letters from home to home were finished; Mrs Fraser went home alone. Within a few weeks of her departure, the armies had gathered themselves, as she foresaw they would in time of crisis, from every part of the Japanese Empire. It was war.

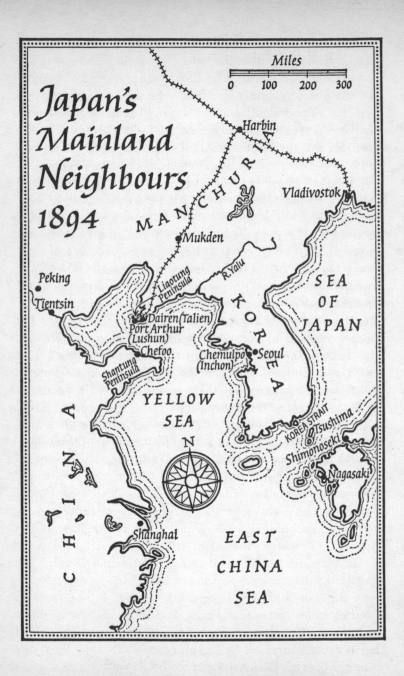

Miles

0   100   200   300

Japan's
Mainland
Neighbours
1894

MANCHURIA

Harbin

Vladivostok

Mukden

Peking

Liaotung Peninsula

R. Yalu

SEA
OF
JAPAN

Tientsin

Dairen (Talien)
Port Arthur
(Lushun)

KOREA

Chefoo

Chemulpo
(Inchon)

Seoul

Shantung
Peninsula

YELLOW
SEA

CHINA

N

KOREA STRAIT

Tsushima

Shimonoseki

Nagasaki

Shanghai

EAST
CHINA
SEA

V

At the extreme end of the Liaotung Peninsula in eastern China there was a town called Port Arthur, named after H.R.H. Prince Arthur, Duke of Connaught. It was a shabby, one-storey sort of place that had grown from a fishing village to a naval port during the last fifteen years or so. In summer, winds whipped its reddish hill dust into vicious spirals and sullen fogs rolled unexpectedly in from the water; every autumn it rained and rained and the wide wheels of the ox-carts turned the dusty streets into mires; then it snowed and snowed, sharp frozen snow which lay for a long time over the rutted streets and athwart the rows of junks, rowing-boats, corvettes, trawlers, coalers and merchant ships in the docks. From the various vessels, in their season, landed shore-eager seamen, from Russia, America, Holland, France, Britain; fishermen from Shanghai, Chefoo, Tientsin; tourists, occasionally; commercial agents and consular officials; silk and tea traders – nearly all of them on their way somewhere else.

For Port Arthur was not, on the whole, considered a very desirable destination. Bleak stony hills rising from three hundred to fifteen hundred feet – 'The White Wolf', 'The Dragon Ridge', 'the Eagle's Nest' – crammed the port along the shoreline and the shoreline was a clutter of dry-docks, cranes and warehouses, the water of its harbour almost landlocked by the Tiger Peninsula, a slim strip of land culminating in the 'Tiger's Tail' which swished to within a few hundred yards of the opposite coast. Landwards, behind and beyond the encircling hills, the empty spaces of Manchuria began, whence blew the snow and the dust; seawards, not so far – about two hundred miles east – was Korea, and south eastwards, down and around the Korean corner, was Japan. In August 1894 Japan declared war on China, an act which was to have dire consequences for the inhabitants of Port Arthur.

The Sino-Japanese war may have seemed to some western observers at the time to be little more than a short, typically bloody, oriental scrap; but for Japan it was extremely important. It was the first full-scale conflict that the country had engaged in outside its own territories for well over two hundred years; the war was, in fact, its military début on the modern scene, and Japan emerged from it as a victorious, energetic David of a nation well qualified to join the catch-as-catch-can game of territory-taking which Goliaths such as Russia, Britain and Germany were already playing in Asia. The Japanese had, for the last decade, watched with particular concern the manoeuvres of Russia and China with regard to Korea – that undeveloped, melancholy country which, they hoped, would act as an independent buffer state separating Japan from her giant neighbours. But neither Russia nor China saw it quite like that. During the eighties, Russia tried, and failed, to gain control of an ice-free port on the eastern Korean coast; then the Chinese went to Korea and tried, in effect, to transform the country into a Chinese province. This more or less peaceful invasion was quite successful, and, by the early nineties, the Korean government was largely subservient to the Chinese – a situation which the Japanese, for political and strategic reasons, refused to countenance indefinitely. An opportunity to challenge China's position came in the spring of 1894, when a faction of rebellious Koreans rose against their corrupt, incompetent government. China, announcing that the country was her 'protectorate and dependency' sent in troops to quell the disturbances, the Japanese protested at the Chinese action and sent a few contingents of their own army to the scene, which reached Chemulpo (now called Inchon), the port nearest to the capital, Seoul, in June.

Disciplined as the troops were, there was inevitable confusion as they landed: transport boats, loaded to the gunwales with pack-burdened soldiers, jostled in the harbour with junks bringing supplies of rice and fish; horses reared and snorted between the shafts of carts, some loaded with forage, others with heaps of shell and shot destined for the walls of the Royal Palace in Seoul; piles of oiled weaponry gleamed on the balconies of commandeered houses along the quay. But, even with all this martial effervescence, many must have stopped to stare at the plump, rather short figure of an elderly Victorian lady who was picking her way, seemingly unconcerned, among the bales of fodder, the knapsacks and the guns. It was Isabella Bird, now 63 years old; who had just spent a pleasant three months having a look at the interior of Korea. She had travelled, mostly by sampan, along the River Han and had stayed in Buddhist monasteries, silent eyries that hung high and cold among the hard rocks of the northern Diamond Mountains. As she had left most of her luggage with friends in Seoul for those three months, she was now on her way back to the capital to collect it.

Isabella had not been idle during the years between her exploration of Japan's unbeaten tracks and her investigation of the Chemulpo quayside. She had, for example, travelled over part of the tableland of Central Asia on the back of a yak and on horse and mule from Burujird to Trebizond; she had married, been widowed and lost the one deep love of her life – her sister, Henrietta. She was tougher by now and her face was tanned and wrinkled by many eastern suns, but her voice was still low and her manner gentle and wherever she went people welcomed her. War was not at all to her taste and she was secretly somewhat disconcerted to find herself, quite by accident, surrounded by a thousand or so battle-ready Japanese soldiers.

More worried than Isabella herself was the British Vice-consul at Chemulpo, a man, probably, with rather more conventional ideas than she of the correct behaviour for ladies. He visited Miss Bird at her inn during the afternoon and told her that she must leave Korea at once, for she was in grave danger – the Chinese might send a force to Chemulpo to resist the Japanese landings, and he could not be responsible for her safety. Isabella did not really believe in this eventuality, but as she wrote to a friend, 'it is one of my travelling rules never to be a source of embarrassment to British officials'. So, wistfully mindful of her supplies of clean clothes and money left in Seoul, she obediently boarded a British steamer which was bound for Chefoo on the Shantung Peninsula and left the war behind her. Her only travelling-dress was torn and faded, her shoes were cracked, she had just about enough money to pay the fare. But such minor reversals caused only a minor delay. The British Consul in Chefoo came to her rescue and she was soon on her way again, for she had much still to do – a journey up the River Liau to Mukden in a pea-boat, a climb over the 10,000 feet high mountain passes of western China and a further visit to her dear Japan. She did not arrive at the more common man's dream of the exotic – Marrakesh – until she was seventy, when she also stayed with the Berbers in their strongholds among the Atlas mountains. But no one ever really harmed her, her luck never really deserted her and she died quietly and peaceably in Edinburgh at the age of 73, finally exhausted.

Back in Korea on that hot, busy day of June 1894, as Isabella prepared to leave, the Japanese officers were sorting out their men and horses and a pontoon bridge was thrown across the River Han in about half an hour. In due course, the men, the carts and the gun batteries trundled over it towards Seoul. The Japanese captured the Royal Palace after a short skirmish and the Korean government, such as it was, fell into their hands. Soon after, there was another skirmish – this time a sea-fight between Chinese and Japanese warships all heading for Korea, and a Chinese transport boat carrying troops was sunk. These preliminary bouts occurred in July and eventually the war, which everyone knew to be now inevitable, was declared on 1 August.

For the Japanese the whole enterprise was astoundingly, gloriously easy, like shelling peas. The Chinese were numerically far superior and both sides were equipped with western-style weaponry and, in theory, trained in western military tactics. But, while the Japanese had really learned to use these new aids to victory, the Chinese seemed incapable of firing straight and were in the habit of turning pigtail when the fighting got fierce. The Japanese were able to establish naval supremacy early in the war, in the battle near the mouth of the Yalu river; the full strength of the Japanese First Army then landed in Korea and surged forward into Manchuria; the Japanese Second Army landed on the Liaotung Peninsula and proceeded to wipe out resistance there. The Chinese strongholds – Fenghuangcheng, Haicheng, Dairen – simply crumbled under the Japanese onslaughts and for the Chinese it was one bitter tale of failure, cowardice, humiliation and death. By November, therefore, when the Japanese Second Army was poised to come down upon Port Arthur, it was hardly surprising that some of its beleaguered civilians, cold with the sick panic of anticipated defeat, were scurrying away towards the hills, while those who remained were hiding in cellars or barricading themselves in the town's prison.

Among those who had tried, but failed, to get away before the holocaust was a certain James Allan, a 'gentleman's son' originally from Lancashire, who had run through his father's textile fortune with great rapidity and was now wanderer, seafarer, adventurer, jack-of-all-trades that were risky, freelance and as lucrative as possible. And Allan's violent, harsh story of his involvement in and miraculous survival from the capture of Port Arthur, which he relates in *Under the Dragon Flag*, characterises the whole Sino-Japanese war – its savagery and its carnage, the ruthless speed and efficiency of the conquerors, the hopeless disorder and spiritlessness of the conquered.

This was the story. Back in late August, just after the war had been declared, Allan and his mate Webster were sitting in a bar in San Francisco one night drinking and minding their own business, when an Australian of their acquaintance, called Francis Chubb, came in looking for a couple of competent, trustworthy and not too fastidious fellows willing to act as mates on the ship he was proposing to take to China. And it so happened that Allan and Webster were out of work and almost out of money. The ship was a two thousand-ton, long, low, sharp-bowed screw-steamer, called, for the time being, the

Columbia, painted dead-grey, capable of twenty knots, fuelled with anthracite (which gave off less smoke) and freighted, under a top layer of innocent rice and salt, with a supply of 'those munitions of which the Celestials were stated to be in want'.

Gun-running through Japanese waters had its hazards and the enterprise nearly foundered off the coast of Korea near Chemulpo where the *Columbia* was spotted by a Japanese patrol and boarded. Just as the boarding-party were finding out what was under the rice-sacks, some of the crew, under Chubb's orders, attacked them and threw them into the sea; the steamer, though threatening to burst her boilers with exertion any moment, made a clean getaway. Five of the crew were killed by Japanese shells fired after them and Allan was depressed by the fact that there was not a single Bible to be found aboard, so that it was difficult for the survivors to give their dead mates a proper burial service.

They reached Tientsin without further bother, turned, presumably, a neat profit on their cargo and were then given a chance to double their money if they would drop a few thousand Chinese soldiers in Korea on the way back to the States. Money was money, so the *Columbia* carried the troops to Korea and finished the assignment by taking back to Port Arthur a Chinese agent who had guided and interpreted for them during the voyage. Port Arthur's permanent garrison of seven thousand men was already on constant alert and its civilians were nervously aware that Japanese warships lurked impudently close to the docks on occasions and that, somewhere on the far side of the hills encircling the town, the victorious Japanese bayonets were already swinging. Allan, who was always curious about war and the exciting preparations for it, decided to take a quick trip round the town while the *Columbia* was in port.

Seldom can a man have paid more dearly for a two-hour sightseeing jaunt ashore. There was what Allan charitably terms a 'misunderstanding' on the *Columbia* during his absence; when he returned to the dock he found that the ship had sailed – it was on the way back to San Francisco without him.

Luckily, Allan had a philosophical nature, and he had money in his pocket and clothes on his back and no master to regulate his working day. So he sat in various dockside bars for a week and then boarded a Chinese dispatch boat bound for Shanghai. But his luck was well and truly out. An hour or so after leaving Port Arthur, they were delayed by bad weather; without warning a Japanese gunboat, cannons blazing, lurched at them out of the fog. The dispatch boat sank almost immediately and Allan found himself a prisoner of the Japanese. The officers of the gunboat, justifiably suspicious of exactly what this unknown westerner was doing there, treated him hospitably, but indicated that he would be partaking of their hospitality for a considerable period, whether this suited him or not. So, for the next month, as the gunboat sleuthed around the Yellow Sea, Allan made friends with his new hosts and bided his time. It came one dark night when they lay a mere mile from the Chinese coast; Allan jumped overboard and swam for his life, bullets plopping in the water behind him. He reached the shore and, six weeks after his departure from Port Arthur, he was back there again, almost penniless, somewhat thinner and somewhat anxious about the future.

And indeed the outlook was not too rosy. During his absence the port's Chinese garrison had increased to twenty thousand; not an allied ship of any kind was in dock to give him a passage out; in the hill-forts guarding the town, unkempt soldiers slumped at the look-out posts, watching for the first enemy bayonet to appear from behind a rock; everyone knew that the Second Army under General Oyama was coming and that there was nothing to prevent it. Often, small miserable bands of Japanese prisoners, captured while on reconnoitring patrols, were herded through the streets; the Chinese mutilated them horribly before killing them.

Soldiers and civilians alike had braced themselves for a siege, but the battle for Port Arthur began and ended on 21 November. Very early that gruesome morning, Allan left the inn where he was staying and climbed one of a cluster of hills called the 'White Boulders' on the town's perimeter, where he proposed to spend a few interesting hours until lunch watching the approach of the enemy. It was a good vantage point. On his left, he could see the north-western forts, the fiery dragons on the Chinese flags rampaging in the wind from every tower; to his right lay the eastern harbour and the sea beyond it was a silent menace of black Japanese warships that had crept closer during the night; in front of him lay the victim town, many of whose inhabitants were waking up to their last day on earth.

The fighting began at seven-thirty; the Japanese attacked the forts in a series of disciplined, systematic, unwavering forays. At noon, the largest of the Chinese strongholds, Pine Tree Hill, was blown into a million fragments of stone, wood, metal, flesh and shredded flags; 'not a solitary Chinaman', wrote Allan, 'stood for a bayonet thrust'. Along the valleys between the hills dark lines of enemy forces converged on the town, 'the sheen of their bayonets glancing here and there through the columns of smoke which had settled thickly in the hollows'.

Once inside the ring of forts, many of which had simply been deserted by the Chinese, the Japanese army divided pincer-wise and the port was held like a nut in its grip; only the way to the sea was open. Realising this, Allan fled towards the water along with several thousand Chinese citizens and soldiers. The latter, he recorded, were in complete rout, tearing off their uniforms as they ran to fight for a place in the small overloaded boats full of refugees that were putting out hopelessly on to a sea torn with shells from the warships. After watching a couple of these little craft sink within a few hundred yards of the shore and all those aboard drown, Allan decided that *his* best hope was to hide at his inn on the other side of town. He armed himself with an axe prised from the grip of a dead man's fingers and hurried away along a back alley. Dusk was falling – a tormented dusk, racked with the crack of bullets, the thud of booted feet, the grunts, screeches and yells of the slaughtering and the slaughtered. Suddenly he came face to face with a Japanese soldier. He dived through an open doorway, the soldier followed, lunged with his bayonet and skewered Allan by his jacket against a mud wall. As the soldier wrenched his weapon out to make another thrust, Allan split his skull open with the axe.

At this juncture there was perhaps just one thing for Allan to do and he did it. Wincing, he bent over the dead man, took off his brain-spattered uniform and put it on. With a little dagger he found in the soldier's belt, he shaved off his own moustache, picked up the man's rifle and bayonet, pulled the bloody Japanese army hat well down over his wide western eyes and went out. Luckily it was now dark. When he next met a group of triumphant Japanese soldiers, Allan waved his rifle above his head, shouted something that he hoped sounded like 'banzai' and hurried on. In this fashion he reached his inn. The headless body of his landlord slumped in the empty courtyard. He crept upstairs and, in a corner of the attic, stumbled upon one of the inn servants and a Chinese mandarin who had chosen the same hiding place. They stayed there together for an hour or so, gibbering with mutual terror, until the sounds of savagery were more distant, and then, fearing that the respite was a brief one, they decided to make a dash for the docks where they hoped to find a boat and escape in it before daylight. To get there, Jim had to lead them back through the town centre and thus to take the most nightmarish, grotesque, harrowing journey of his entire life.

James Allan was not really much of a writer. There is no record of his ever writing anything other than *Under the Dragon Flag*, and parts of this one book seem very ponderous and colourless when one considers the vitality of his subject-matter. It is clear from it however that what lived branded deep in his memory for the rest of his days was that three hours between ten o'clock and one o'clock on the night of 21 November, when he and the mandarin and the servant crossed Port Arthur from the inn to the docks.

At that time, Chinese and Japanese alike used coloured lanterns to hold back the dark – pretty globules of orange, blue or yellow that bobbed along the back streets in their owners' hands or swung in the breeze above shop doorways.

That night the lanterns were all lit and their coloured rays bobbed and swung over bundles of hacked corpses chucked on top of each other, squelching from open doorways like liver from a bag. Some were headless, their necks like severed red branches; some were armless, hands lay alone in gutters; some were gutless, their guts making the pavements slippery. Once, the three fugitives came upon a group of Japanese soldiers roaring down an alley. They waved their victorious weapons at Allan, who waved back while his companions fell among the dead pretending to be dead. Once, they came upon a group of Chinese women wailing and screaming as they found among the anonymous heaps of carnage the faces they had known. Once, rounding a corner, they cannoned head-on into a high-ranking Japanese officer who was walking alone. A long sword glistened from his belt and his gloves were still white. Allan killed him and took the sword – it was a beauty. Once, they all three hid from some soldiers by rushing inside a large, silent building. When the threat had passed and they re-lit their lantern, they saw that the place was a post-office. Heads were stuck on every spike of a row of railings across the counter, their distended eyes glazed but still bleeding; the floor was a mass of entrails; impaled, spreadeagled across the counter was the body of a child.

And yet they reached the docks and were still just able to remember that they had come for a boat. And they eventually found one – a shabby rowing boat that lay on the deck of a junk some distance down the shore. The junk had been full of Chinese soldiers trying to escape when the Japanese caught up with it. When Jim and his companions climbed aboard they found it reeking with corpses that were jammed in the hatchways and slung like rag-dolls across the decks. The rowing boat was also full of the dead; they had to drag each one out and scrape a bit of the mess off the planks, then they lowered it over the junk's side without making a splash, and climbed into it and slid quietly away from the harbour.

At that point Allan's luck came back to him. About two miles out they came upon a larger junk which was full of live

Chinese also trying to escape. The mandarin, remembering his authority, managed to fix his quivering lips sufficiently to call for help and the three of them were taken aboard. Miraculously, this vulnerable vessel evaded every Japanese warship, gun and patrol boat in the area and so Allan lived to tell his tale – to the seamen of Shanghai, where he left the junk, to his casual mate Webster with whom he was eventually reunited in Australia, to the various proppers-up of San Francisco bars where he spent the remainder of his gun-running proceeds, to all these and many more, he told his special ancient mariner's horror story about the battle of Port Arthur. Later still, in one of his periods of chronic insolvency, he took the Japanese officer's war-sword to a Liverpool pawnbroker and, in the course of the transaction, explained how and where he had come by it. The pawnbroker found Allan's story impossible to believe – the sword was such a work of art, its hilt so delicately carved, its lustrous blue blade so beautiful.

Like many of man's most bloody conflicts, the battle of Port Arthur was to little purpose. The Japanese continued to march over crumbling China, though they did not again behave with such gratuitous brutality and the general who had allowed it was later severely censured and cashiered. Following their next victory, at Weihaiwei, the Japanese were chivalrously lenient towards the defeated, as if to make amends. But whatever they did, the Chinese – butchered, maimed or simply cowed – put up scant resistance and by March of the next year the invading armies were almost within hailing distance of Pekin and the Chinese government sued for peace at almost any price.

The terms of the original peace treaty of Shimonoseki concluded between the two antagonists were, therefore, to the disadvantage of the Chinese: Korea was granted independence, most of the Liaotung Peninsula, including Port Arthur, and also the island of Formosa were ceded to Japan, and China had to pay a substantial war indemnity. However, the ink of the treaty signatures was barely dry when three western powers, Russia, Germany and France, made their 'Triple Intervention'. Under the hypocritical guise of offering 'advice' in order 'to further the interests of peace in the Far East' (a hollow phrase indeed, in the light of later events) they made it very plain that if Japan did not at once retrocede the Liaotung Peninsula to China, the country would run the risk of their considerable displeasure – a displeasure that could easily take a quite violent form. The 'interveners' were by no means the disinterested peace-lovers they pretended to be; for years, they had all been pursuing their own plans for territorial expansion in China and were not prepared to let a young dog like Japan jump in and snap up such a tempting morsel as Port Arthur from under their noses. Just to emphasise the point, a large force of Russian warships happened to be concentrated in the Yellow Sea area; there were further reserves at Vladivostok; Germany and France were reported to be on the alert.

And so, bitterly aware that they could count on no ally and that even sturdy Japanese soldiers were not yet ready to take on, single-handed, three Goliath-size bullies at once, Japan was forced to return the Liaotung Peninsula to China. It was a resounding diplomatic defeat after such a crushing military victory and one that both humiliated the Japanese and made them angrily contemptuous of the motives of the 'peace-loving' western powers. They neither forgot nor forgave an intervention that was so patently the result of cynical self-interest – particularly when, within three years of Japan's returning the Peninsula to China, Russia, one of the interveners, had extorted the lease of this strategic territory for itself!

'The national pride has been deeply wounded,' said Lafcadio Hearn, describing the mood of the country at the time. And he recalled the belief of the Japanese that the souls of their soldiers killed overseas return to their camps when the bugle sounds at dusk in the garrison towns. Restless below the stone fortresses at Weihaiwei, the gulf of Pechili, the deeps of the sluggish Yalu, the grim hills of Port Arthur, the sad souls respond to the bugle-notes and flock homewards – 'And they will hear them again', Hearn prophesied, 'in that day when the armies of the Sons of Heaven shall be summoned against Russia.'

Part Four
1896–1905

Of writers and consuls, war and peace

Lafcadio Hearn, who wrote about the legendary excursions of Japan's warrior souls, about the condition of Tokyo's streets in the rainy season, about climbing Mount Fuji and about so much else typically and traditionally Japanese, was a strange man. An elusive figure, literary pundits explain, an odd one – odd in Japan's 1890s, odd probably anywhere, any time. When he arrived in the country he was forty years old, shortish, squarish, with a soft American-Irish accent, an abrupt yet tentative manner and a great eagerness for anything genuinely oriental. He was a man of literary talent who yearned for literary excellence; words, their exact nuances, their shapes, textures, stresses, endlessly tantalised him; he accomplished much, but he kept arranging his life in expectation of greater recognition than he actually received.

His early life had, unfortunately, been arranged for him in a series of unsettling and unsatisfactory ways. His mother, Rosa, was the beautiful, moody, illiterate daughter of a landowner on a small Ionian island where Charles Bush Hearn, an Anglo-Irish surgeon, happened to be stationed. The result of their stormy affair was two sons, the first, born before their marriage, died soon afterwards; the second, legitimate, was born on the island of Lefkas, or Lafcadio. Following the marriage, Rosa spent a couple of sunless years with her son in her husband's Dublin home, where she nearly went mad. Then she returned to Greece, the marriage was annulled and Charles Hearn went off to India where he later died. The young Lafcadio was left in Dublin and brought up by a rich aunt. While at school he lost the sight of one eye during a game – a disfiguring accident, which had a permanently adverse effect on his emotional balance and personal confidence. Soon after this misfortune he was told that his aunt was bestowing her lucrative attentions elsewhere; he was not to be the favoured heir after all. At the age of eighteen he received a small cheque from the man who had secured his aunt's favours and with it a curt note telling him to take himself off to a distant relative who lived in Cincinnati, Ohio, and there make his fortune for himself, if he could. Lafcadio had nothing to lose, so he went.

Cincinnati in the 1870s was a tough, thrusting, ugly place and the role young Hearn found for himself in it was that of a tough, thrusting reporter who told the readers of *The Daily Enquirer* all about the ugly lives that were lived on the dark underside of their city. Lafcadio soon became adept at making the hair of respectable citizens stand on end as they ate their breakfast oatmeal and read his stories: the one about the shredded remains of a man thrust into a furnace and burned to death by his brothers; the one about the sickening stinks and brutal killing methods of the slaughter-houses; the one about the white girls in the negro brothel; the one about the opium-takers in the riverside shacks, the body-snatchers who lurked near the cemeteries and the knife-quick feuds of the boatmen on the waterfront.

The violence and disorder of these years stimulated his fascination with the bizarre, the supernatural and for the emotional maelstroms of people who were unrespectable, uninhibited and unpredictable. It was a fascination that caused him to marry, while in Cincinnati, a mulatto girl who soon left him and returned to her former life as a prostitute and, later, to leave the city in search of yet more exotic pastures. He went first to New Orleans, where he studied the dialects and customs of the Creoles, and then to Martinique. The lush colours and sensuous careless tempo of the island delighted him, and his abilities as a writer sharpened and expanded. But he was still a minor figure on the literary scene, translator of Gautier and Maupassant, admirer and emulator of Edgar Allan Poe, author of several serialised stories and collections of folk legends.

Hearn returned to New York in 1889 and spent an unhappy period quarrelling with publishers and old friends. It was during a stormy session at *Harper's* Magazine that one of the editors suggested he might like to go to Japan – a country that was becoming very fashionable (and might provide good copy), an exotic place certainly, full of beautiful, obedient women, somewhere different and – a long way off. Hearn still had little to lose, he went.

It was good that he did so because, in a sense, Japan needed him. He was the first western literary figure of any stature to establish a permanent relationship with the country and to write, to the exclusion of all else, a considerable body of work about all he found there. He took Japan very seriously, very intimately and expended a great deal of intellectual effort in trying to understand the 'heart' of its people. He married (legally and permanently) a Japanese woman, he had Japanese children, he became a Japanese citizen, he lived and worked there for the rest of his life. Few western men before him had done as much. Nevertheless there is the smell of near-failure about Lafcadio Hearn; the relationship between him and his adopted country became almost rank in the end. Part of the reason, perhaps, was that any of his later responses could not but fall short, in some respects, of the supreme joy he felt when he first discovered the land.

Among the globe-trotters' reluctantly-published batches of journals, sketches and letters there are a considerable number that could fit under the umbrella-title of 'My First Day in Japan'. Most of the writers were thoroughly exhilarated by the experience, yet most of their descriptions of it are bricked over with platitudes, stuccoed with clichés. Hearn, however in the opening essay of the earliest of the fourteen books he wrote about Japan – called, ingenuously, 'My First Day in the Orient' – conveys all his delighted surprise at the country which he first saw during a thrilling, day-long, not-long-enough *jinrikisha* ride. Ahead of him, the white bowl-shaped hat of his runner swayed rhythmically against the sky, a limpid, luminous blue sky, its breezes cool with 'wind-waves from the snowy cone of Fuji', its air clear with the 'soft white witchery of the Japanese sun'. Everything charmed him, 'even a package of toothpicks of cherry wood bound with a paper wrapper, lettered in three different colours; even the little sky-blue towel with designs of flying sparrows upon it which the *jinrikisha* man used to wipe his face. The bank bills, the commonest coins are things of beauty. Even the piece of plaited coloured string used by the shopkeeper to tie up your last package is a pretty curiosity.'

For the next week or so Hearn hurried eagerly from one shrine to the next, pleading, humbly, to see the wisest of the wise priests, the most sacred of the sacred statues, the most revered of the revered scrolls, peering hungrily with his one over-strained bulging eye at the subtle textural harmonies of ochre-lichened stone, rain-tinted wood, cloth of shredded blue and silver. *Shaka* he saw, 'colossal, black-visaged, gold robed, enthroned upon a giant lotus'; 'weird *Sodza Baba*, she who takes the garments of the dead away by the bank of the River of the Three Roads which flows through the phantom world. Pale blue her robe is; her hair and skin are white; her face is strangely wrinkled; her small keen eyes are hard'; the Goddess *Benten*, with sea-serpent in flaked gold-leaf, peeped at him from a dusty corner; withdrawn in the courtyard he discovered a fiercely beautiful wooden figure, 'red as with the redness of heated iron cooling into grey ... a tiger frown and nightmare eyes'; inside the inmost shrine he stood stunned with awe as a priest slowly raised a curtain before him to reveal a goddess with 'golden robe ... columnar thighs under chiselled drapery, a Face golden, smiling with eternal youth ... and a tiara of divinity'.

Bemused by the delicate elegance of these pine-shaded shrines with their frail, ever-courteous attendants, their placid, dusty gods, their low-toned rituals, Hearn felt like some blundering monster from a cruder uglier world. And he relates, with wry self-disgust how, when he was preparing to leave one particularly exquisite shrine, a smiling priest approached and held out a bowl. Hearn, assuming it was a begging bowl, dropped some coins in and then saw that it was full of water –

for him to drink. Oh crass occidental mistake! How he writhed while the priest, still smiling, took the bowl away and returned bearing another into which he poured water for Hearn to see and again offered the pure liquid to his embarrassed visitor.

During these first days in the country Hearn felt that such misunderstandings were entirely his fault; he was the defective, ungainly stranger whereas 'Japan, in very truth, with its magical trees and luminous atmosphere, its cities, towns and temples was filled with forty million of the most lovable people in the world'. Naturally, having stumbled into such an earthly paradise, Hearn wanted to remain, and so, through the good offices of his new friend, Basil Chamberlain, he secured a post as English teacher in Matsue, an old-fashioned city in the western province of Izumo, not so very far from Kyoto and the Inland Sea. It was a mild, lush landscape where oranges, yams and tropical red lilies ripened during the long summers; vine-hung forests still held large numbers of deer, stag, badgers, chamois occasionally, and grizzly monkeys; green snakes wriggled in the warm paddy mud; edible green turtles, octopus and huge crimson and yellow spider crabs drifted through the tepid waters along the coast and the village women, stripped to the waist, dived for fresh seaweed in spring and, in late summer, thrashed apart the kernels of the berries on the wax-trees to make their own rush-wick candles.

His new resting-place fitted Lafcadio. He appreciated its quiet rhythms: 'The first of the noises of the Matsue day comes to the sleeper like the throbbing of a slow enormous pulse exactly under his ear,' Hearn wrote. 'It is a great, soft, dull buffet of sound – like a heart-beat in its regularity, in its muffled depth, in the way it quakes up through one's pillow so as to be felt rather than heard. It is simply the pounding of the ponderous pestle of the *kometsuki*, the cleaner of rice ... The measured muffled echoing of its fall seems to me the most pathetic of all sounds of Japanese life – it is the beating indeed of the Pulse of the Land.' The machine to which Hearn refers operated on a primitive see-saw principle. The pestle was fastened on the end of a wooden lever suspended above a large mortar of rice. The labourer, who both pounded and cleaned the rice, had the dreary task of continually climbing on and jumping off the end of the lever. Every time he jumped off, the pestle made its 'soft dull buffet of sound' as it fell.

Soothed into wakefulness by this gentle cadence, Hearn rose, slid open his paper window and looked out on – 'a soft green cloud of spring foliage rising from the river-bounded garden', on 'long nebulous bands' that swathed the lake below so that it looked like a 'spectral sea'. As the day grew, he saw 'sunward up the long Hashigawa, beyond the many-pillared wooden bridge, one high-pooped junk, just hoisting sail'. It seemed to him 'the most fantastically beautiful craft I ever saw – a dream of Orient Seas, so idealised by the vapour is it; the ghost of a junk, but a ghost that catches the light as clouds do; a shape of gold mist, seemingly semi-diaphanous and suspended in pale blue light'.

A 'dream of Orient', a misty world with its harshest edges bandaged – this Hearn craved and this he found for a time in Matsue. He was an excellent teacher and was admired by his students. Wrote one of them, Mr Otani, in a later tribute, 'He impressed us with his earnestness and sympathy ... He was patient to correct our English accent carefully; and he went minutely over our compositions and it was our greatest joy that he wrote even a criticism on them.' Otani goes on to recall an occasion when 'we invited him to a certain Buddhist temple when we had a musical entertainment ... He sat as we did from two o'clock until evening attentively; and we were surprised to see him not even palsied in his legs as any other foreigner would be after even a half-hour's experience ... He tried to absorb, when off-duty from school, everything Japanese and strange and he, with his students made many little excursions almost everywhere in the city.'

And in this fashion Hearn grew to know and love the place. He often visited its massive castle, a feudal grey stronghold bristling above the town, and 'from under the black scowl of its loftiest eaves,' Hearn wrote, 'looking east and south, the whole city can be seen at a single glance as in the vision of a hawk'. After the heights, a return to the humble human ways below – along 'fishermen's street' where nets were strung high on bamboo poles 'like prodigious cobwebs against the sky' and across the curved wooden bridge of Ohashi, where, all day, the pattens of the townsfolk made 'a rapid merry musical clatter like the sound of an enormous dance'.

Lafcadio expressed his grateful sense of belonging at last by 'going native'. He learned not only to sit cross-legged on the floor for hours, but to eat Japanese food, enjoy blister-hot baths and wear loose *yukata* when at home. He began too his collection of Japanese pipes, those slender-stemmed little instruments of brass, silver or ivory, quaintly carved with demons muttering the holy name of Buddha, or badgers beating their drum-round bellies, or hares cleaning their rice on the moon. 'What heavenly delight he felt with his pipe,' recalled one who often watched him. 'He looked so happy already even to touch the pipe; he would pull out one from a hundred and look on its *ganbuki* (wild-goose neck) and mouthpiece with the quick glance of a connoisseur ... He used to sit as a Japanese; and when he smoked he put his left hand mannerly upon his knee and swayed his body back and forth.'

The person who wrote that was his wife, the twenty-two-year-old daughter of an ex-*samurai* whom Hearn met and married in Matsue. Her name was Setsu Kozuimi and Setsu means 'true' which was an appropriate name for their marriage. Not for Hearn the ephemeral bargains of a Pierre Loti and his Chrysanthemum or the fictional sentimentality of Clive Holland and his porcelain-pretty Hyacinth; he took his marriage and later his children by that marriage as earnestly and devotedly as he took all things Japanese. And so he soon found that, in true Japanese fashion, he had inherited along with his wife a miscellaneous assortment of ageing relatives who all expected him to support them and give them houseroom. It was, mainly, therefore, to meet the increasing demands on his salary that Hearn moved, with his new family, to Kumamoto, on Kyushu, where he took up a more lucrative teaching post in the town's new university.

But Kumamoto was the beginning of the end of the golden dream, and while there Hearn took the first of the long swings on the pendulum which, as he ruefully admitted, now attracted him to and then repulsed him from his adopted country and its people. While Matsue, even in the last decade of the nineteenth century, had remained sufficiently rural and isolated to preserve, almost intact, the patterns of old Japan, Kumamoto hummed with growing industries and ambitious students straining to pass as many examinations as possible. 'There is no religion here,' Hearn complained in one of his many letters to Basil Chamberlain, 'no poetry – no courtesy – no myths – no traditions – no superstitions. Beastly modernisation!' For Hearn, myths had ever been more real than the realities of everyday; he was deeply dismayed to see that the Japanese had, seemingly, chosen to reject the artistic richness, the decorous patterns of their past in order to participate wholeheartedly in the competitive, ugly, hybrid process of industrialisation. 'What is there to love in Japan,' he asks, 'except what is passing away?' He found too that not all the country's forty million inhabitants were as lovable as he had once thought. In Matsue, the ordinary people were 'soft, gentle, old-fashioned. Here the peasants and the lower classes drink and fight and beat their wives and make me mad to think that I wrote all the Japanese were angels.' Typically, Hearn began to torture himself with hopeless envy of his own first joyous innocence and delight. One day he turned up the notes he had made a few years before for that lyric book *Glimpses of Unfamiliar Japan*: 'I find I described horrible places as gardens of paradise and horrid people as angels and divinities. How happy I must have been without knowing it. There were all my illusions facing me on faded yellow paper . . .'

The vision was turning sour; he seemed to have lost the knack of happiness; he might as well move to Tokyo, hub of the modernisation he loathed, 'saddest hole in the world,' he once called it. 'In this horrid Tokyo I feel like a cicada, I am caged and cannot sing,' he wrote to a friend. In 1896 he became Professor of English at the Imperial University where he was a venerated, if eccentric, figure on the academic scene. There are many recollections of him at this time – his slight body bent inside an old mouse-coloured coat, a floppy broad-brimmed hat shading his weak eye, under his arm a large purple kerchief bulging with the works of the Eminent Victorians. He seldom went to the staff-room between lectures, but sat on a rock by the garden pool and silently puffed a favourite pipe. 'The students', wrote a Japanese colleague, 'did not dare to come near to him for fear lest they might disturb his solitude, but admired him from a distance as if he were some old china vase which might be broken even by a single touch.'

The absorbed, aloof fragility of the man was impressive, if rather daunting. He was totally dedicated to his writing and, when not at the university, devoted his whole energy to the self-imposed task of trying to explain Japan – to himself and to the rest of the western world. Yet, 'what a horribly difficult thing it is to write about Japan,' he complained. 'I can't venture to imagine its soul-play. The motives and thoughts escape me as individualities. I get glimpses of them in generalities only.' With rather pathetic credulity he asks his friends to send him winsome tales of the everyday life of the 'common people': 'any "heart-thing" I would like to know. I collect all I can and write them and put them in drawers. In time they work themselves out.' Precious as gold-dust was this apparent evidence of purity of soul among old-fashioned servants, children, gentle grandmothers – a relic from the integrated, wholesome morality of the past.

So naturally, every summer, Lafcadio shook off the modern complexities of Tokyo and retreated to Yaidzu, a small fishing village off the old Tokaido highway. Yaidzu was a row of weather-worn timber houses – 'Lizard-like it takes the grey tints of the rude grey coast on which it rests, curving along a little bay.' The bay was protected from the full force of the waves by a great stone wall littered with nets, buoys, ancient wooden anchors 'like ploughshares' and round six-feet-high bait baskets of split bamboo which, when stood out to dry, looked like little native huts. Hearn used to sit on the wall for hours listening to the thump of the sea, watching the outline of mist-wrapped Fuji fade or glow on the horizon. He rented two shabby rooms in the village for himself and his two elder sons and his friends were the local fishermen, the barber and the priest. The villagers declared he was 'borne from the water' and each evening he would swim away from them like a small pale fish and when they thought he had gone for ever, they suddenly saw a flare on the water's surface as he lit a cigar and lay far out, floating and smoking. The comparison between Hearn and a fish was often made by friends who saw his normally defensive, angular little body relax and cavort in the waves. One of them, W. B. Mason, taxed him with the thought one day and records, 'the sad smile characteristic of Hearn passed over his face for a moment as he replied, "Oh yes, and I can drink sea-water."' This was not a joke; it must have been true; Hearn's most oppressive defect is that he totally lacked a sense of humour. Nevertheless, when he returned from his prolonged marine submersions, he was, decided his friend, for a short time, 'the happiest man in the world'. He wrote simply-worded letters to his wife – describing the creaking frogs under his veranda, the dragonflies and crabs his son had caught, the night-fishermen, unloading a huge haul of bonito from their high-prowed boats. And he wrote essays in praise of the village and its inhabitants, 'frank and kindly as children – good children – honest to a fault, innocent of the further world, loyal to the ancient traditions and the ancient gods'.

But, summer ended, the ancient gods withdrew and Hearn returned to his teaching and his task of explaining that complicated phenomenon – Japan. *Japan, an Attempt at an Interpretation*, was the title he gave to his last major work on the subject published in 1904. In it, he tries to analyse such problematical issues as the structure of moral obligation in the Japanese family, the enigmatic responsibilities of ancestor worship, the pull of the country's feudal past on its thrusting present; yet, the more he wrote, the more he doubted. A foreigner, he felt, must learn 'to think backwards, upside down and inside out', if he was to follow the tortuous subtleties of the Japanese mind; between the intellect of a modern western man such as himself and that of a Japanese there was, he despairingly concluded, 'a psychological interval as hopeless as the distance from planet to planet'.

It was a bitter judgement to make at the end of a fourteen-year exercise in cultural intercommunication, and, because most of Hearn's efforts to explain the underlying forces in Japanese society end on a similar note of uncertainty and dissatisfaction, he is probably most admired nowadays for his essays on what he called 'the queer, the curious and the artless' aspects of the national life. He wrote about the evocative, plangent chant of a blind street-singer who came to his door one day, about the wraiths and nightmare hobgoblins that haunted the countryside – such as the *Tengu*, creatures with the beaks of eagles or crows who dined off corpses in the dead of night – and about the musical insects that the towns-folk bred and kept in cages, bribing them with slivers of melon, cucumber and aubergine in return for their song. There were the bell-ringer insects, the 'weavers' whose notes were like the shuttling of a hand-loom, one rarity called the Black Lark, crickets – demon, shrimp and horse variety – the water-melon-seed insect and the *Kutsuwamushi*, the Bridle-Bit insect. This latter was so called because its sound was like that of a bridled charger in full gallop, as Hearn illustrates by quoting the song of a wistful wife-in-waiting:

Listen, his bridle rings – that is surely my husband
Homeward hurrying now, fast as his horse can bear him.
Ah, my ear is deceived – only the *kutsuwamushi*!

The insect-world's unholy combinations of the lovely and the hideous obsessed him: 'Even the little that we have been able to learn about insects fills us with the wonder that is akin to fear,' Hearn wrote. 'The lips that are hands; the horns that are eyes and the tongues that are drills; the multiple devilish mouths that move in four different ways at once, the living scissors and saws and boring-pumps and bracing-bits; the exquisite elfish weapons which no human skill can copy . . .' He refused to kill a fly or a mosquito, his wife remembered, even if it crawled over his writing paper or sucked his blood; he crouched in his garden for hours watching ants invade a new mound; when the city was heavy and noisy around him he longed only 'to think the slow thoughts of the long grey crickets, and the thoughts of the darting shimmering dragon-flies and the thoughts of the basking, trilling cicadae and the thoughts of the wicked little crabs that lifted up their claws from between the roots of the pines'.

The antennae of Hearn's senses reached towards and were at one with his natural surroundings. 'I never saw such a person as Hearn,' said his wife, 'whose heart was disturbed terribly by a single shiver of a roadside weed.' He fretted over the health of his pomegranate tree; when a morning-glory flowered unseasonably he was lost in admiration, 'Oh what lovely courage, what a serious intention,' he exclaimed to his family. To the bulbous bullfrogs near the pond he would quote a favourite *haiku*: 'Putting his hands so politely, Oh look, the frog is offering his own songs.' Sometimes in sudden bursts of glee he imitated the slappity-hop of the comic creatures to please his children; but then he became grey and quiet again and, his wife said, 'once he felt sad I believe that with him he thought the whole world was going to disappear'.

In a sense, Hearn must have wanted the world to disappear. During his last year of life he withdrew almost completely into himself. He resigned from the university over a question of money and broke with his remaining friends, 'bolting his door right against their faces,' as a Japanese colleague put it. With his wife and children he was increasingly distant, melancholy, dreaming himself away, to them it seemed, melting rather than dying. He died of heart failure in September 1904 and was buried beneath bamboo trees and soft moss transplanted from his own beloved garden. His tombstone was engraved with the Japanese name he had taken several years earlier, when he became a citizen of the country: Kozuimi, 'Little

Spring' (the name of his wife's family) and the appropriately elusive first name that he had chosen for himself – Yakumo, which means 'Eight Clouds'.

After his death Hearn's work was, for a time, in vogue. Some of his books were translated, biographers and critics evaluated them, there were plans for a Hearn Society in Tokyo. Then the enthusiasm evaporated abruptly as such post-mortem enthusiasms tend to, and he has since been allotted a fairly minor literary niche. Nevertheless, Hearn's life in Japan and what he wrote about the country were important because he took such pains to emphasise and elucidate the value and richness of the country's traditional culture and its lasting effect on the present. By so doing Hearn was, perhaps, more in the mainstream of modern thought at the time than he realised. For, during the 1890s a growing number of Japanese in various fields of endeavour began to criticise openly and thoughtfully the indiscriminate aping of the West. The time had come, they felt, for rejection as well as for selection and adaptation; perhaps it was time also to reconsider the older verities of Confucianism, Shintoism and Buddhism as the Imperial Rescript of 1890 had suggested.

And with this trend there naturally came a revival of interest in the arts and crafts of old Japan – its writing, painting, pottery and carving – skills that had attained an extremely high degree of sophistication several centuries before Commodore Perry arrived on the Japanese scene. And in this movement back to national sources of inspiration, the Japanese were encouraged and applauded by a number of prominent westerners who were very appreciative of and knowledgeable about the native culture. Hearn of course was one of these; another was Ernest Fenollosa, a Bostonian who became Professor of Philosophy at the Imperial University and who roundly declared that the visual arts of Japan were far superior to those of Paris or New York, and that the main thing the Japanese lacked was a national academy to foster interest in them. Another connoisseur of the indigenous culture was Captain Brinkley, prickly, erudite editor of *The Japan Mail* for many years and such a fervent and dogmatic admirer of everything Japanese that he had almost as many occidental enemies as oriental friends.

Men such as Brinkley and Fenollosa were proficient linguists who lectured in Japanese colleges, read papers to the Japan Society and were in contact with leading politicians and scholars in the capital. They were often fairly scornful of western business men and traders who, they felt, remained wilfully unappreciative of the cultural resources of the country around them. And the business men, predictably, sometimes retaliated by making snide comments about 'starry-eyed, hypocritical Japan-lovers'. Two of Osman Edwards's *Residential Rhymes* neatly mock those on either side of the question. First, the merchant of Yokohama, shown riding in a pretentious carriage and saying:

> When I first came to live in Japan
> My duty was simple and plain,
> To dazzle the nation with civilisation
> Implying more money than brain.
> In mansions as big as the Bluff
> I had servants and horses enough
> While the native possessions
> Outside the concessions
> Appeared to me very poor stuff.

And, on the next page, 'The Professor in Nirvana' – who is shown in the accompanying illustration reclining in beatitude on a bier encircled by Buddhist saints and saying, as he melts Nirvana-wards:

> I draw the breath of old Japan
> New vistas fade and modern voices cease;
> My soul on wings cerulean
> Attains to perfect wisdom, perfect peace.
> In vain the self-deluded students prate
> In accents loud of western lore,
> In vain of commerce and of Rights debate,
> Forgetting what they learned of yore.

Let them spurn an alien creed,
Shun the European fold
... Unless of course they chance to need
Mere perishable gold.

The animosity was fairly mild, a reflection of differences commonly-felt everywhere between the world of learning and the corridors of commerce. Both worlds flourished in the Japan of the period – the former centred mainly in the capital around the principal educational institutions and the foreign legations; the latter still centred in the treaty ports, where the glitter of 'mere perishable gold' led some, as it always had, to ruin, but more, in these palmier days, towards success.

II

The man who came to Tokyo as British Minister after Hugh Fraser's sudden death and who, by virtue of his position, at once became a prominent figure in all foreign circles – business, academic and diplomatic – was Sir Ernest Satow, and it is doubtful if there was any Englishman alive and available better qualified for the post. For Sir Ernest had begun his association with Japan thirty-three years earlier, when, as a student-interpreter at the British Legation, he had arrived in Yokohama a few weeks prior to the murder of an English merchant, Charles Richardson, by warriors of the Satsuma clan – an affair which had stormy international repercussions at the time. In those tentative, exploratory, riskier days, the linguistic aids available for the study of Japanese were few, and the young interpreter more or less made up his own dictionary as he went along. But Ernest had the gift of languages and, obviously, of a disciplined intelligence. He soon became the most competent and informed secretary at the

Legation, then under Sir Harry Parkes, and was actively and most profitably concerned in both weaving and wriggling among the various webs of diplomatic intrigue strung between the western representatives, the last Shogun and the clan-leaders of the Imperial party at the time of the Emperor's restoration to power. He quickly became one of the handful of scholarly foreign linguists who explored with enthusiastic appreciation the rich cultural life of the country; he was an indefatigable reader of papers to the Japan Society; native intellectuals and politicians were among his best friends. And yet, in 1882, he left the country as if for good.

Propelled like a ball in a pinball machine on to the totally unpredictable Foreign Office circuit, he was bounced first to Bangkok (as Consul-General), then as Minister to Uruguay and to Morocco; he also continued his earlier law studies and took silk in 1887. When he returned to Japan in 1895 he was fifty-one years old, newly elevated to the rank of K.C.M.G. He was a fair-minded, knowledgeable, very competent man who was generally respected and trusted by both Japanese and foreigner. During Satow's six years of office, Japan was at peace, and it was a propitious time for the initiation of informal talks, the taking of friendly diplomatic soundings that were to result in the Anglo-Japanese Alliance, eventually signed in 1902. Satow was also, like the Japanese themselves, very anxious about Russia's expansionist policy in Manchuria and Korea and encouraged the working out of a *détente* over those inflammable areas, though without much success.

In his capacity as diplomatic 'Chief', Satow seems to have gained the confidence of nearly all those who worked under him, for, in addition to the dispatches from the Foreign Office, letters from Japanese ministers and officials, the reports on trade and domestic affairs, the requests for audiences and pleas for his attendance at innumerable functions which poured across his ministerial desk every day, there arrived a tream of chatty, frank letters from his consuls in the treaty orts. Sir Ernest rightly encouraged the sending of these letters, which were often richly illuminating. For example, they often provided the stories behind the local trade figures, the details, often unintentionally revealing, of the pressures and conflicts within the foreign communities, items of information which could have political significance and finally, but no less important, little pointers to the characters of the writers themselves, whose careers it was one of Satow's many tasks to make or hinder, largely on the basis of his own judgement.

From northern Hakodate, and only from there, the story Sir Ernest heard from Mr B— was still one of a land and people full of promise but undeveloped. Consuls still languished there, feeling under used, neglected and lost in the emptiness of it all. 'Never was there such a "sleepy hollow"', wrote Mr B— 'and it is only the prospect of the arrival of some of the fleet that keeps me going.' Well, the fleet came and brought a spurt of excitement with it – a few rows to settle (out of court if possible) between the 'blue-jackets' and the local police, and a vice-admiral to entertain and take on a shooting trip ('It is the responsibility of consular officers to be on good terms with officers of the navy', Sir Ernest admonished another member of his staff, who once neglected the stint.) In the absence of the navy, Mr B— found that John Batchelor, who was still preaching among the Ainu, made a congenial companion for a hunting expedition. The consul and the missionary wore Canadian moccasins and snow-shoes, shot deer and geese mainly, and developed quite a taste for falcon curry. Batchelor, who could make enquiries with much more seeming innocence than Her Majesty's Consul, kept an informative 'watching brief' on continuing Japanese troop movements in Hokkaido, and also reported an increase in the number of Russian coalers that chugged along the wild coast on the way to Sakhalin. Every summer, 'those delightful gentlemen, the sealers,' tramped into Mr B—'s office, some of them, nowadays, from British Columbia; but there were no foreign otter-hunters any more. For over twenty years otters had been slaughtered indiscriminately by Mr J. H. Snow and his fellow sharpshooters, until now few remained – and those that did were being polished off by the Japanese themselves.

Clearly, compared to their counterparts in the other treaty ports, the consuls at Hakodate led a trouble-free, slow-tempoed life; their main problems, according to Mr B—, were 'clothes and teeth'. After eighteen months in that back-of-beyond, he was 'really in rags' and his wife's plight was even more dire. And now that they were being posted to some muggy little consulate on the China coast, could Sir Ernest see his way to allowing them a few days' leave to buy some light clothes? And teeth were similarly tattered, could they go first to a Yokohama dentist? And, er, he was not entitled to a new 'outfit allowance' just now, was he, perhaps? So the B—'s left Hokkaido gladly, as most consular families did and came south to the dentists, outfitters and other sophisticated amenities of Yokohama, a booming, busy place whose consul was, presumably so overworked and close at hand, that he was released from the duty of writing chatty letters to the Chief about its progress.

But if the consuls did not write about Yokohama, many others did, though not always with charity. 'Anything duller and narrower than these English communities in the East it is difficult to imagine...' judged a British woman journalist. 'They [the foreigners of Yokohama] did not know anything about Japan except pony racing, nor did they wish to, a fact they very soon let you know.' A visiting American concurred, 'The contents of the mailbags, social events and a perfection of their physical comfort comprise the interests of most of the residents of Yokohama.'

Both writers were describing the port during the second half of the nineties, by which period it had well over two thousand western residents, plus the uncountable Chinese. About half of the westerners were British, a quarter American and they had all managed, by this time, to rearrange and subdue the various native intractabilities of the land to approximate that desirable 'perfection of their physical comfort'. The Public Gardens were orderly with neat paths; the streets were well-lit and the road round the bay was macadamised to smooth the passing of carriage and pair. Trains ran every half-hour between Yokohama and the capital (late night specials for Gala Balls) and prices of 'rickshas were posted in English at every stand. On the Bluff, among clean little roads that reminded one visitor of the outskirts of Tunbridge Wells, withdrawn along tree-shaded drives and shrubberies of camellia and rhododendron, stood the houses of the wealthy merchants and the professional men. They came in various styles – mock Tudor, Queen Anne, American Colonial or serviceable Victorian red-brick; their wrought-iron balconies, wistaria-entwined verandas, porticoed entrance halls, double french windows overlooked swathes of trim lawns and tennis-courts (all summer there was usually someone for tennis). And the houses contained, not simply the foreign families, but staffs of servants grown Legation-large: house-maids, cooks and waiting amahs, gatekeepers and grooms in suitable liveries, laundry amahs, nurse maids and sewing girls, gardeners and sweeping boys. And all these menials were properly trained in the mysteries of western domestic rituals – the arranging of table napkins and finger bowls, the ironing of dress-shirts and ruffle-fronts, the polishing of fish knives and grandfather clocks, the serving of roast beef and sherry trifle.

No coolie was permitted to rupture the Bluff's quietude with raucous cries of effort – *ho, ho, huida, hai* – as he hauled his load up the hill; no layabout was long allowed to loll beneath the bandstand in the Gardens; all the scavengers' carts and buckets had tight covers over them – by order. Compared to twenty years before the streets were less muddy, the canals less fetid and rat-infested; there were more banks, churches, burglar-proof godowns, shops and respectable women to patronise them. And so the shops stocked many more pretty, comforting, home-like things: chandeliers, doe-skin gloves and moustache brushes for instance, tallboys and knickerbockers, beaded curtains and Ball Programmes with Pencils and Tassels attached. National speciality shops thrived – the German confectioners for pepper nuts and marzipan whisk figures, the

English vintners for porter-in-cask and Carpy's Californian Claret, and 'Nouveau Printemps' on Main Street sold superior veilings and children's corsets.

During the summers, the same steamy, torrid summers, many more residents could afford an escape to the mountains or the sea. At least, it was fashionable so to escape, even if one could not afford it. Growled one of the long-suffering local moralists: 'In many cases households have been established whose expenses are out of all proportion with the business that supports or is supposed to support them. The few days that were spent in some modest country resort twenty years ago once a year have grown into weeks and months, and the country trips are made with a family of five or six and two or three servants. The modest country resorts adapted themselves to circumstances to the extent that they have disappeared altogether and their place was taken by hotels where people sit down to a dozen courses and dress for dinner.'

In short, as they all said, 'money talked'; money meant dinners and houses and staffs and, to a considerable extent, money meant status – a most important accretion in a society where the inclusions and exclusions of status, sex and nationality were most painstakingly defined. Ladies meeting in the Ladies Reading Room knew exactly whom they could or could not, must or must not invite to tea; gentlemen knew which of the several clubs in the community their position and jobs entitled them to join. These clubs were genial centres of the port's social life and Rudyard Kipling was among several visitors to describe the Yokohama United Club with affection: ship's captains from all ports east of Suez swung in for a few drinks and 'the veranda by the sea where the big telescope stands is a perpetual feast of the Pentecost'. There, 'consuls and judges of the consular courts meet men over on leave from the China ports or it may be Malaya, and they all talk tea, silk, banking and the exchange, with its fixed residents. Everything is always as bad as it can possibly be and everybody is always on the verge of ruin.' It is easy to fill in the details from that – the bewhiskered large-waistcoated gentlemen equipped with their 'b & s', sitting along the sunny veranda overlooking the ship-loaded harbour and grumbling to visitors about the cupidity of Japanese customs men, the slothfulness of native government officials, the extortionate price of coolie labour. The same themes, the same complaints, the same underlying nostalgia for those good old touch-and-go days when things were simple and a fellow could take a risk and perhaps make a fortune in five years. But those days were gone, there was too much red tape now, too many tariffs, too much local competition.

And it was certainly true that prevailing business trends were steadier now and duller too. The national currency was firmly based, there was more capital available for industrial expansion and, in 1897, Japan made the important shift from the silver to the gold standard, and so allowed for further development of overseas trade. The men who succeeded in the foreign settlements these days were usually cautious and persevering, with a good grasp of large-scale commercial transactions; such men often feathered their nests quite lavishly, but the process probably took twenty years or so of their lives.

But – what if you were a woman, a frivolous, pretty woman married to a man who was neither steady nor persevering nor capable in any other way of feathering as luxuriant and opulent a nest as your beauty and charm obviously entitled you? There was your husband, leaning at the bar of the United Club and drinking as usual, a tall, fine-looking man, popular with the members, always good for a whisky and a shady joke, a regular sport – when his 'old liver wasn't playing up' – that was Mr Walter Carew. Mr Carew was always at the Club because he was its manager; he had been for five years until, late in 1896, 'The Carew Case' blew up, the spiciest, vilest, most scandalous scandal that had ever rocked the foreign community of Yokohama in all its years of existence.

It is a pathetic, singular story, a 'melodrama set in foreign parts', a morality tale without hero or heroine that provides an illuminatingly detailed cameo-picture of the effortless, rather fallow lives of the local social set. The prevailing tone is of perfunctory insouciance, a certain spiritual seediness of those whose pleasures had become as predictable and almost as tedious as their duties, whose fantasies were as circumscribed and conventional as those available in the novels they borrowed from Main Street's subscription library. This was not true of all the settlers – few of the top-rank professional families, the missionaries or teachers floated around this leisurely lackadaisical circle – but of the many people who wrote about 'The Carew Case' at the time, none suggested that the Carew household's way of life was particularly unusual or atypical of its time and place.

The drama's first scene was typical enough: 10 October 1896, Yokohama's Regatta Day. Grouped across the green sward near the boathouses were the community's wives in their flowery high hats and pinched-waist dresses, carrying parasols, their men, in blazers and light trousers with field glasses dangling round their necks, and their children, in frilly clothes, bowling hoops or being dragged from the water's edge by chiding amahs. And in the boats on the water were the day's heroes, the brawny, hairy-armed young men chaffing each other, buying winning or losing drinks after each race. Walter Carew was there, drinking, telling his rusty stock of risqué stories and racing his yacht *Cocktail*, crewed by Reggie Porch, his brother-in-law. Reggie had come East two years before, hoping that something would turn up for him; he was still there, hoping; he was a good yachtsman. Walter's wife Edith was there too, small, brown-haired, pretty, flirting, as usual, with her select admirers. Three there were, who rode with her several afternoons a week. Edith looked sweet on a horse; they did not seem to have any more urgent occupation. In private she called them The Ferret, the Organ Grinder (a certain dashing foreign Consul) and the Youth. The latter, the sorry youth, was little Harry Dickinson, a clerk at the Hong Kong & Shanghai Bank with whom, for several months, Mrs Carew had been sharing a passionate correspondence and several clandestine rendezvous in a secluded teahouse. For want of a better, little Harry had been cast by her in the role of knight errant who was to rescue her from the stale, besotted cruderies, the financial insufficiencies of her uncaring husband. 'My life is drear and empty of happiness,' she had wailed in one letter, and Harry had responded, grown big with chivalry, 'Divorce at all hazards. Keep up your heart my dear one, and do not give in now under his cruelty and coarseness.'

Looking after the two Carew children at the Regatta, as on other days while Mummy flirted and Daddy drank, was Miss Mary Jacobs, governess. There were no amorous swains at the beck of plain envious Mary or of her one friend and confidante, Elsa, a Swiss governess in a similar plight. Mary and Elsa were starvelings in such a society, bound by its conventions to be unfailingly decorous, self-effacing, usually out of sight, forced to feed on the crumbs from other women's cakes and ale. And so the most thrilling nourishment of the two governesses' days was the scattered scraps of Harry Dickinson's love-letters, which Mrs Carew threw carelessly in the waste-paper basket – whence they were retrieved by Mary and, at a suitable opportunity, taken to share with Elsa. Elsa was handy with her needle apparently, and she sewed all the scraps most carefully together again, so that, guilty and eager as voyeurs, she and Mary could read in one piece the whole story of Harry's little passion. 'I sewed the letters together,' Elsa told the court a few months later, 'I never pasted them. I only sewed letters in Yokohama.' A grotesquely amusing distinction without a difference – yet the picture of the two young women so avidly relishing the discarded fragments of someone else's second-rate extra-marital affair, is a sorry, almost a touching one.

The Carews' home at 169 The Bluff – 'a green, glabrous house in a gloomy hollow', as a journalist ghoulishly described it, after the event – was staffed with the usual over-supply of underpaid menials. There was a cook, a groom, two amahs, a 'boy' – whose names Mrs Carew did not even know and with whom she spoke no word of Japanese – in addition of course to Miss Jacobs and a Eurasian maid for the mistress's personal use. All that summer the members of the household had drifted in and out, Edith and admirers rode and played tennis, Walter drank and got liverish, Reggie mooched and sailed, the children took *jinrikisha* rides with their unhappy governess, in the evenings, in a house farther along the Bluff, Elsa sometimes sewed.

And nothing untoward seemed to be happening until, on that Regatta Day, Edith, following the line of a plot apparently suggested to her by a novel in the library, arranged for her husband to receive a note in an unknown hand which said that a certain 'A.L.' must see him urgently. The ramifications and contradictions of the 'A.L.' letters confused lawyers, jury and eventually Mrs Carew herself, who seemingly wrote them in an effort to create an imaginary killer for the husband she was planning to murder. At about the time Edith was creating 'A.L.' (the initials of one of her husband's long-discarded mistresses) as a pale woman veiled in black who spoke in low, desperate tones, but only to her creator, the Carews had their last bitter quarrel over money. This concerned both the money which came from Edith's father but which Walter spent, and the additional money they needed but did not have in sufficient quantities to pay off their accumulated debts or buy the grander house to which Edith felt herself entitled. Two nights after the Regatta, Carew came home very late and very drunk from a carouse at the United Club and behaved as boorishly as usual. The next day he was nauseous and drowsy, a condition which he blamed either on his liver, for which he took Mother Siegel's Syrup, or his recurrent bouts of malaria, for which he took Fowler's Solution of Arsenic in controlled doses.

For the whole of the next week Walter Carew remained either in bed or tottering feebly about becoming sicker and sicker and drowsier and drowsier – which was not surprising because the wife who was so devotedly 'nursing' him was, with a singleness of purpose surprising in one so light-minded, pouring down his dry throat large quantities of arsenical solution mixed with barley-water or milk. The doctor came two or three times, examined the usual bodily discharges, went away puzzled. On 22 October, eight days after Carew took to his bed, those two shadowy bats-in-the-wings, Mary and Elsa, their suspicions aroused by repeated purchases of medicinal arsenic, decided to act. They showed the sewn letters to Elsa's employer declaring that wicked Mrs Carew was killing her husband with arsenic so that she could marry Harry Dickinson. On the same morning the doctor, whose suspicions were by then also aroused, ordered Mr Carew's removal to hospital, where he died that afternoon.

There was an inquest and, as a result of it, a trial which lasted for several weeks. Mrs Carew had to tell the packed courtroom how she used to write to Harry about the cruelty and extravagance of her husband (a spendthrift he certainly was, the cruelty charge was not proved); silly Harry had to tell how he admired and pitied poor Edith (but could not have married her anyway, because the Bank would not let him marry until he reached an accountant's rank); Miss Jacobs had to tell how she retrieved the letters and Elsa how she sewed them together. The 'Organ Grinder', that mysterious foreign consul, skipped away on leave the day Mrs Carew was arrested; the veiled 'A. L.' who was supposed to have written letters confessing to the crime, never materialised; in spite of the length and complexity of the proceedings, the jury took just twenty-five minutes to decide that Mrs Edith Carew had murdered her husband with repeated, deliberately administered doses of medicinal arsenic and deserved to be hanged by the neck until she was dead.

At which point – 3 February 1897 – Sir Ernest Satow, who had undoubtedly read every word of the court reports as keenly as every other foreigner in Japan, came to a sound conclusion, given all those wretched circumstances: he would use the power vested in him as Minister to commute the death sentence to one of life imprisonment. He did so, and among the letters on his desk a day or so later was one from his friend Judge Mowat, who had heard the case. 'I was glad you saw your way to commutation,' the judge had written, 'and relieved at not having had to express an opinion.' The last one hears of pretty, elusive, strange Edith Carew is that she would be on her way to Hong Kong gaol as soon as a female warder could be found to accompany her.

The other treaty ports were not as sophisticated (cynics said 'decadent') as Yokohama; they could not boast of scandals on the Carew scale, nor of as many social clubs, libraries, societies and general recreational facilities; but foreign trade was expanding elsewhere too, and Kobe, in particular, was expanding with it. Therefore, among the numerous entreaties which reached Sir Ernest's desk every morning, were regular pleas from his man in Kobe for the appointment of a vice-consul to share the burden of the work. In 1896 the poor Kobe consul, Mr E— was quite incapable of coping because he had an abscess of the liver, from which, wrote his assistant, Mr P—, 'doctors say patients seldom survive'. Here, perhaps, Mr P— paused, looked guiltily round his office, chewed his pen, coughed uneasily, wrote quickly, 'In the event of the worst happening, and more promotions arising accordingly, I hope you will not think me too presumptuous if I solicit your good offices with the Foreign Office...?' Satow surely shuddered with distaste; everyone knew the consular service was a dog-eat-dog fight in which the fittest survived, but it was not often expressed quite so crudely. In his reply, the Minister icily informed Mr P— that the question of promotion was somewhat premature, and in any case, Mr P— had not passed his interpreter's examination, without which qualification no promotion could at present be contemplated. Mr P— writhed: he had been toiling with Japanese for years and could not pass that damnable exam, and now here was poor old E— about to pop off with his liver and then some young punk would come in over his head and order him about, most likely. 'You must resolve to conquer the Japanese Language,' the Chief had ended, and that was that.

The Consul died soon afterwards and a younger man Mr G— arrived, a good speaker of Japanese, as it happened. Mr P— hissed through his teeth and got down to work – work which included several prickly problems in addition to that of conquering the intractable language. Most pressing was the matter of 'coolie violence'. The port coolies, a tattered, under-fed, footloose bunch of men who lugged rice into godowns, swept roads, scrubbed decks, pushed handcarts, loaded freight were becoming increasingly angry about their miser-ably underprivileged lot in life. The nearest dogs to kick to relieve their frustrations were the Chinese labourers who worked with them and who – as the recent war had shown – were a mere bunch of spunkless chickens. So the native coolies started kicking the Chinese coolies whenever they could and pulling them off ladders by their pigtails and throwing coal-dust in their egg-noodle soup. And, as they seemed to get away with this lightly (anti-Chinese feeling was still quite prevalent) the coolies started to attack other foreigners also. One or two sailors were beaten up, a visiting gentleman was tipped out of his *jinrikisha*, and insolent unwillingness was generally wide-spread among the labouring classes. Sir Ernest, hearing of the disturbances, which were not confined to Kobe, asked for a Report on Coolie Violence. Mr G— and Mr P— laboured for many hours over this document, too many, it seemed, for when it eventually reached the Chief's desk it was too late to be of much use, though it read well enough, Sir Ernest added.

On the social level also, local relations between the foreign community and the Japanese were becoming somewhat touchy. The committee of the Kobe Club actually tried to pass a resolution to exclude Japanese from membership and Mr P— had to resign from it forthwith, as the consulate would not be associated with such a policy. The motion was eventually with-drawn, but, as the consul wrote to Sir Ernest, 'It will take some little time to blunt the edge of race prejudice at this port.' The Consul also tried to create a warmer relationship between the Japanese and the Foreign Chambers of Commerce in Kobe. Some of the members of the former chamber were, it seemed, remembered as 'mere stripling office boys' by some of the age-ing worthies of the latter chamber, who thus felt it below their dignity to fraternise. A short-sighted view, as the Consul told his chief, but hard to alter.

Underlying these spurts of inter-commercial malice was a growing feeling of insecurity among some of the foreign merchants who knew that the good old days of extraterritoriality in the treaty ports were almost over. Britain had been the first of the western powers to reach an agreement with Japan that extraterritoriality should end once the country's new legal code came into force; it had been signed in July 1894, a month after the death of poor Mr Hugh Fraser, who had worked so hard on the matter. During the next four years, similar agreements were made between Japan and other countries concerned and, in addition, revisions of all the foreign treaties were worked out and adjustments made to the tariff system so that it would be weighted less heavily against the Japanese.

The new treaties were to be promulgated in 1899 and this meant that, during the two years before, the foreign consulates received at least four calls every week from their worried nationals asking what the revisions would mean in terms of hard cash, when they would become operative and – if extraterritoriality was to end – who was going to protect foreigners' property and persons against coolie rowdyism and so on? The Kobe Consul himself was anxious and wrote to Sir Ernest that Japanese preparations for the implementation of the new laws seemed 'woefully behindhand'. But in the event all was well. The treaties came into force in the July and with them the 'treaty ports' as such ceased to exist; they were just ports now where communities of foreigners, subject like everyone else to the laws of the land, happened to live. In exchange for the surrender of extraterritoriality foreign merchants were, from then on, free to trade in many other parts of the country. The ports' municipal affairs passed entirely into Japanese hands and continued to function, in spite of some predictions to the contrary, and Japanese policemen were issued with language booklets telling them how politely to detain in custody drunken foreign sailors. It is fascinating to speculate about what a

Japanese judge and jury would have made of the Carew Case, if Edith had delayed her murder for three years.

While these developments were keeping the Kobe consular staff very busy, Mr P— was also still battling with his Japanese verbs and was at length ready to take his interpreter's exam. Well, not exactly ready, for, as he told Sir Ernest, 'I assure you I approach the ordeal with fear and trembling. I never had any penchant for languages.' But the hurdle was jumped; he passed and was soon given the consulship of Hakodate – where, Sir Ernest probably thought, the resources of the foreign community were so limited that Mr P— would be forced to make use of his newly-acquired fluency in the native tongue.

More worrying to Sir Ernest than the reorganisation of his men in Kobe were the almost continuous difficulties of the Nagasaki consulate. Here too the volume of work had increased and Nagasaki's *dolce far niente* days were over. A naval arsenal had been built near the docks and the harbour resounded to the crump of machine-tools, the clank of derricks; coal-mining and other local industries were being developed so that more ships now called there; plans were afoot to enlarge other port facilities. The consequent expansion of business would have presented a challenge to a healthy and ambitious British Consul, but poor Mr Q— at Nagasaki was neither.

He has been 'beastly ill' for months he tells Sir Ernest, when he can stand it no longer; he had been 'on a diet of rice and milk' for five weeks, but it did nothing for him; he must ask for sick leave. This granted, Mr Q— went to Shanghai where the doctors found that his 'intestines were full of a sort of fungoid growth' and they 'have cleared tons of it away they say'. Soon, he was able to totter round the hospital grounds, 'weak as a cat', but he 'managed to keep down half a mutton chop, the first solid for ages'. So Mr Q— returned to Nagasaki, confident and joyous, 'It is so jolly to feel well again,' he told the Chief happily. But alas, very soon, as Sir Ernest probably guessed from his disjointed, irritable letters, the trouble all returned – the nausea rising in the throat after every attempt at food, the spongy lassitude of a body already flaccid in the heat, the queasiness of a milk-sop-churning stomach, the writhing of the intestines. 'But the climate isn't so bad, I don't know *why* I can't pick up,' he writes in fretful misery to sympathetic Sir Ernest. The doctors couldn't discover the cause, perhaps the 'fungoid' was growing again; he'd heard of the death of poor old E— in Kobe, another one gone then; perhaps a cool climate would fix him up – what about Hako-date?; he didn't look so bad, though he'd lost an awful lot of weight; people kept pestering him so, but no one could help him; he needed to see a specialist, a London specialist; he'd tried everything the local doctors advised, but he just got worse and worse – oh so tired, so feeble, so sickeningly, hope-lessly, revoltingly seedy. He had to get away, he was down to a skeleton, and 'the doctors wouldn't vouch for me otherwise'. He boarded the *Empress of Canada* for home and was too ill to leave the ship at Yokohama to see the Chief, though he had wanted to discuss his future prospects, after all, he'd be back in a year, surely, wouldn't he? Or perhaps some cooler place . . . Mr Q—'s obituary appeared in the local papers be-fore his death and the mistake was admitted the next day; but he sounded a doomed man, past the help of even the most skilful London specialist.

During the last sorry year of Q—'s consulship and for some time after it, most of the work at Nagasaki fell on the broader shoulders of the young assistant, Mr F—. Mr F— was so eager to prove his sterling worth to Sir Ernest that he wrote frequent and voluminous letters detailing everything of any possible significance. Merchants were complaining because a firm of English shippers were storing kerosene in a godown that wasn't properly fire-proofed, he explained. A few days later, some Japanese officials arrived on an inspection tour, and the foreign community wanted to hold a reception for them; but, in the absence of Mr Q— they could not decide on the consu-lar doyen, so there was no reception and, finally, he had simply called on the officials 'in white undress uniform semi-offici-ally', for Sir Ernest should understand that 'The heat entirely precluded the wearing of frock coat and high hat.' And then, a junk was accidentally sunk by a British vessel in the Shimonoseki Strait and the captain was 'frightfully cut up about it', and then a Mexican Admiral called asking him to accept Mexican consular interests – there were no Mexicans in Nagasaki of course, but one never knew, what did Sir Ernest advise? Worst of all, he had just heard, in strictest confidence, that an English employee of a local trading company, a Mr X had 'made *enceinte*' a sixteen-year-old Russian orphan, the adopted child of some American missionaries. And the orphan had told the doctor it all began with Mr X when she was *thirteen*! And that wasn't all, because Mr X was engaged to someone else, and so then his official fiancée had rushed along to the same doctor in tears and the doctor found that Mr X had 'made her *enceinte*' too!! And what *was* to happen? Mr F— had to follow up this letter with a hasty telegram of apology: it was a matter for the judge of course; he was so sorry to have bothered Sir Ernest with it; the fact was that he'd got a bit carried away.

Soon after this the new Consul Mr L— arrived to take over, an older, seemingly more easily ruffled man, who was appalled by the general disorder and burgeoning demands of the Nagasaki office. Q—, the poor sick fellow, 'had let things accumulate'; F— had done his best, but could not keep abreast and now Mr L— proceeded to inform his Chief in great detail how many merchants inquiring about tariffs, tourists asking silly questions, Admiral's ladies wanting guides for shopping-sprees and business men bothering about land-titles kept interrupting his work – not to mention the suicidal 'pauper-lunatic' someone had brought in last week, who was raving mad in the cell below-stairs and needed an escort to the Shanghai asylum. In short, Mr L— must have additional reliable clerical help; he 'couldn't write twenty lines a day' under these conditions and the 'whole place was pandemonium' sometimes; there had been thirty-six ships in the harbour on one day recently, causing terrible congestion at the entrance, all wanting coal and clearance at once and too many Russian warships about – that was one of the main troubles.

Those Russian warships, thick-sided, grim, black, gun-studded ironclads, cruisers, torpedo boats and sloops, trundled in and out of the pretty port in greater numbers each year. It was a consular duty to find out about their movements, but this was difficult, for Russian captains often sailed under sealed orders, 'cloaked all in mystery' and if you asked too many questions you could be taken for a spy. There were rumours of course, duly reported to Sir Ernest: that 15,000 Russian troops had just passed through on route to Vladivostok; that others were massing near Mukden; that a regiment of Cossacks had arrived in Fusan. But no one knew for sure what was happening or, worse yet, what would happen. It was 1899 and war was still five years away, but it was already being talked of as inescapable.

Inescapable in 1899 and equally so two years later apparently, when Pierre Loti revisited Japan. Loti was still a naval officer, with a few more celebrated books and affairs behind him, and, walking round Nagasaki after a fourteen-year absence, he decided that 'War proclaims itself inevitable and imminent. It may even burst without a declaration, perhaps tomorrow, through some impulsive folly of outposts, so firmly has each little yellow brain decided upon it. The most insignificant porter in the streets talks of it as though it had begun and reckons insolently upon victory.'

Loti of course had never liked the land and now he liked it less than ever. Even the languorous, exquisite grace that had been its principle charm in his eyes was now wilting under the onslaught of so much aggressive industrialisation. The waters round Nagasaki had become positively crammed with immense flotillas of warships – German, British and French as well as Russian – and the mantle of tropical vegetation that used to swathe the harbour sides like curtains of green velvet, had all been torn down when the docks were enlarged. Former tea-houses along the front were bars now, reeking of absinthe and gin; you tramped inside wearing military boots and sat at a grimy table, instead of removing your shoes at the entrance and reclining on clean, straw-gold mats. Across the hillside facing the harbour, white letters ten yards long advertised an American food-product; all day, smoke from the arsenal and a nearby munitions factory belched into the blue air; at night, electric lights supplemented or replaced the dancing lanterns. And, worst of all, 'Where now are those beautiful great junks, bird-winged, that had the grace of swans? The bay of Nagasaki was once peopled with them; majestic with their trireme poops, supple, light, one saw them come and go on every breeze; little yellow athletes, naked like antiques, used leisurely to manoeuvre their thousand-pleated sails as they glided in silence amid the green of the banks. Some few remain, but decrepit, dejected; lost today, astray in the crowd of hideous iron craft, the tugs, lighters, patrol boats like those of Havre or Portsmouth.'

Loti briefly visited other parts of the country and found it everywhere the same. Townsfolk, he said, had become 'pride-puffed', quick to take offence, soldiers and business men wearing 'suits the colour of puce or rats' tails' strutted through streets made hideous with electric lines, telegraph wires and tram-cars. Journeying through the spring countryside, he looked uneasily at the hard-working coolies in the paddies and decided that 'these little super-muscular peasants will make astonishing soldiers with their wide low obstinate brows, their sideways cat-like glances, sober from father to son, from the very beginnings without nerves and so without fear of the running red blood, having besides but two dreams, two cults, that of their native soil and that of their humble ancestors'.

Loti prophesied correctly: they had no fear of the blood, they did make astonishingly courageous soldiers. He felt a distant sympathy because so many of them would have 'to go to die on the plains of Manchuria' and that prophecy too was fulfilled. What he did not foresee, however, was that they would win the coming war.

III

At the end of the Liaotung Peninsula stood Port Arthur, wind-swept and stormy, encircled, still, by backing forts along ridges called 'Dead Head', 'Quail' and 'Wolf' and, on the seaward side, by the same fortified 'Tiger's Tail' that lashed towards the Old Town. The Old Town was now so called to distinguish it from the New Town, the area of western-style offices and barracks where many of the Russians lived.

After the Japanese had been forced to relinquish Port Arthur, its remaining Chinese inhabitants had scarcely time to lick their wounds when they learned that their Empress had been forced to sign a convention which leased the Liaotung Peninsula to the Russians for the next twenty-five years. The peaceful acquisition of this ice-free port (and Russia was always looking for an ice-free port) was a happy triumph for the Czarist government, which was still pursuing its policy of expansion in both Manchuria and Korea; for the Chinese it was another loss in a bitter deluge of territorial losses to the various western powers. In 1898 then, less than three years after the Japanese left, the Russians arrived.

Cossacks kicked the mud from their heavy boots and hurried into Saratov's, the new restaurant on the harbour-front, for a plate of steaming purple *borsch*; cabarets and a circus came to town and, as there was the usual eastern seaport shortage of western women, every equestrienne felt like a sequinned beauty, who could command a dozen admirers by raising a spangled finger. Each night the Big Top trumpets blared up to the walls of the hill-forts; grog-shops were full and empty vodka bottles floated in the oily waters of the dock; rooms at the one hotel of any size – Efimoff's – contained a camp bed, a washstand made from an old packing-case, a cracked mirror, a petrol tin for slops and, at extra charge, a comfort-seeking guest could hire a lumpy pillow, a frowzy coverlet and be served with dirty cups of greasy tea. In spite of its amenities, Efimoff's was invariably full, because the number of Russians arriving in Port Arthur continued to increase.

The Boxer Rising of 1900 had given Russia an excuse to pour troops into Manchuria 'as reinforcements' – a pretext which looked particularly suspect when contingents of other foreign troops withdrew from China after the trouble was over, but the Russians remained. They not only remained but consolidated their military position. A branch line from the main Trans-Siberian railway was pushed down the Liaotung Peninsula, another strategic triumph for the Russians because it enabled supplies and men to be brought to Port Arthur from both Europe and Vladivostok. Seawards too, the traffic into the port increased and the Russians tried to deepen the harbour by constructing a huge breakwater. When it was finished they found to their dismay that the breakwater did not merely deepen the sea-level, it also obstructed the outflow from the largest river behind the port and deflected the direction of a warm ocean current. As a result, the harbour waters froze for the first time, and the Russians' delight in their 'ice-free port' was chilled. However, for most of the year, the warships of the Czarist First Pacific Squadron still came lumbering in to stock up on provisions, refuel and allow their disconsolate crews a taste of the tinselled nightlife.

And when the Japanese sailors stared at the town from the darkened ships of Admiral Togo's fleet on the night of 8 February 1904, the nightlife was even gayer than usual. It was the name-day of the port's commander, Admiral Starck, and the battleships in the roadstead and the entire centre of the town were lit up in celebration. 'The Russians', wrote William Greener, a British secret agent, who arrived in Port Arthur the following day, 'had for several months been dancing under the sword of Damocles, though they could not be made to believe it.' They still could not believe it when they heard the first reports from the enemy guns that February night or when they rushed out from the dance halls in their military dress uniforms to see the warning rockets snaking across the sky from the signal station on Golden Hill. But the next morning they had to believe it, when they went to the top of Quail Hill to watch the opening round of the first full-scale naval engagement of the Russo-Japanese war which was taking place just off shore and in which four Russian cruisers were severely damaged. And later that same day they had fully to face the fact that the dancing was over and that the sword had fallen as they gazed incredulously into the first of many hundreds of shell-holes that were to gouge the Port Arthur waterfront – this one alone, estimated Greener, 'large enough to hold an omnibus and team'.

For disbelief was no longer tenable. In Japan there had been much coming and going between the Russian Embassy and the Foreign Office and now the Russian Ambassador was hastily packing his bags; Russian-Chinese banks remained shuttered; five hundred 'Japanese females' in the brothels of Vladivostok were herded into a home-going steamer; the English-language newspapers in Tokyo, which, for weeks, had given alarming details of 'The Situation', announced on 10 February (forty-eight hours after the first shots had been fired) that 'The Emperor of Japan, seated on the Throne occupied by the same Dynasty from time immemorial' had made a grave Proclamation to his loyal subjects – 'The War' read the new headlines.

Why the war? For the last hundred years or so Japan and Russia had intermittently harassed and snapped at each other angrily and then rubbed noses in reconciliation, like a couple of bad-tempered dogs in neighbouring kennels. Russians, notably Nikolai Rezanov, the Czar's envoy and Vasilii Golovnin, captain of a survey vessel, had been among the very few westerners to penetrate Japan's period of Tokugawa seclusion, and Rear Admiral Putiatin, with some vessels of the Russian navy, had arrived in Nagasaki and later in Shimoda, very soon after Commodore Perry's arrival, to make sure that whatever concessions America wrung from the Japanese, Russia could secure also. Though Japan had signed trading agreements with the Russians during the 1850s as she had with other western powers, commerce between the two countries did not greatly develop and snarling-contests continued to erupt from time to time – over possession of the northern Kurile Islands for instance and, as at the time of the Sino-Japanese war, over the position in Korea. And, of course, the Japanese never forgot their humiliation and fury at the Triple Intervention of Germany, France and Russia following that conflict.

Since 1895 Japan had enjoyed a period of economic prosperity during which it had built up, through extensive conscription, a strong, disciplined modern army and navy, which no nation aspiring to world-power status could afford to be without. And the way to use these military forces was, as Japan had rapidly learned from the West, to invade another weaker country with them and so lay the foundations of an Empire. Considering that the Western European powers were busy annexing territory on the opposite side of the globe from their own countries, Japanese initial ambitions in the Empire game were relatively modest: mainly to exert control, or at least to prevent others having control, of their near neighbours, Korea and Manchuria. But it was no use battling with the Chinese over these areas any more, because the Russians were there, dominating Manchuria and interfering as much as they could in Korean affairs. So Russia was the chief enemy.

Japan was not the only nation worried by Russian expansionism; Great Britain too feared a check to her own development of her 'spheres of influence' in China. This mutual concern was a major incentive towards the signing of the Anglo-Japanese Alliance in 1902, whereby the two countries agreed to protect each other's interests in China and remain neutral if either nation was engaged in hostilities against a single power in the Far East. The Alliance was a new high-water mark in British-Japanese relations which had been improving ever since Britain had refused to align herself with the three other major European powers at the time of the Triple Intervention.

It was an important alliance to both countries – to Japan because it implied increasing prestige in a world where Britain was still one of the top dogs, and to Britain because it heralded a gradual withdrawal from the policy of 'splendid isolation' which it had been allegedly pursuing for the previous eight years or so. Thus supported by Britain and also by increasing American concern, Japan made vigorous protests to Russia about its continuing occupation of Manchuria. At one point (soon after the signing of the Alliance) Russian troops began to withdraw, but in 1903 (soon after the opening of that precious rail link with Port Arthur) the troops returned in greater numbers than before; moreover, the Russians began to send soldiers into North Korea, under cover of their monopoly right to cut timber there. Given this inflammable situation war, as most observers in Japan had been saying for years, had to come.

But the Russians, at least the ones on active duty, had not really believed this, and back in Port Arthur where it all started, there was shock and chaos. Bakers ceased to bake, butchers ran out of meat, tradesmen could not deliver because their carts were requisitioned, shopkeepers hoarded their stores and thousands of coolies simply disappeared, leaving no one to clean the houses, sweep the roads, carry water, scavenge and perform all the other necessary chores which foreigners assumed that someone else always did. There was a terrible mess at the Russian military headquarters: ships in port with precious provisions were allowed to sail away still carrying them; two Russian destroyers collided with each other and two others were struck by their own mines; torpedo boats were ice-bound – in the newly frozen harbour – and orders sprayed like bullets from the office of the general in charge, Stoessel, many of them contradicting each other. A hopeful order issued on 16 February read 'The Staff Commander will institute performances of high-class MUSIC on the Boulevard from three o'clock until five o'clock twice a week'. This particular order, it was said, had a most unsettling effect on the circus horses that had been commandeered by the army a few days previously – a rider was liable to find himself doing the polka whether he would or no as soon as his steed came within earshot of the cheerful trumpet.

Most of the town's civilian population – Poles, Americans, British, Germans and especially Chinese with long memories – were not fooled by the sound of music. They queued all night and fought outside the railway station to get the first train out and away – away anywhere. And yet, even with shells landing in the town itself, the Russians did not seem to take the threat of the 'yellow monkeys', as they usually called the Japanese, completely seriously. When, about a month after his arrival, the British agent, Greener, was forced by the military authorities to leave the town, he recorded that Russian ladies and children were still promenading along the Boulevard at sunset to listen to the band, the bar-pianos tinkled each night, corks popped by the hundred and in busy Saratov's 'cards and chalk, glasses and crisp rouble notes crowded the green-cloth tables. That was Port Arthur.'

Ugly, battered Port Arthur, a suffering town. Ten years before the Japanese had captured it in a single day; this time it was to take them three hundred and twenty-seven times as long. Night after weary night the port's drab buildings shook as the naval barrage thundered in from the Japanese gunboats and destroyers that were trying to complete the blockade of the harbour. Day after day more shell-holes were discovered, along the waterfront, in the house-walls, the hospital roof, the hillside forts. In May, troops of the Japanese Second Army under General Oku and the Third Army under General Nogi landed on different parts of the Liaotung Peninsula, their aim being to sever Port Arthur's rail link with the rest of Manchuria. Owing to bad weather these landings were spread over three weeks, but the optimistic mood of those taking part in them is suggested by an observer who wrote that the men were 'fastened to their steam launches like beads on a rosary. Rolling and tumbling, these rosaries of boats would whistle their way to the shore.'

In Port Arthur, by the middle of that hot, wet July, the bands had stopped playing and no one was whistling. There were

42,000 men in the Russian garrison with 450 horses, flour supplies for about 200 days, meat for twenty days but no salt to preserve it with, tea for 320 days and forage for 150 days. At the end of the month the Japanese armies' pincer tactics succeeded and the port was completely cut off, 'as isolated as Ladysmith', judged one historian, 'and with far less chance of relief'. On Sunday 7 August, when many of the town's Christian population were gathered in the one unwrecked church to pray for safety, the first shell to reach the town from the Japanese batteries on land thudded in the street outside.

To those Russians who realised the remorseless proximity of the Japanese troops, who were aware of the political and economic disarray prevailing in their distant homeland and who hopelessly watched the administrative muddle over the provision of their own supplies, that thudding shell must have sounded like the beginning of a long tough end. Worst of all, as they may also have known, their enemy was not beset by any of these problems.

From the first Japan had been completely united in its aim to win the war at whatever cost in men and money. The ritual self-sacrifices of the wealthy had long ago been performed: the Empress had 'disposed of her gold ornaments' and ordered economies to be made in the imperial cookery expenses; aristocrats sold their private carriages and rode in the despised *jinrikisha*. The preliminary indoctrination of the next generation, in case it was required for cannon fodder, was in full spate that summer and the 'War Song of General Fukushima' was fiercely chorused in every schoolroom:

> Up and forward, steeds and warriors,
> March, already spring is here!
> Righteous war admits no foeman,
> Joy is ours with nought to fear!
> Break the ramparts of Port Arthur
> Tear the walls of Harbin down!
> On the heights of Ural mountains
> Float the Banner of the Sun!

Every Japanese officer who asked for men for suicidal missions, such as blowing up torpedo boats or gun emplacements, was deluged with offers, some written in the volunteer's own blood. A War Fund had been started in Tokyo and contributions poured in from business men who sold their art collections, from street beggars, babes in arms, students dying of consumption, criminals condemned to execution. Britain and America both supported 'the gallant little Land of the Rising Sun'. In Yokohama an organisation to alleviate the sufferings of war victims was quickly formed by the foreign residents; free hominy grits were sent from the United States to feed Japanese soldiers (whether the soldiers were grateful is not recorded); foreign ladies joined their Japanese sisters in knitting socks for soldiers and Anita McGee arrived from Philadelphia with eight American nurses to tend the wounded. These young women caused a sensation in Tokyo where they were greeted with huge banners proclaiming 'Welcome to the American Angels of Mercy' and presented with a red crêpe flag with the crest of the Women's Temperance Red Cross Society embroidered thereon, together with a plum-blossom design worked by the fair hand of a cousin of the Princess Imperial herself. In London the Japanese Embassy was besieged by people offering gadgets to help win the war – food in the form of white pills, airships and a submarine guaranteed to approach the Russian ships underwater and, according to a local newspaper, 'drag them over to the enemy by a mysterious force of magnetic attraction'.

But no hominy grits, nurses or magnetic submarines were offered to the Russian garrison immured in Port Arthur and the August which had begun with that ominous shell was an odious, hot ordeal. Soon, the remaining civilians were living in cellars as the noise from howitzers, mortars, field and naval guns crashed above them and reverberated among the surrounding hills. Water supplies were rather low and thirsty Russian soldiers looking seawards for help, were dazzled by the sun's glare on the water's surface; looking landwards, they saw only the hillsides increasingly torn and scarred with trenches, the valleys soured with corpses, an occasional dazzle of sun on the polished guns of the Japanese batteries. From about the middle of the month onward, an observant Russian with good field-glasses might have vaguely wondered about a large black umbrella which mushroomed every day on the summit of one of the small hills just behind the Japanese firing line. He may have lobbed a shell or two in its direction; if so, they missed, which was fortunate for the men who were using the umbrella as a shelter from the sun's scorching rays.

There were three men usually: a photographer named Ricarlton, whose immediate ambition was to get the best shot ever taken of a shell exploding in mid-air, an enthusiastic young reporter from *The San Francisco Chronicle* known only as Barry and a rather less enthusiastic journalist from *The Illustrated London News*, Frederick Villiers. Villiers was an old hand at the war correspondent's game and was thus no longer moved to cries of excitement when shells crumped into the earth near his rucksack or guns blew up behind him. He had been at the Battle of Plevna with the Russians in 1877; he had gone through the Khyber Pass into Afghanistan with the British; he had been on the bridge of H.M.S. *Condor* when she fired the Egyptian Fort Marabout near Alexandria during one of the Middle East's 'minor dust-ups'; he had gone up the Nile with Wolseley's expedition in the attempt to relieve Gordon at Khartoum. Moreover, he had been at a look-out post a few hundred yards to the east of the umbrella under which he now sat just ten years earlier, when he had watched the same sort of guns pounding the same forts as the Chinese were routed and the Japanese ran down easily into Port Arthur, while the same hillsides rang with their 'banzais'. 'I never saw so many heads rolling about the streets,' he wrote in his description of the massacre that had followed. So, all in all, there wasn't much you could tell Frederick Villiers about war. Most of its brutal combinations of blood, steel, bone, earth, stink and sweat were familiar to him; he had seen the futilities and the heroics and the shifty manoeuvres of the doomed, and now he was content to stay put under Ricarlton's black silk umbrella and drink as many cups of tea as the billy-can would run to while Barry zealously rushed about and fragments of flesh and soil spurted up in the valleys below every time a shell found its mark. In any case, the ten or so western correspondents who were then present at the siege were not permitted to send out dispatches during this most critical stage of the fighting and were, as Villiers later wrote, 'really prisoners of the Japanese, though held with a silken cord of courteous goodwill'.

The siege, as the correspondents described it, was of the classic copy-book style: the permanent forts along the ridges had honeycombs of smaller redoubts connecting them, and the ground in front was spiked with mines and barbed-wire entanglements and riven with trenches; these forts the besiegers had to capture. So, in classically suicidal fashion, thick columns of Japanese soldiers flooded across the valley and up the opposite hill that was topped by two of the forts from which a jagged cannonade of steel and slug beat down into them. 'The dead', said Villiers after one such engagement, 'are sprinkled on the shell-pitted slopes like flies in summer time on treacled paper' and he could trace in an outline of corpses the frozen still-life of their effort 'in a zigzag up the glacis, bunching in the centre and thinning to one man who was in the act of springing over the parapet of the fort'.

At last the stained sun went down on that particular massacre, and Villiers hastily cooked himself a snack over an improvised stove. It was a pity to leave yet, for soon the night attacks would begin and these were his favourite spectaculars: ' ... the deep purple of the mountain, the pale lemon moon, white rays of searchlights, incandescent glow of star-bombs, reddish spurt of cannon's mouth, yellow flash of shell all mellowed by a smoky haze'. Almost exhilarating it was, when the shadows veiled the bleeding slopes, the sun ceased to rot the putrid flesh and, in among the searchlight beams, dodged stretcher-bearers, crawling among the dead to rescue the merely wounded, feigning death themselves when the lights flashed near them, edging their oozing burdens across the valley towards safety.

As days reverberated into weeks and neither side gained more than temporary advantages, Villiers came almost to like the life. He shared a tumbledown cottage in a village behind the front line with young Barry and they had a Chinese boy who cooked stews for them over a corn-stalk-smoky fire. The village was ringed with Japanese divisions and so a natural observatory – 'there is not a shell fired down in the valley that I cannot see,' Villiers noted happily. In spite of the stray fusillades that spattered the nearby crops and the ammunition trains and lines of stretcher-cases which slowly filtered through their village in opposite directions, the peasants stolidly toiled at their customary tasks. They harvested buckwheat, maize and the purple-brown heads of the millet and their children who rolled around naked on the threshing floors had pieces of shrapnel and shell-cases as toys. Villiers' landlord, who lived next door, thought it an auspicious time to get married and the thumpety-thump of pom-pom guns punctuated his wedding music. Every so often Barry rode a donkey to Dalney, the port some twenty miles to the north east which the Japanese had captured in June, and brought back supplies of goodies – pots of strawberry jam (Barry consumed one a day), Bologna sausages, buns and champagne. Villiers also took a few trips on the donkey, a 'poor little brute' with legs so short that he (a large man) used him as a 'kind of hobby-horse' and punted the animal over the hills with his alpine stock.

Villiers visited General Nogi's headquarters for lunch in this fashion and decided that Japanese morale was still amazingly high, as indeed it was. While the Russians in the beleaguered garrison were, by this time, eating mule flesh and the occasional snared night-hawk, the Japanese were well supplied with sweet potatoes, Nestlés milk, kidney beans and pickled plums for a treat. And victuals, as both sides knew, were important. Early in the siege the Russians had set up a cooking-station within clear view, and easy reach, of the enemy batteries, but it was never shelled. The reason for this was not humanitarian but was because the Japanese could see, through a powerful telescope, what the Russian cooks were giving the men and thus gauge the state of their food supplies. Like all westerners who observed the Japanese infantry under battle conditions, Villiers praised their cleanliness (the soldiers had a horror of being killed while wearing dirty underclothes) and remarked that their one absolutely indispensable 'weapon' seemed to be the long-handled toothbrush they all carried in the crown of their hats. Villiers also paid a fleeting, most uncomfortable visit to 'The Thirty Minute Trench', a stinking, shell-racked hell-hole on the very front of the front line less than a hundred yards from Russian sharpshooters. The trench had changed hands five, ten, twenty, nobody knew how many times and a continuous spray of bullets ricocheted madly from its rock sides and stout timber frames like balls round a pin-ball machine. Sentries guarding its shattered parapet moved about 'like caged animals from one loophole to another' and were relieved every half-hour – if, indeed, death had not relieved them sooner, as was usually the case – for no man could be expected to bear more than thirty minutes at a stretch of its ear-splintering noise, the stench of its unburied bodies, its endless, filthy chaos and gut-twisting terror.

By the middle of the autumn the very shells which, for weeks, had come 'humming along the valley like mighty malignant wasps' now thumped down near Villiers' cottage with a rather dispirited air. One he describes as 'creaking and wheezing on its path . . . as if it had a very poor send-off from Port Arthur and, in its humiliation, buries its head in the heavy soil with a low wail'. Russian supplies of powder as well as food were dwindling; icy winds began to whip in again from the north and further stiffened the perpetually-aching limbs of the soldiers. Villiers himself caught the ague and shook so much during the frigid evenings that he could not stand upright; his Chinese boy was ill too and the food was getting ghastly; his one precious blanket fell from the freight train on which he was travelling from Dalncy and he could not get a replacement. The ban on foreign correspondents leaving with their dispatches had been lifted, and Villiers felt it was time to go. He was certain of the outcome of the siege – Port Arthur must fall to the Japanese, probably, he thought, within three weeks. The only contingency that could possibly help the Russians would be if their Baltic Fleet, which had been hastily assembled and had left the Gulf of Finland for the East early in the autumn, could reach Port Arthur before it fell and defeat Admiral Togo's blockading warships. This was most unlikely and Villiers decided to assume that the show was finished. Early in November he punted himself out of the village on his donkey for the last time, his knapsack crammed with blood-curdling copy and sketches for the readers of *The Illustrated London News*.

Villiers, like most other observers and the Japanese themselves, under-estimated the obstinate endurance of the Russian defenders. In December the cannons were still crashing and the Japanese, after a week of to-and-fro fighting, managed to capture '203 Metre Hill', one of those melancholy, barren protuberances on the earth's surface which suddenly become a blood-soaked, ravaged graveyard for thousands – its name shudderingly remembered by all who survived its horrors, its cross-scarred outline reproduced in the sad sepia of military history books. '203 Metre Hill' cost the Japanese over 10,000 men, but from its summit they could shell into final annihilation the remains of the Russian squadron which had been trapped in the harbour for so many months.

During the next three weeks one hill-fort after another fell as the Japanese tunnelled, sapped, mined, lobbed grenades and fought bayonet to bayonet over every redoubt, sandbag and slippery stair. At last, on the afternoon of New Year's Day 1905, a little white flag came fluttering towards the Japanese lines borne by a messenger from Stoessel, the Russian commanding general. He brought proposals for truce negotiations. A strange silence cloaked the place, broken only by muffled explosions as the Russians unostentatiously demolished the engine-rooms of their few remaining ships. Delegations from the two armies assembled in a small thatched hut to the north of the town incongruously called 'Plum Tree Cottage'; in the open space before the house a group of glum Cossacks stood holding their horses' heads, waiting for nothing. Soon, the Russian surrender was announced; that night Japanese soldiers lit bonfires on every hill and corner and danced and sang till dawn. The next morning the Russian newspaper *Novy Krai* which had appeared every day during the entire siege – though towards the end it had been hand-written on one very small sheet of brown paper – failed to materialise.

Russian losses in killed and wounded during the ten months of siege totalled about thirty thousand men; the losses of the Japanese were much higher, and, to the survivors dancing round their bonfires, it must have seemed like the end of the whole war. But it wasn't. Port Arthur was efficiently occupied, the Russian garrison (a considerable number, some 22,000) were formally disarmed (except that its officers were allowed to retain their war-swords in recognition of their gallant stand) and shiploads of prisoners were taken to Japan (where they were well treated). And then the reorganised Japanese divisions were hurried northwards by their tireless and determined General Nogi, so that many a veteran who had survived months of besieging Port Arthur was killed at the Battle of Mukden, the key city on the route across Manchuria which the Japanese captured after three weeks of hard fighting during February and early March. Mukden was really the end of the land-struggle; it now remained for the sailors of Admiral Togo's fleet that had successfully blockaded Port Arthur, to give the *coup de grâce* to the Russian navy, whose Baltic Fleet was still steaming eastwards in an effort to reach Vladivostok.

The Russian ships had got as far as Madagascar when the news of Port Arthur's fall reached their admiral-in-chief, Rozhdestvenski – tidings which meant, in effect, that this unwieldy, hastily-assembled armada was its country's last hope. Morale, which was already low, sank to zero: 'we shall have about as much chance as a game cock would have in a battle with a vulture,' glumly prophesied one

Novikoff-Priboy, a steward on board the ironclad *Oryol* when discussing the news with his friend Vasilieff, an engineer of Marxist leanings. All Priboy's sympathies veered in the same direction for he, in company, he says, with the great majority of his shipmates, had completely lost faith in the ability of the squadron's senior officers, in the battle-worthiness of its ships and in the judgement of a government that had sent them on such a hopeless, ill-planned mission. Priboy, whose book, *Tsushima, Grave of a Floating City* is an angry tirade against the stupidity and horror of the war and against the incompetence with which the Russian military establishment handled it, later became an active revolutionary against the Czarist regime, and his account is doubtless coloured by his political affiliations. It is, however, well authenticated that the men of that Russian fleet who sailed eight thousand miles across the world to meet their doom in the Sea of Japan were ill-trained, poorly-equipped and with no heart for the fight, their confusion and despair a reflection of the political discontent that was seething to the surface back in their homeland. During the months of voyaging eastwards, acts of insubordination and fist-fights were common on all the vessels; drunkenness increased among officers and men – some of the former performed a war-dance on the repairing ship one day, while midshipmen crouched under tables and barked like dogs; when gunnery practices were held, some men refused to take part, having already decided that they could not aim the old-fashioned guns properly.

For Admiral Togo, the celebrated 'Nelson of Japan', the battle against the Russian fleet which took place in the strait between the island of Tsushima and the coast of Korea in late May 1905 was the consummation of his career. It was, wrote a biographer, 'his masterpiece', 'elegant' in its assured timing, its purposeful celerity, like the one deadly stroke of a *samurai*'s war-sword; for the Russians that battle was a nightmare of pain, death and humiliation. Priboy lived through it and he makes the nightmare throb with his terror from the first moment of that spring day when the bugler on the *Oryol*'s upper deck sounded the reveille – his cheeks puffed out, his instrument sparkling in the early sunlight – to that moment, some thirty-five hours later, when the ship's engines, surprisingly, stopped.

For the first hour or so of that most unpleasant day, the Russian ships steamed lemming-like towards the Tsushima Strait, determined upon the one route north which nearly all the men, except the commander-in-charge, Rozhdestvenski, considered to be the most dangerous. Aboard the *Oryol*, crew members played draughts, read Gorky, drank tea from huge copper samovars; during the morning the anniversary of the coronation of the Czar and Czarina was uneasily celebrated by the hoisting of flags and the holding of a service. At noon, they came abreast of the southernmost point of Tsushima Island; it was misty now and the rear vessels of the grey, dispersed squadron were hardly discernible from the *Oryol*'s conning-tower. At one-thirty p.m. the Japanese fleet appeared on the starboard bow, action stations were signalled and Priboy went to his post as assistant in the sick bay.

The ship became very quiet, the only sound a faint slithering hiss of water from the fire hoses which were kept playing upon the bridge and the upper deck. In the sick bay no one spoke. The enamelled walls shone; piles of sterile gauze and dressings were neatly wadded in boxes; surgical instruments gleamed on immaculate lint; along the glass shelves of the cupboards stood rows of bottles and jars – camphor, morphine, iodine, chloroform, ointment for burns – and under the operating table were clean white pails ready for the blood. There were still only three sounds: that distant hiss of water, the rhythmical heart-thud of the engines and the ventilator fans which had been switched on overhead and made 'a buzz like that of a huge bumble bee'. When the 75 mm. guns crackled for the first time and the first two shells thumped against the ship's side, the bay remained white and silent; the surgeons in their clean overalls shifted restlessly and looked at each other over their masks. Then came the first victim – the ship's cook who had been deafened by a shell's explosion and could only lip-read enquiries about his condition. But he looked so unharmed and funny, everyone suddenly laughed hysterically at the comedy of it.

Then the battle began in earnest. Midshipmen, officers, the quartermaster, gunners and engineers came pouring down the narrow stairway into the bay, some on stretchers, some walking, some crawling, some holding their own intestines, some without eyes, some so badly burned as to be unrecognisable and calling out 'I'm so cold, so bitterly cold'. Priboy cleared the soiled linen off the operating table, cut clothes from injured limbs, handed morphine, found himself holding the remnants of a leg and boot which had just been amputated from a writhing body. The pails under the table were full, emptied into the sea, filled again. News reached him in gasps and shouts and it was all bad. The warship *Oslyaba* had 'turned turtle', shells from the *Oryol* itself were all falling short of their targets, the flagship, *Suvoroff* was disabled by fire. And still the ships pressed blindly forward into the mouths of the Japanese guns trying to force a passage through to Vladivostok. Vladivostok is not usually thought of as a Promised Land, but for the men of the Baltic Fleet it had become a heartbreakingly distant, yearned-for Mecca, haven of silence and safety, a dream of home that only a handful of them were to see that year. For, though the battle raged throughout the day, its outcome was rapidly assured: '... an hour sufficed', wrote Priboy bitterly, 'to transform our squadron into a floating caravan of death'.

Aboard the *Oryol*, a battered, shattered remnant of that deathly caravan, the sickening trail of disasters continued: Lieutenant Pavinoff at his post in the observation tower firing again and again while blood streamed over him from his burst eardrums; the stern deck cracking open 'like stretched paper struck by a fist'; sheets of fire engulfing a gun-turret and turning to cinders the men inside; a gunner crawling towards the bridge on all fours crying out 'Brothers where am I wounded?' while the red blotch between his shoulder blades grew larger and he died. The horrors multiplied, the sick bay overflowed, new grotesqueries of pulped flesh and bone fell upon and sank under the piles of corpses, the *Oryol* like a torn whale, floundered from one failure to the next, riven by shells, blackened by fire. Surely the only white thing left aboard was the handkerchief belonging to Priboy which, towards dusk, he took from his pocket to wipe the stains of others' wounds from his face as he wondered briefly, how and why men endure so much.

As darkness fell the shelling moderated. Priboy resumed his 'ordinary evocation as paymaster's steward' and doled out emergency rations in the stern torpedo room. On the main deck some blue-jackets, 'moving jerkily with pallid faces and sunken eyes' tried to plug holes in the vessel's sides with hunks of wood, mattresses, rolls of greased canvas; on the battery deck about fifty men with buckets and brooms tried to sweep some of the water towards the bilge pumps. Miraculously, the ship survived the night, wallowing through the waves with about two hundred tons of water on its decks and empty magazines below so that she was in danger of turning turtle, as the *Oslyaba* had, at any moment.

Dawn, which none of the men had ever expected to see, brought breakfast of bully beef and a temporary surge of hope as they surveyed the calm sparkling straits, blessedly empty of enemy ships. And then, along the horizon fluttered a grey pennon of smoke 'drifting slowly, slowly down wind, like the reek of a bonfire'. It was from the foremost of twenty-seven Japanese warships all apparently unscathed after the previous day's battle. As they drew nearer, surrounding the *Oryol* and four other surviving Russian ships in 'a deadly ring of iron', a priest on the poop deck gabbled a few prayers over the already dead; each man received a tot of vodka. The ailing iron-clad could only limp along, half its guns were out of action and four-fifths of its ammunition had already been fired. In the event of attack, Priboy reckoned she would stay afloat about ten minutes. He looked up at the spring sunshine; most of the lifebelts were burned; all the small boats had been shot to pieces. The action signal resounded across the shattered decks and as the guns roared Priboy walked heavily towards the sick bay.

But, in addition to Priboy's handkerchief, there remained one white thing aboard the *Oryol* – a large white tablecloth. And, there not being an appropriate flag to hand, it was this that flew from the bridge just as Priboy made to go below deck for, as he thought, the last time. The Russian flagship ahead had surrendered; the *Oryol's* officers followed suit and messengers ran round to the gun-turrets shouting, 'Don't shoot, the battle is over.' The engines slowly stopped and the ship rolled like a cradle in the quiet water. Priboy looked up at the sun again and at the cloth fluttering from the bridge in the spring breeze. He was alive, unhurt.

Priboy was very lucky. Of the 18,000 sailors aboard the Russian ships in the Straits of Tsushima it was estimated that some 12,000 did not survive the battle and the Baltic Fleet, Russia's last hope was, in fact, practically annihilated. When the news reached St Petersburg governmental disorder increased and full-scale revolution threatened; in Tokyo, though huge crowds celebrated the victory, the war leaders were forced to realise that Japan was on the brink of financial exhaustion and her armed forces were dangerously depleted. President Roosevelt, who for months had been in touch with both sides urging the cessation of hostilities, was now invited by the Japanese to arrange for peace negotiations.

Two months later, after the customary diplomatic bickerings, a conference between the envoys of the two belligerents opened at Portsmouth, New Hampshire. Japanese terms were stiff, for Japan was clearly the victor and she demanded, among other concessions, the payment of a substantial war indemnity. This Russia absolutely refused to consider and, when negotiations came dangerously close to breaking down, the Japanese gave way and on 5 September the Peace Treaty of Portsmouth was signed between the two countries. By its terms the Russian lease of the Liaotung Peninsula was ceded to Japan so that the Japanese could, at long long last, remain in Port Arthur. The troops of both sides were withdrawn from

Manchuria, but Japan was allowed a protectorate over Korea – which it annexed five years later. These gains were less than the Japanese had hoped for and there were riots of disappointment in Tokyo when the details of the Portsmouth settlement were announced. Nevertheless, Japan had achieved a great deal: for the first time in modern history an Asiatic power had defeated a western power in a full-scale military conflict; as a result the country's territorial rights and influence in the Far East were greatly extended; the nation's blossoming status as a world force to be reckoned with was underlined by the formation of a closer alliance with Great Britain the same year.

It had been less than forty years since the young Meiji Emperor had proclaimed the Charter Oath of Five Articles which promised that 'the absurd customs and practices of the past' would be discarded. The idealistic progressivism embodied in the Charter had been much modified in the light of later developments, but, broadly, its intentions were being fulfilled. During those exciting and convulsive years between Japan's restoration of its Emperor and its victory over Russia many mistakes had been made, many false lights followed. Undoubtedly however, the modernisation of the country opened many doors that had been too long shut and the foreigners who visited, lived and worked in the country at the time helped to widen Japanese horizons by demonstrating and exemplifying new possibilities of thought and action.

The teachers who went had introduced challengingly unfamiliar disciplines, technologists and engineers had developed improvements in technical efficiency and communications, merchants had opened larger areas for trade, missionaries had revived the spirit of religious enquiry, scientists and travellers had awakened scientific curiosity in fresh fields, writers and linguists had described startlingly different political and social theories, military experts had displayed the effectiveness of modern weaponry, doctors had taught more proficient ways of controlling disease, diplomats had imparted the conventions of international negotiation, even the globe-trotters had contributed their mite – by just being there, independently and freely, moving easily and sociably around the land with their unexpected questions, criticisms, approbations.

Throughout this period Japan had responded eagerly to all these challenges and had proved itself to be the most apt, willing and enterprising pupil the West had ever found in the East. In 1905 however the country's term of apprenticeship in world affairs was truly over. And so much had been learned, so much accomplished, that the nation was surely justified in looking forward hopefully to a period of further expansion and prosperity as a full and equal partner with the western powers. But, unfortunately, other tactics would be adopted, other false lights followed, other obstacles encountered. The next forty years of Japan's history would tell a very different and, in many ways, a very much sadder story.

Bibliography

Allan, James, *Under the Dragon Flag* (London, 1898)

Allen, Bernard, *Sir Ernest Satow, a Memoir* (London, 1933)

Arnold, Sir Edwin, *Japonica* (London, 1892)

Bacon, Alice M., *Japanese Girls and Women* (Boston, 1891)

Batchelor, Rev. John, *The Ainu of Japan* (London, 1892)

—*Sea-Girt Yezo* (London, 1902)

Beasley, William G., *The Modern History of Japan* (London, 1963)

Bickersteth, Mary, *Japan as we saw it*. (London, 1893)

Bird, Isabella, *Unbeaten Tracks in Japan* (London, 1880)

— *Korea and her Neighbours* (London, 1898)

Black, John, *Young Japan* (Yokohama and London, 1880)

Blacker, Carmen, *The Japanese Enlightenment* (London, 1964)

Blond, Georges, *Admiral Togo* (London, 1961)

Bond, Catherine, *Goldfields and Chrysanthemums* (London, 1898)

Brownell, Clarence, *The Heart of Japan* (New York, 1902)

Carmichael, Amy Wilson, *From Sunrise Land. Letters from Japan etc* (London, 1895)

Cassell's History of the Russo-Japanese War (London, 1904–5)

Crow, Arthur, *Highways and Byeways in Japan* (London, 1883)

Culty, A., *Yokohama Ballads* (Yokohama, 1890)

De Becker, J. E., *The Nightless City* (Yokohama, 1899)

Dixon, William G., *The Land of the Morning* (Edinburgh, 1882)

Duncan, Sara J., *A Social Departure* (London, 1890)

Edwards, A. H., *Kakemono* (London, 1906)

Edwards, Osman, *Residential Rhymes* (Tokyo, 1900)

Farrer, Reginald, *The Garden of Asia* (London, 1904)

Faulds, Dr H., *Nine Years in Nippon* (London, 1887)

Fraser, Mary C., *A Diplomatist's Wife in Japan: Letters from Home to Home* (London, 1899)

— *Further Reminiscences of a Diplomatist's Wife* (London, 1912)

Greener, William, *A Secret Agent in Port Arthur* (London, 1905)

'Grenon', *Verdant Simple's Views of Japan* (Yokohama, 1890)

Griffis, William E., *The Mikado's Empire* (New York, 1876)

— *Verbeck of Japan* (New York, 1900)

Handy Guide to the Japanese Islands (Yokohama, 1888)

Hargreaves, Reginald, *The Siege of Port Arthur* (London, 1962)

Hawks, Francis L., *Narrative of an American Squadron's Expedition to the China Seas and Japan* (Washington, 1856)

Hearn, Lafcadio, *Glimpses of Unfamiliar Japan* (Boston and London, 1894)

—*Out of the East* (Boston, 1895)

—*Exotics and Retrospectives* (Cambridge, Mass., and London, 1898)

—*Kotto* (New York, 1902)

—*Japan, an Attempt at an Interpretation* (New York, 1904)

— *Life and Letters* (ed. E. Bisland) (Boston, 1906)

Holland, Clive, *My Japanese Wife* (London, 1895)

Holtham, E. G., *Eight Years in Japan* (London, 1883)

Houghton, Bishop F., *Amy Carmichael of Dohnavur* (London, 1953)

Howard, C. H. D., *Splendid Isolation* (London, 1967)

Jansen, Marius (Editor) *Changing Japanese Attitudes to Modernisation* (Princeton, 1965)

Jones, Francis C., *Extraterritoriality in Japan* (New Haven, 1931)

Kennedy, Malcolm D., *A Short History of Japan* (London, 1963)

—*Some Aspects of Japan and her Defence Forces* (London, 1928)

Kipling, Rudyard, *From Sea to Sea* (London, 1900)

Kipling, Rudyard, *Letters of Travel* (London, 1920)

La Farge, John, *An Artist's Letters from Japan* (London, 1897)

⊕ Landor, A. H. S., *Alone with the Hairy Ainu* (London, 1893)

Lockwood, William W., *The Economic Development of Japan* (Princeton, 1954)

Long, John Luther, *Madame Butterfly etc.* (New York, 1898)

Lorimer, Norma, *Japan from a Woman's point of view* (London, 1904)

Lorrimer, Charlotte, *The Call of the East* (London, 1907)

Loti, Pierre, (Louis Marie Julien Viaud) *Madame Chrysanthème* (Paris, 1888)

—*Madame Prune* (Paris and London, 1905)

Maclay, Arthur, *A Budget of Letters from Japan* (New York, 1886)

Mason, Clara, *Etchings from Two Lands* (Boston, 1886)

McWilliams, Vera, *Lafcadio Hearn* (Boston, 1946)

Nish, I., *The Story of Japan* (London, 1968)

Noguchi, Yone, *Lafcadio Hearn in Japan* (Yokohama, 1910)

Norman, Henry, *The Real Japan* (London, 1892)

Novikoff-Priboy, A., *Tsushima, Grave of a Floating City* (London, 1930)

Page, Jesse, *Japan, its people and Missions* (London, 1895)

Paske-Smith, M. *Western Barbarians in Japan* (Kobe, 1930)

Pearson, George, *Flights inside and outside Paradise* (London, 1886)

Peery, Rev. G., *The Gist of Japan* (Edinburgh, 1897)

Pidgeon, Daniel, *An Engineer's Holiday* (London, 1882)

Purcell, Theobald, *Our Neighbourhood* (Yokohama, 1874)

Reischauer, Edwin O., *Japan Past and Present* (Tokyo, 1946)

St John, Capt. H., *Notes and Sketches from the wild coast of Nippon* (London, 1880)

Sansom, Sir George, *The Western world and Japan* (London, 1950)

—*Japan, a Short Cultural History* (London, 1931)

Satow, Sir Ernest, *A Diplomat in Japan* (London, 1921)

— *Observations*, ed. by George Lensen (Florida, 1966)

Satow, E. and A. G. Hawes, *Handbook for Travellers in central and northern Japan* (London and Tokyo, 1884)

Scherer, James, *Japan Today* (London, 1904)

Scidmore, E. R., *Jinrikisha Days in Japan* (New York, 1892)

Sladen, Douglass, *Queer Things about Japan* (London, 1903)

Snow, H. J., *In Forbidden Seas* (London, 1910)

Stoddart, Anna, *The Life of Isabella Bird* (London, 1906)

Tamba, Tsuneo, *Yokohama Ukiyoe* (Tokyo, 1962)

—*Meiji Tenno to Meiji Jidai* (Tokyo, 1966)

Villiers, Frederick, *Three Months with the Besiegers* (London, 1905)

—*Villiers, his five decades of adventure* (London and New York, 1920)

Wagatsuma, George, *Japan's Invisible Race* (Los Angeles, 1966)

Wetmore's Guide to Japan (Yokohama, 1878)

Williams, Harold S., *Tales of Foreign Settlements in Japan* (Tokyo and Vermont, 1958)

—*Foreigners in Mikadoland* (Tokyo and Vermont, 1963)

Wingfield, Lewis, *Wanderings of a Globe-trotter in the Far East* (London, 1889)

Yanaga, Chitoshi, *Japan Since Perry* (Connecticut, 1966)

Newspapers and Periodicals

Chrysanthemum Magazine (Yokohama, 1881–3)

The Eastern World (Yokohama, 1892–1905)

The Far East Magazine (Yokohama, 1870–6)

The Japan Mail (Yokohama, 1871–1905)

The Japan Punch (Yokohama, 1873–83)

The Japan Times (Tokyo, 1897–1905)

The Japan Herald (Yokohama, 1870–6)

The Kobe Chronicle (Kobe, 1900–1)

The New East Magazine (Tokyo, 1917–18)

The Russo-Japanese War Illustrated Record (Tokyo, 1904–5)

The Tokio Times (Tokyo, 1877–80)

Also consulted

Transactions of the Asiatic Society of Japan 1872–1900

Letters of Sir Ernest Satow 1895–1900 in the Public Record Office, London.

Letters in the Jardine Matheson & Co. archives for the 1870s and 1880s.

Acknowledgements

Acknowledgement is due to the following who have kindly allowed us to quote passages from the following works: Edward Arnold, Ltd, publishers of *In Forbidden Seas* by H. J. Snow; Mrs George Bambridge for the extracts from *Letters of Travel* and *From Sea to Sea* by Rudyard Kipling; Chatto & Windus, publishers of *A Social Departure* by Sara J. Duncan; the Church Missionary Society, publishers of *Sea-Girt Yezo* by the Rev. John Batchelor; Harper & Row, publishers of *The Mikado's Empire* by William E. Griffis; Hutchinson & Co., Ltd, publishers of *A Diplomatist's Wife in Japan: Letters from Home to Home* by Mary C. Fraser; T. Werner Laurie, Ltd (Bodley Head), publishers of *Madame Chrysanthème* by Pierre Loti; The Lutterworth Press, publishers of *The Ainu of Japan* by the Rev. John Batchelor; The Macmillan Company of New York, publishers of *Kotto* and *Japan, an Attempt at an Interpretation* by Lafcadio Hearn; Marshall (Horace) & Son, publishers of *From Sunrise Land: Letters from Japan etc.* by Amy Wilson Carmichael; Methuen & Co., Ltd, publishers of *The Garden of Asia* by Reginald Farrer; John Murray, Ltd, publishers of *Korea and Her Neighbours* and *Unbeaten Tracks in Japan* by Isabella Bird; Oliphants, Ltd, publishers of *The Gist of Japan* by the Rev. G. Peery; Fleming H. Revell Co., publishers of *Verbeck of Japan* by William E. Griffis.

We have been unable to trace the copyright holders of a number of works quoted and would like to apologise for any inconvenience caused.

Index

FOR THE BEST IN PAPERBACKS, LOOK FOR THE

In every corner of the world, on every subject under the sun, Penguin represents quality and variety – the very best in publishing today.

For complete information about books available from Penguin – including Pelicans, Puffins, Peregrines and Penguin Classics – and how to order them, write to us at the appropriate address below. Please note that for copyright reasons the selection of books varies from country to country.

In the United Kingdom: Please write to *Dept E.P., Penguin Books Ltd, Harmondsworth, Middlesex, UB7 0DA*

In the United States: Please write to *Dept BA, Penguin, 299 Murray Hill Parkway, East Rutherford, New Jersey 07073*

In Canada: Please write to *Penguin Books Canada Ltd, 2801 John Street, Markham, Ontario L3R 1B4*

In Australia: Please write to the *Marketing Department, Penguin Books Australia Ltd, P.O. Box 257, Ringwood, Victoria 3134*

In New Zealand: Please write to the *Marketing Department, Penguin Books (NZ) Ltd, Private Bag, Takapuna, Auckland 9*

In India: Please write to *Penguin Overseas Ltd, 706 Eros Apartments, 56 Nehru Place, New Delhi, 110019*

In Holland: Please write to *Penguin Books Nederland B.V., Postbus 195, NL–1380AD Weesp, Netherlands*

In Germany: Please write to *Penguin Books Ltd, Friedrichstrasse 10–12, D–6000 Frankfurt Main 1, Federal Republic of Germany*

In Spain: Please write to *Longman Penguin España, Calle San Nicolas 15, E–28013 Madrid, Spain*

In France: Please write to *Penguin Books Ltd, 39 Rue de Montmorency, F-75003, Paris, France*

In Japan: Please write to *Longman Penguin Japan Co Ltd, Yamaguchi Building, 2–12–9 Kanda Jimbocho, Chiyoda-Ku, Tokyo 101, Japan*

BY THE SAME AUTHOR

The Coming of the Barbarians

A Story of Western Settlement in Japan 1853–1870

Nineteenth-century Japan was pristine, inviolate and feudal, ruled by the legendary Shogun and the sacred puppet-Emperor, the Mikado.

Foreigners were despised and feared as 'hairy barbarians', and for more than two hundred years Dutch merchants had been the only settlers, interned on the tiny island of Decima.

The advent of a US naval force in 1853 heralded a new era of drama and upheaval as foreign consuls, merchants and travellers established a risky presence on its shores, opening up a new frontier for both East and West. Pat Barr's sparkling and vivid narrative spans these twenty years and captures the excitement and wonder, beauty and adventure of Japan at its moment of entry into the modern world.